Nick Da[...] was born i[...] an English mother. After schoo[...] Chelsea Art School, later becom[...] a visiting lecturer at art schools and universities and holding one-man exhibitions of his work in London and New York. His photographs have appeared in many newspapers and magazines worldwide. In 1982 he was awarded a Winston Churchill Memorial Trust Fellowship to follow ancient trade-routes. He set off in 1984, and out of the experience came his first book, *Danziger's Travels*, which described his hair-raising adventures during an eighteen-month journey 'beyond forbidden frontiers' in Asia; he journeyed in disguise as an itinerant Muslim, on foot and using traditional means of local transport. The book became an immediate bestseller.

In June 1991 Nick Danziger's documentary video film *War, Lives and Videotape* (based on the children abandoned in Marastoon mental asylum in Kabul) was shown as part of the BBC's 'Video Diaries' series.

Danziger's Travels is also published by Flamingo.

Non fiction Gift Aid
£

0 031140 028364

KT-153-297

By the same author

DANZIGER'S TRAVELS

DANZIGER'S ADVENTURES

From Miami to Kabul

NICK DANZIGER

Flamingo
An Imprint of HarperCollinsPublishers

Flamingo
An Imprint of HarperCollins*Publishers*
77–85 Fulham Palace Road,
Hammersmith, London W6 8JB

Published by Flamingo 1993
9 8 7 6 5 4 3 2 1

First published in Great Britain by
HarperCollins*Publishers* 1992

Copyright © Nick Danziger 1992

The Author asserts the moral right to
be identified as the author of this work

ISBN 0 586 09081 9

Maps by John Callanan

Set in Palatino

Printed in Great Britain by
HarperCollinsManufacturing Glasgow

All rights reserved. No part of this publication may be
reproduced, stored in a retrieval system, or transmitted,
in any form or by any means, electronic, mechanical,
photocopying, recording or otherwise, without the prior
permission of the publishers.

This book is sold subject to the condition that it shall not,
by way of trade or otherwise, be lent, re-sold, hired out or
otherwise circulated without the publisher's prior consent
in any form of binding or cover other than that in which it
is published and without a similar condition including this
condition being imposed on the subsequent purchaser.

CONTENTS

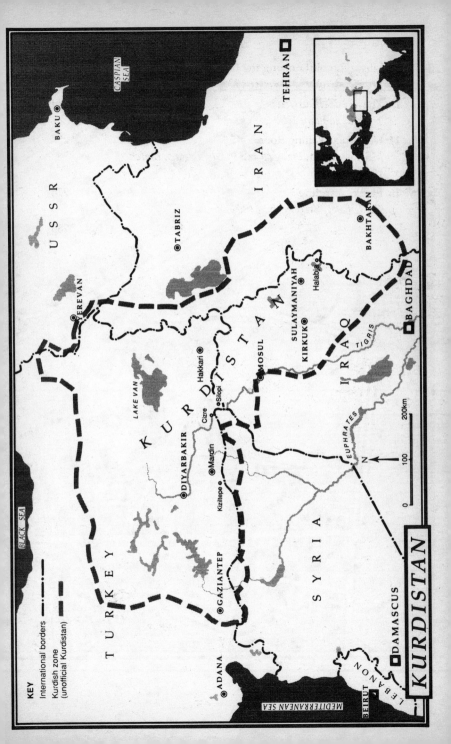

KURDISTAN

KEY
International borders ———
Kurdish zone ▬▬▬
(unofficial Kurdistan)

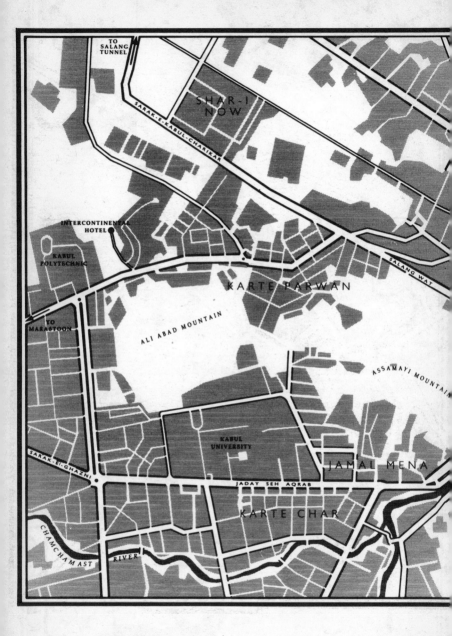

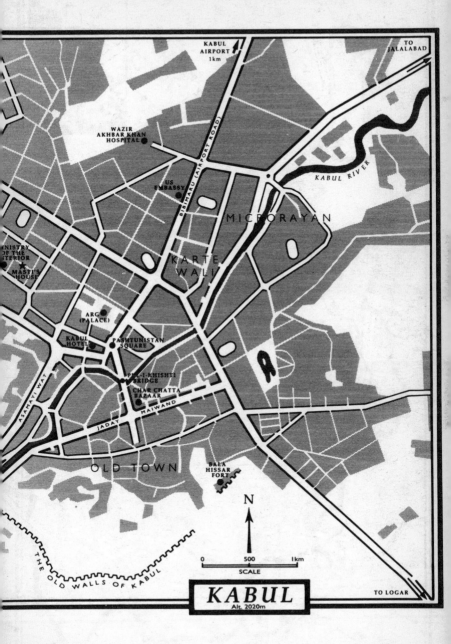

TO
JALALABAD

KABUL
AIRPORT
1 km

WAZIR
AKHBAR KHAN
HOSPITAL

US
EMBASSY

KABUL RIVER

MICRORAYAN

KARTE
WALI

MINISTRY
OF THE
INTERIOR

MASTI'S
HOUSE

ARG
(PALACE)

KABUL
HOTEL

PASHTUNISTAN
SQUARE

ASAMAYI WAT

PUL-I-KHISHTI
BRIDGE

CHAR CHATTA
BAZAAR

JADAY
MAIWAND

OLD TOWN

BALA
HISSAR
FORT

N

THE OLD WALLS OF KABUL

0   500   1 km
SCALE

KABUL
Alt. 2020m

TO LOGAR

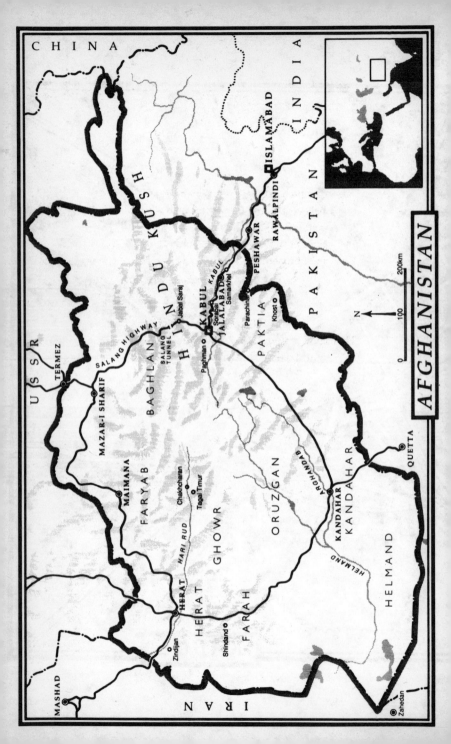

. . . then madness was very near, as I
believe it would be near the man who
could see things through the veils at
once of two customs, two cultures, two
environments.

T. E. Lawrence, *Seven Pillars of Wisdom*

This book is dedicated to those who helped me
and asked for nothing in return.

ACKNOWLEDGEMENTS

I would like to thank my mother and stepfather for giving me the space to write this book and my father, my brother Richard, Aline, my aunt Leonore and the many other members of my family for their support. I would also like to thank the following friends who have helped me: Gordon Adam and the BBC Pashtu Service, Charlie Bourn, Alex Bowling, Edward J. 'Barney' Brown, Tania Cagnoni, Mary Chamberlain, Cormac, Caroline Crippen, Richard Cronk, Lisa Cuscuna, Louisa Czartoryska, Bernice Davison, Daisy Decazes, Rifat Dedeoglu, Lyse Doucet, Richard Duncan and Juliette, Diana Faust, Mastaneh Firouz Notz, Charlie Gore, Ginny Jenkins, Ann Jousiffe, Eddie Lederer, Lelei Le Laulu, Tracy Lerman, Bob Long, M.M.M., Marvin Singer, Jinous Vaziri.

Marianne Taylor read my first draft and helped in the selection of the pictures. Robert Pledge and Trisha Ziff cast a critical eye, but also offered encouragement and inspiration. I hope my American lecture agent Nancy Nelson will forgive me for certain indiscretions, and I would like to extend this apology to the women's groups, corporations and other institutions I have lectured to who have presented me with many opportunities I would not otherwise have had. Christa Paula's hard work and corrections to the final draft were invaluable. Thanks also to my literary agent Mark Lucas for his guiding advice, and his assistant Kirsty Ackland Baring for all her help; Pete Morgan, who for two years was my invaluable assistant and informal office manager; Janice Robertson, for her editorial skills; Barry Taylor and Olympus Cameras for their continuing support, and Fuji Film for supplying me with film; my publisher Richard Johnson, who has once more given me the opportunity to record my experiences in one of the few ways I can find to repay those whom I am unable to mention by name but who have shown me tremendous kindness, hospitality and generosity. I apologize for inevitable errors of omission.

In memory of Stephen Abis.

Finally, I would like to thank one young Kurdish man who at great risk to himself helped me in life-threatening circumstances. I neither know his name nor have I described the events surrounding his heroic act for fear of compromising him with the local authorities. I shall always be in his debt.

1

YOU KILL ONE PERSON
AND THEY CALL YOU
A MURDERER

The organised cult of machinery [is a]
monster that can transform man into a
passive, purposeless animal.

Lewis Mumford,
writer and social philosopher

Poplar, London's East End, Spring 1987

It was one of those winter mornings when the cold and wind
combine to drive sheets of rain across the city under a bleak grey
sky. It had taken me over an hour to reach Poplar in the East End of
London on the Number 15 bus. I stood in front of the ground-floor
flat in the housing estate, drenched to the bone, fumbling in my
pocket for the keys to the front door. The rain dropped off me in
rivulets onto my sodden plimsolls soaked from stepping in puddles
of water that camouflaged broken paving stones. As the door
opened I was horrified by what I saw before me. The furniture in
the flat was floating across the living-room floor in six inches of
water.

The previous day I had arrived in London from my family's
comfortable home in Wiltshire in search of lodgings. Cormac, a
friend of mine who had escaped to the sunnier climate of Los
Angeles, suggested I take over his hard-to-let council flat in one of
England's most depressed neighbourhoods. Steve, the previous
occupant, was moving out; all I had to do was keep the rent book up
to date and pay for my electricity, gas and telephone bills.

'There's only one other condition,' said Steve, handing me the
keys to the flat. 'You must take good care of Cormac's wicker

furniture; it belongs to Jackie Collins.' I stood there wondering whether Jackie Collins was rhyming slang.

As Steve and I parted he wished me good luck. 'You'll need it,' he said. 'There's bound to be trouble, the kids are always looking for it.' He advised me to catch one of the bastards and give him a lesson he wouldn't forget – 'It's the only language they understand and that's the only way they are going to leave you alone,' said Steve, referring to the violence with a disarming smile which he used sparingly.

I prepared to barricade myself against vandalism. But the first challenge on my arrival the following morning was provided by the six inches of water on the living-room floor.

I was beset by a host of problems. Cormac had agreed I could take over the flat for an unspecified time. He was, however, unaware that Steve had failed to pay all the quarterly service bills; they had remained unpaid for months and the council was owed three weeks' rent. The gas and electricity boards were threatening to cut off supplies and take legal action. British Telecom had long since disconnected the phone. There seemed no end to my misfortunes. When the water finally receded, the flat reeked of dampness, the curtains were stained by a watermark and more than a hint of mould, and the furniture smelt as if it had been lying in Thames mud next to a raw sewage outlet. The water supply to the council estate was cut and I had to join a long queue to collect water from a single standpipe.

It was an alien landscape to me. Ironically Poplar was less familiar to me than Peking. The tourist sights of the British capital never included the inner-city housing estates, psychopaths, loners, junkies and homeless. It quickly became obvious why the flat was hard to let. My view from the front window was limited to a pre-World War II gas storage tank; articulated lorries rumbled past my front door *en route* to the North, kicking up a constant shower of rubbish as they passed. My ground-floor flat did have the benefit of a back garden, but six floors of tenants and pedestrians had turned it into a rubbish tip. It was littered with everything from an empty butane gas canister to chicken bones and an abandoned frying pan. It was a miracle that grass continued to grow between the refuse.

The car park beyond the garden was a mausoleum for grime-covered cars on cinder blocks or exhausted tyres. Parts of the estate were built like a rabbit warren: faceless corridors and unlit passageways haunted by the spectre of predators where young cannibals wait to prey on hapless victims. Rhyming slang was laced with threats of grievous bodily harm; a man routinely pinned against a wall was offered a choice by his assailant: a raised left fist – six weeks in hospital, or a raised right – sudden death?

At the local pub my sense of being from another world was highlighted.

'What will it be?' asked the publican.

'A glass of red, thanks.'

I thought he was going to choke. He raised an eyebrow, thinking me a pretentious nancy. Shaking his head, he said, 'Lager or Bitter?' his arm at the ready to pull a pint.

Slowly the flat began to dry out. Living conditions were made easier by the surprising promptness meeting my request to have the phone reconnected. Without prior warning two British Telecom engineers were at my front door.

'Where's the dog?' they asked.

'I don't have one,' I reassured them.

'It says here you've got one,' said one of the engineers, pointing to his worksheet.

'I don't have one,' I repeated, a little confused.

The taller of the two men looked at his worksheet. 'This *is* 15 Braithwaite House?' It was. 'We've got instructions to check your dog and bone.' Which I now understood was rhyming Cockney for phone.

The flat in Poplar wasn't the artist's studio I dreamed of, but it was a start. For the last year I had been writing about my experiences during an eighteenth-month journey across Turkey, Iran, Afghanistan, Pakistan and China. I felt very lucky and fortunate still to be alive. Surviving wars and local insurrections in Afghanistan, Iran and Kurdistan had made me think twice about continuing my travels, reasoning that, according to the law of averages, the odds for survival were bound to diminish with each close call with death. I no longer wanted to run the gauntlet across some god-forsaken field under fire or jump into some make-do foxhole. I wanted to listen to music, put my feet up in front of the television and visit exhibitions. Above all, I wanted to find a studio to paint in. It had been over three years since I had had my last one-man exhibition at a London gallery. I even hoped to return to the art schools that had once employed me as a visiting lecturer.

Since an early age I have travelled to Third World countries, most of which have been caught in a perpetual cycle of wars and revolutions, bombings and pogroms, earthquakes and famines. The troublespots I have visited were located in the grinding poverty of parts of South and Central America, the Middle and Far East. I was often shocked by repressive and authoritarian regimes and their crimes against humanity. I was horrified by the atrocities, the internecine wars and cultural clashes. In travelling to some of the more remote and inaccessible parts of the world I had observed what it meant to be born in the wrong place; a world without access to schools, doctors and hospitals, a world where freedom and choice were dreams. But something was about to change; this new experience was bringing me close to the realities and deprivations not of far-away places but of my own society.

Although I was born in London I had never been more than an observer of Britain's inner-city slums. Poor buildings infested by cockroaches and rats, overburdened hospitals, the hopelessness, rage and frustration I had seen in the faces of young people were in the slums of *favelas* and *barrios* I had visited in Latin America.

Unawares, I had stumbled into a kind of war. My neighbours remained barricaded into their flats. At night as the temperature dropped so the tension mounted in the poorly lit streets. I watched a man and woman wrestling in the street. I wasn't sure who had been chasing whom. As they grappled with each other their embrace was both a dance of death and a dance of love; she clutched him, out of affection or fear, but definitely to avoid being hit. He grabbed her brutally and shook her while struggling loose to reject her affection. I was not alone. I could feel dozens of eyes witnessing the scene but like myself they probably also felt it was none of their business. He began to yell at her; tears were streaming down her cheeks. I could only hear his violence over her pleading.

'I DON'T GIVVA SHIT ABOUT NO FUCKIN' COMPLIMENT. It don't mean nothing if I give yer a fuckin' compliment. You're not saying SHIT. If I say yer got fuckin' nice clothes IT DON'T MEAN FUCKIN' NOTHIN', LISA. You hear me. DON'T YOU TELL ME YOU'RE GOING OUTSIDE AGAIN.'

He slammed the trembling woman against the wall. 'BITCH! FUCK YOU! FUCK YOU! FUCK YOU!' he cursed and walked off.

She slid to the pavement and squatted on her haunches, arms over her head, sobbing heavily.

The violence was everywhere. The only public pay phone in a quarter-of-a-mile radius had been brutally dismembered, each window pane systematically smashed. The caretaker to the block of flats had been driven out, his flat bolted shut with an iron bar across the front door. The housing estate's lifts seldom worked; when they did they provided a crude tableau of the latest gossip – MARY SUCKS COCK – and gave expression to frustrations: DON'T MUG ME MUG A YUPPIE, Ⓐ CLASS WAR Ⓐ, QUEER IS BEAUTIFUL, and warnings from a local East End gang calling itself 'THE INTER CITY FIRM'. The volatile concoction of graffiti in the lifts merged with the stale odour of urine. At night the battle raged between Heavy Metal and Garage music, the intrusion like the jarring sound of a helicopter gunship hovering overhead. The noise droned on through the night like the heartbeat of an earthquake – loud enough to measure 8 on the Richter scale. If the hi-fi stack had been wired to the building we'd have had major structural damage, if we didn't already.

My new world was inhabited by people whose faces were so frightened and intimidated that little remained of their dignity, and self-respect was lost in sorrow, anxiety and a siege mentality. The old and infirm were trapped in their tenements. Single women had the choice of venturing out at night or staying locked in their flats – prisoners of their environment. Local voluntary groups offered tenants, especially women and the elderly, advice about securing their homes and warned them to restrict their travel to safe areas at safe times and to safe types of transport.

It was difficult to meet people let alone get to know them. Like everybody else I was separated by only six inches of concrete wall from my neighbours, but we rarely met. If I stopped someone in the street to ask directions the first reaction was fear of violence, which gave way to suspicion.

The air was stale with resentment and resignation. Aggression was fuelled by bitterness and frustration. Hope and jobs were a long way from drugs and decay. Gentrification and prosperity, the development of Docklands, had by-passed this part of Poplar and anyway they didn't want it – the graffiti on a Light Docklands Railway bridge read EAST END FOR US NOT YUPPIE FILTH. Escape might figure in people's imagination but the West End of London, only a bus ride away, was another land, the distance immeasurable. For some just to get there would cost ten per cent of their weekly dole money.

For some young women, to escape from an awful home situation or to live independently was almost impossible. A pregnancy and a child might give them the independence and a space of their own, but one form of tyranny often begets another.

I met Maria through her weekend job at a market stall. She was tall and slender. She had light auburn skin, crimson fingernails and long, thick black hair which she tied into a single braid. She had a wide mouth, fine lips and wore lipstick that matched her nails. She stood out from the crowd, and was an easy target for men's sexist remarks; she rarely rose to the bait – but when she did she gave as good as she got. At first she seemed easygoing but an inner tension was always ready to explode. At twenty-eight she already had four children; well, as she put it, 'How was I to know that the third would be twins?'

I never asked her about the father of her children; she just told me to telephone her at work or early in the evening. 'He's always out drinking' – that was the only reference she ever made to another presence in her life. She asked me over for dinner one evening; we sat on the sofa or, more precisely, I sat on the sofa with her girlfriend, two years her junior but neither married nor a mother. Maria sat in an armchair, the only other piece of furniture except for the television and a glossy poster. She offered me a piece of meatloaf; it was delicious. We drank beer. We watched television. We didn't talk much. It was getting late and she was having a battle getting the kids to bed. Matter-of-factly she told me that two of the children slept on the floor. 'I can't afford another two beds.'

The children fought, screamed and were defiant to the last; every one of Maria's demands was met with angry shouts and verbal abuse. Maria had a full-time job as a scanner at a food-packaging plant. I didn't know where she got the energy to work and run her family. She was consumed by a life that was devouring her; from work she had to collect the kids from school, do the shopping, fix the dinner, do the dishes, wash the clothes . . .

This was poverty; not the hard, barren life of Afghanistan but the nondescript struggle in an appendage to a rich city.

It was around the time of the first break-in to my flat that Steve, the previous occupant, showed up. He wanted to know whether his lover's child benefit book had come through the post. 'She's having a hard time,' he told me of his girlfriend, 'what with living in this flat where she couldn't face going out and now we've been fire-bombed in Hackney – you should have seen the smoke, but I'm sure it was meant for the Asian neighbours.' A flicker of doubt flashed across his face when he thought about his unpaid debts. Steve had been a mini-cab driver until his car got stolen and was later found, totalled, on the side of a road. To get back on the road, so to speak, he had expanded his dope-dealing network. He reasoned, 'Why should I work forty hours a week breaking my neck in a boring dead-end job when I can earn the same amount in a few hours?' The idea of getting a regular job didn't really enter into consideration. He failed to mention at this second of our encounters that he was combining his dope-dealing with a job as a private detective.

Before Steve left he tried to interest me in some Bob Hope. I couldn't think why, I didn't have a stereo; but what he meant was as in Bob Hope – a line of rope – rhyming Cockney for dope. 'Of course, I'm going to give up dealing,' he would tell me each time I saw him.

I remembered the piece of advice Steve had given me before taking over the flat: 'There's bound to be trouble, the kids are looking for it. You want to catch one of the bastards and give him a lesson he won't forget – it's the only language they understand and that's the only way they are going to leave you alone.' The only precaution I had taken was not to move anything of value into the flat, and to walk on the other side of the street from trouble.

I had seen the roaming mobs before I came to live in Poplar, usually every other Saturday when I went to watch my football team. Drunk and violent, Chelsea's Headhunters stood on the stadium's terraces or waited to taunt rival supporters like Birmingham's Zulus and Arsenal's Gooners with chants of 'WE HATE HUMANS!' as they emerged from the local tube or train station. Millwall's Nutty Turn-Out's answer was, 'No one likes us, WE DON'T CARE!' They never looked for trouble individually; they always marauded in packs. Bunched together, they seemed like modern-day pirates, with their initiation rites and death-do-us-part allegiances indicated by home-made tattoos etched onto fingers and occasionally foreheads. Their trophies were destroyed trains, smashed stadiums and shopping precincts; their enjoyment was gained in kicking the shit out of rival fans and in confrontations with the police. Sometimes they used petrol bombs and sometimes they killed people. They sniffed glue, smoked and were brave with beer, although many hadn't even reached the legal age to buy fags or alcohol.

A small local group of adolescents always hung out at a derelict house with a council 'dangerous structure' notice attached to the boarded-up front door, and the local fish-and-chip shop near the Blackwall Tunnel where the air was thick with lead and carbon monoxide from the belching exhaust fumes of heavy traffic. They were young, bored and looking for a bit of fun at someone else's expense. They had a certain look which appeared either casual and cool or hell-bent on intimidation and destruction. Their faces declared a lack of feeling, an absence of commitment and disregard for rules other than the courage to be first in and last out when it came to a fight: maximum viciousness combined with minimum conscience.

It was easy to understand their inability to feel any affinity with the immediate environment. Life was becoming more anonymous. Tarmac, concrete, sterile architecture, tunnels, passageways, artificial lighting, automobiles formed a distant world completely divorced from nature. They were surrounded by artificial barriers and it was almost impossible to break out of the maze.

Everyone felt threatened and every day the big world outside the home grew more hostile. Television and the papers brought it into the living room and the pub. The talk was of terrorists, Third World dictators and communists, muggers and pimps. Mind you, every threat gave rise to a budding Attila the Hun. Answers to the world's problems came at the end of a pint: 'Send the immigrants back', 'Bring back conscription – put the young into the army' and 'Bring back capital punishment' were the stock solutions. This was not the lucid dream of the process of becoming, but rather survival and the conservative safekeeping of property or what was left of it. Some tenants never had money. They did have chequebooks and credit cards. Credit was everything. It was like Third World debt in that they were struggling to make the interest payments on what they owed. If you happened to get a paycheque the money had already been spent. They were hooked on payments for the car, the television, the stereo and the video.

Some residents were driven if not hounded from their homes and places of work. The local high street was an armoury of steel rabbit fencing welded protectively over the shop façades. One Asian shop owner had been forced to close. FUCK OFF PACKS had been scrawled across his front door. The South Bromley Community Shop was also padlocked and fenced off because of cuts and staffing shortages. Its posters were based on the rules for survival in the inner city: Racial Attacks Are Against The Law; Beware of The Bogus Caller; Women's Safe Transport; Kung-Fu Self-Defence Classes for Kids from 6 Years Old; Stranger Danger awareness campaign for schoolchildren. Fear and paranoia were embedded at an early age; and suggestions for teachers included, on school bullying: 'Tell the children from day one that bullying (verbal or physical) is *not* tolerated in the school.' Note: 'in the school'. I discovered there were hundreds of children who didn't attend any school because of lack of places.

For those who needed to run the gauntlet to the bus shelter, every alleyway was a reminder of an invisible presence: 'Dev is a wanker', 'Tracey is horny', 'Babs is a fucking shit', 'BEWARE girls cos i'l FUCK ya', read the graffiti, and 'KILL'. The dilapidated shelter featured drawings of penises and burst Durexes to a chorus of scrawled tirades: BAN BABY FARMING; DUREX IS OXYMORON. This last had been altered to read YOUR MUM IS OXYMORON; 'Mum' was crossed out and not replaced by anything. Children were pre-

vented from playing in the streets; pensioners feared to cross them.
If you ventured out, to return home was to be haunted by the
spectre of an uninvited intruder, possibly still there; you might
catch him by surprise.

My flat was broken into regularly. They could easily have got in
through the front door which was only protected by a Yale lock.
However, they always insisted on smashing the windows to gain
access to the all but empty flat. On each of their rampages they left
an object-cum-weapon presumably lifted from some other luckless
fellow – such as a heavy rubber underwater torch (with batteries
inside, it could be used as a lethal cosh, but torches unlike knives
had the advantage of not being classified as dangerous weapons –
in other words, you couldn't be prosecuted for being caught in
possession of a torch), a vacuum cleaner extension tube and a large
carving knife. There was nothing to take but they did smash a
mirror above the bath with a portrait of Marilyn Monroe etched
onto it. Her effervescent smile had been smashed between the
eyes.

The only time I confronted a mob of young adolescents making a
racket while rummaging through disused building materials near
my front door, the leader of the pack, who couldn't have been more
than sixteen years old, picked up a piece of metal conduit tube and
waved it at me. Taunting me, he shouted, 'What's it to you?' I felt
like saying go stick it in your ear, but I thought I'd better not. Even
though it might have been too early for them to be high on
amphetamines or beer, they were dangerous enough when they
were sober. Perhaps for my cowardice – according to Steve's logic
about meeting violence with violence – for my failure to strike out or
for my audacity in raising my voice at them, or perhaps for both, I
received a brick through my kitchen window later in the day.

It was after the fourth break-in that I finally decided to leave
Poplar. I was returning home from dinner in Hackney. I waited for
the last bus, but when it arrived the driver explained he wasn't
going any farther than the depot. There were no night buses along
this route, but the bus driver took pity on me. 'If you wait while I
cash in the takings at the garage I'll give you a lift as far as the
Commercial Road.' Driving towards his home we discovered we

had much to talk about. He was married to a Colombian woman and he had also travelled out to Nepal in the sixties across Iran and India.

The delight at getting an unexpected lift down to the Commercial Road was in stark contrast to the misery I felt when I reached my front door. In one aspect it was worse than usual; burglars had not only smashed the flat's windows, they had also left excrement on the living-room floor. For the first time I called the police to report the crime. I doubted their ability to catch the perpetrators, and supposed their report would be filed away to become just another statistic. After three hours of waiting and several irate phone calls later, I spoke to the duty sergeant and complained about the time it was taking for the police to arrive. He told me to stay on the line whilst he made some enquiries. Moments later he returned to the phone and explained: 'I've just spoken to the patrolman. He's chasing a suspect towards your premises at this very moment.'

After the break-in I received several letters. The first was from the Tower Hamlets Victims' Support Scheme. In the letter they offered sympathy but no help: 'We are sorry to learn from the police that you have recently become the victim of crime. Normally one of our Volunteers would call on you to give sympathy, understanding, help and practical advice, but regrettably the number of incidents occasionally exceeds the volunteers available, and we are unable to call automatically on victims in every case.' I thought 'occasionally exceeds' was the understatement of the year. Tower Hamlets Council sent a letter in five different languages: Bengali, Cantonese, Urdu, Somali and Vietnamese. I couldn't tell whether the council was offering helpful advice or serving an eviction notice.

The police referred to my break-in as E 413. Their letter said, 'The information which you have provided has already been acted upon and will form the basis of our investigation.' I was not hopeful. The only information I had been able to provide the police was that the break-in had occurred some time during 31 March.

The next morning I called Maria. I thought of her resigned face, tired eyes and take-it-or-leave-it attitude. She didn't want to talk. I could sense something had happened.

'What's wrong?' I asked.

'He's lost his job – that's the second this year.' It was only April. Maria had lost track of the number of jobs the father of her children had lost through absenteeism and lack of interest.

'How will you manage?' I enquired.

'He will get his unemployment cheque, I won't see any of that. He just wants to get drunk as much as possible, sleep long hours and get up late. I will have to take a second job that isn't part-time.' There was no bitterness or self-pity in her voice; she was not a dweller but a doer. She asked me not to call her again. I realized the gulf that separated me from her and the rest of the council estate was enormous. I came from the comfortable class. I had grown up with hobbies, an education, a foreign language, but most important of all I had choice. I could leave here. Maria, the unmarried young mothers, the pensioners, had nowhere else to go and for their future only decay and destitution; for neighbours the squalor, the rage and the frustration. They had about as much hope as a climber might trying to dig his way out from under an avalanche. They were victims of a social system that offered choice only to those who could afford it; their future was as predictable and hopeless as mine offered variety and adventure.

I hadn't found a studio to paint in, but I was no longer sure that painting was the best way to express the issues that had touched me. Bolivian tin mines, the homeless children of Rio, war-ravaged Afghanistan and Poplar seemed a long way from the art galleries of Western capitals. Besides, the advance for my first book was all but spent. Before I could decide whether I wanted to return to painting, continue to write about my travels or capture events through my photography, I needed to get a job.

I went to a local pub to mull over my future. If you lived where I lived you too would have stayed away from home as much as possible. In this, I don't think I was alone, but others in the neighbourhood might have had different reasons. The atmosphere in the pub was heavy and silent. The musty carpet smelt of a decade of spilt alcohol and spent nicotine.

'What will it be, darlin'?' said the woman behind the bar. Her hair was permed and shiny and beginning to turn grey at the roots. Her make-up failed to hide the deep scar on her chin, I imagined the possible result of a bad marriage, a violent customer or a threat.

'A pint of lager.' I looked around the half-filled pub. Everyone had a story to tell.

''Ere you are, luv,' she said as she placed the glass on the varnished hardwood surface. I extended a handful of change.

As I crossed the saloon a fat man making his unsure way to the lavatory nearly knocked the drink out of my hands. He paused to glare at a woman who looked as though she had put her make-up on without the benefit of a mirror.

I found the only empty seat next to a gentleman sitting in a corner on his own, who nodded gently when I asked if I could sit down. He was in his early sixties and he still looked powerful. He smoked his roll-ups until the tips of his wrinkled fingers could no longer hold the end. I was not keen to encourage him to talk because he might not know when to stop. But without much encouragement he began his life story from gas fitter to prison inmate. I asked him why he had done time.

He dipped his cigarette end into the ashtray swimming in stale beer and butts. 'You kill one person and they call you a murderer,' he said plaintively.

I walked home across another drab and peeling housing estate along partly lit streets. Mashed condoms and broken glass crunched underfoot like pebbles on a beach. At the end of an underground passage I had to step over two skinheads clutching a paper bag and a bottle of glue. They lay so motionless in the urine-stinking tunnel they might have been dead. When I got home I called Cormac in Los Angeles to tell him I was going to leave the flat. I left a message on his answering machine. I called Steve; he didn't sound surprised. 'What are we going to do with the furniture?' he asked worriedly.

'What's the problem?'

'Cormac isn't going to be pleased.' I thought of the wicker furniture that had once floated in six inches of water across the living-room floor; it was stained and the musty smell of damp fabric still remained after all these months. 'What's he going to say to Jackie Collins?'

By now I had decided that Jackie Collins must be rhyming Cockney slang, but Steve went on to explain that Cormac's sister

Anne had told him that Cormac had been living in the States with one of Jackie Collins's daughters.

America seemed like a good place to look for work. I picked up a copy of *Time Out* and turned to the travel ads. The richest city in the world, the American Dream and land of milk and honey beckoned. I left the residents of Poplar facing warning letters and eviction notices, dole queues and social security payments bound by complex regulations, delays, unavailability and bureaucratic red tape. In addition to the constant worry and the need to borrow money to feed, clothe and provide for their families, the residents also faced increasing violence and racist attacks, lack of repairs, permanent dampness and a lingering asbestos threat.

2

I SHOP THEREFORE I
AM*

In America's toughest city, even
Mother Teresa tries to get a little edge.

Time magazine

When I moved to New York, back in
1961, I remember saying that 90% of the
people walking along the street in
Manhattan would be interviewed in
any other town, and the other 10%
would be arrested. It's got a lot weirder
since then.

Calvin Trillin

New York, Summer 1987

With no prospects, I bought a Kuwait Airlines ticket to New York in
search of work and the American Dream. I boarded the 747 and
decided to celebrate my decision to start a new life.

'*Assalamu aleikum. Wa-rahmatullahi wa-barakatuh* [Greetings.
God's mercy and his blessing]. What would you like to drink?' the
stewardess asked.

'Champagne, please.'

'Orange juice or water,' she replied.

I should have known better. Even over the Atlantic from London
to New York the Arab airline was 'dry'.

Nowadays each airline likes to stress its individual identity.
Kuwait offers an in-flight mosque service. Every announcement by

*The title of a painting by Barbara Kruger.

the cabin staff or pilot was preceded by the Koranic invocation, '*Bismillah Rahman i Rahim* – In the name of Allah, The Most Merciful and Benevolent', and so before landing, as before take-off and at mealtimes, Allah was invoked to protect us from bad food and turbulence.

On our final approach to J. F. Kennedy Airport the captain made his last announcement, 'In the name of Allah The Most Merciful and Benevolent, we will be landing at New York's John F. Kennedy Airport.'

We arrived in the middle of the night and the international arrivals terminal was populated by every sort of tout: hotel agents and so-called 'gypsy cab' drivers who for sixty dollars, nearly three times the regular fare, would drop you in Manhattan. With not enough money for a ticket on the airport bus, I had to make my way to Queens where I could catch the E or F train into town.

To arrive in Manhattan at night is to be confronted by a dramatic and glittering skyline reaching to the heavens, home to the richest city in the world; to take the subway is to descend into a subterranean hell. At 2 A.M. the subway is a dormitory for the homeless, each carriage and station filled with people either slouched over the seats or stretched across a bench. I bought my token from the bulletproof kiosk. Smart New York subway riders, I have been told, carry two guns, in case one is stolen. At Queens Plaza where I had to change I noticed that each train had its quota of policemen or Guardian Angels, a vigilante group noted for their adept use of the martial arts. Whereas JFK had been lacking in bilingual signs, the subway trains' advertisements are more often than not in Spanish. We came to a stop under the East River in the tunnel. I surveyed the panoply of Help-line telephone numbers for Hispanics, Blacks, children, the disabled, single women, foreigners, gays and The Coalition for the Homeless, The Food and Hunger Hotline, The Drug-Alcohol Hotline, same-day hernia surgery by a Board Certified Surgeon and an advertisement for roach killers called COMBAT. As a Ms Lee Rubenstein told us: 'A roach crawled across my son's birthday cake. Everybody saw that roach on the cake, my mother, my in-laws, my friends, my neighbors. I was so embarrassed I dropped the cake and burst into tears. That'll never happen again thanks to Combat . . . COMBAT

. . . THE REAL SOLUTION.' 'Round the clock killing for three long months', read the ad for another specific *'contra las cucurachas, GARANTIZA MATARIAS todos los dias . . . 24 hora al dia'*. I guessed there were a lot of cockroaches in the Big Apple.

Twenty minutes later the train still hadn't moved. Over the crackling PA system our driver informed us that a man had committed suicide by jumping into the path of the train in front of us. We would have to return to Queens Plaza and take a different line. As our driver passed through our carriage I asked what had happened. He told me, 'I guess some people prefer to go by train.'

At 4 A.M. I finally arrived at my aunt's. The combination of jet lag, tiredness, but also the fear and excitement of being in a new city with the daunting prospect of finding work, made for a sleepless night, and I set out from my aunt's after an early breakfast. My first stop would be at Paul Smith's, the recently-opened shop of the English clothes designer from Nottingham and Covent Garden in London where Ginny, the sister of my ex-girlfriend Noo, worked as manageress.

I strode purposefully down Fifth Avenue towards the corner of Fifth and 16th Street. It is along Fifth Avenue that you can buy a fur coat with a bulletproof lining; other shops require you to make an appointment to gain entrance. But for every Cartier or Gucci there are a dozen street vendors selling imitations of the latest status symbol for a hundredth of the cost. I passed beneath the fantastic skyscrapers, homes to millionaires, which create vast crevasses, canyons of streets where the homeless and destitute lie. The American Dream is and has always been, for many, something of a nightmare.

It was a stroke of good luck that when I reached Paul Smith their cashier had just decided to walk out. There was no time to ponder the offer of this job, debate the terms and conditions. I was down to spare change, and even though I had never been a cashier was prepared to try my hand at anything.

I settled into the job quickly. Ginny, Pam, Naomi, Richard and Al had all defected *en masse* from another fashion designer's shop to join Paul Smith. And Steve, an ex-student from the Brighton School of Art, had been flown in from the Covent Garden shop to be in charge of fitting men's suits. From what I understood about the opening night, the crush from the throngs of fashion victims resembled a much coveted artist's private view, with the crowds pressing to get into the shop which was decorated with display cases and cabinets imported from old Newcastle chemists and herbalists.

The shop had quickly become something of a cult. Not only were the clothes for sale, including stylish 1940s gabardine suits and waistcoats, but also the Billy Bunter and Biggles books as well as a book on semaphore using Indian clubs, the paintings and Fornasetti neo-classic plates, and the furniture. Paul Smith had cleverly pinpointed his clientele: those who seek out designer toothpaste, Dinky toys, antique tie-pins, ostrich-, shark-, elephant- and snake-skin Filofaxes and hand-generated torches (Steve recommended this last item as a present for a Polish cat-burglar). The purchase of any of these small, frivolous fashion statements was intended to help the purchaser out of his or her depression. But more important to the success of the shop was the unorthodox sales pitch from Michael, who joined the team at the same time as myself.

Michael J. Fox was from Providence, Rhode Island. He dressed in schoolboy shorts, black shirts and a BOY baseball cap with the peak jutting to the side. Michael liked to stroke the cashmere sweaters: 'It's better than sex with myself.'

Although Ginny constantly reprimanded him for 'Bad Attitude' – his late arrival was usually heralded by the thumping House music from his shoulder-carried boom box – his honest approach, not to say his disarming sales technique, could not be faulted. He soon had a list of devoted clients. When one of Michael's customers tried a shirt on for size and asked: 'Does it fit?', if the shirt was too big Michael answered – 'You'll grow into it', or if too small – 'Well, you could lose a bit of weight.'

If a customer, unable to make up his mind in front of a mirror, looked for reassurance or needed advice, Michael, with a coy glint of mischief in his eye, told them: 'It's a look.'

The success of the shop had an unexpected and sinister side effect. At night, when everyone had left, one of the large plate glass display windows was regularly smashed, but inexplicably the most expensive items on display weren't always stolen. With no clues, we were left to guess whether the regular pattern of vandalism was a veiled signal from organized crime asking us for protection money; a junkie from the nearby methadone clinic; or an insurance scam involving a glassworks company. In the absence of any answers, the only solution to be adopted before the sturdy metal shutters could be installed was to hire a couple from a security service. I say couple, because Frank, the security guard, called his partner and companion Big Bertha. Big Bertha, or Kaboom, as we nicknamed her, was in fact a 'piece' – a pump action rifle made for riot control. Frank would arrive before closing time with his metallic guncase, his TV set and, unknown to us at the time, an addiction to a telephone chat line that was to cost the shop $4,000. Before we left the shop at closing time Frank, cradling Big Bertha, would assure us, 'No one is going to mess with me and if they do they're going to meet Jesus.'

The shop opened at ten o'clock in the morning (by which time Big Bertha had been carefully packed away and taken home). However, if you arrived early enough Omar, the cleaner – as well as being coach to Coquinbo United of the New York Chilean Indoor Soccer League and The Wanderers of the Oyster Bay Park Long Island League – did a great line in massages. He would have us stretched out on the large table used for selling clothes to retailers and would then proceed to relieve pressure from our tired bones and muscles. Omar told me his magic concoction was a good cure for arthritis. You may well ask what the magic ingredients were to Omar's particular potion.

'You must crush two Cuban cigars into neat alcohol,' Omar told me.

'But what happens if you can't find Cuban cigars?' I asked. After all, Havana cigars are contraband in the States.

'That's not a problem,' Omar said; 'if you can't find Havana cigars just use pot [marijuana] instead.'

Tiredness was a major problem for most of us – or, more accurately, the real problem was getting to work on time after the previous night's partying. In New York, to find yourself at home without an invitation is to question your existence; paranoia and loneliness set in quickly in a big, impersonal city with energy enough to devour all but the strongest. Too many invitations for the same evening is almost as undesirable as none, because you worry that you might have chosen the wrong party; there might be something better and more exciting going on at the invitation you turned down. The art was to hedge your bets, keep moving from one party to another as if moving through the different courses of a meal.

Elaborate strategies were employed to make parties memorable. Caesar, a movie producer, had rented an inflatable plug-in fountain and hired caterers dressed as Hawaiians in wild sport shirts or skirts with *leis* for his engagement party. It was attended by the stylish and expensively dressed sons and daughters of Soviet and Eastern European diplomats and Politburo members, or Yummies – young upwardly mobile Marxists. Later that evening, at another party, Steve and I were brushing up our rhyming Cockney when a most unattractive woman rushed straight across the room towards us.

'Do you recognize me?' she asked. Neither of us did.

'I'm Joan Crawford.' We nearly choked on our drinks; it was Michael in drag, dressed as Joan Crawford.

'How do I look?' Michael asked, hopefully pursing his lips and swinging his hips.

Steve had to admit that Michael or Joan Crawford, or rather Michael as Joan Crawford, was the ugliest woman he had ever set eyes on. Michael was despondent. He had just quarrelled with his girlfriend Billy, now Billy the Bitch.

If parties were the *hors d'oeuvres*, clubs were the *entrées*. The culture of the city's clubs and bars may be young, but they are framed in a rich history of debauchery, drunks and brawls, cokeheads and coitus. The New York club scene is a surreal journey through a post-nuclear landscape of warehouses and tunnels decorated with stuffed Dobermans, fishtanks and psychedelic gadgetry. In the meat district, home to pretty boys, rough trade and leather-clad crypto-Nazis, one club featured a human horse – a man bent over with a saddle harnessed to his back, mounted by women with their feet in the stirrups, their hands on the reins riding the bucking bronco around the dance floor. In several clubs, the androgynous nature, the exchangeability of gender of the revellers, makes it all but impossible to decipher one sex from the other – an

X-rated Disneyland from the dungeons of the imagination – clothes from a theatrical wardrobe with men dressed in frocks and skintight tights to look feline and svelte.

At many of the most fashionable clubs – their lifespan measured in nanoseconds – I went through the humiliating process of being vetted by the doorman. If you were neither distractingly attractive nor obviously rich you remained amongst a sea of clamouring, desperate masses held at bay by velvet ropes and bouncers dressed in black.

On entering the shop in the morning, Ginny never failed to remind us of the dangers of casual sex without a condom.

'Give us a break,' said Pam; 'using a condom is like taking a shower wearing a raincoat.'

'Or your socks in the bath,' Steve added.

AIDS wasn't the only danger; another more ancient plague, a chemical-dependent one, was slowly but surely eating its way through the fabric of society. Desperately, Al had succumbed to the euphoria of a 'hit'. He sometimes skipped work. When he did show up he suffered from bouts of depression and paranoia and tried to conquer his depression by getting high again. And so began his compulsive bingeing or 'chasing the high', drugs to fly or to fall, to electrify or motorize you. The only built-in defence for many is running out of money. First it's the draining of your savings account, then the charge-card credit lines, then the household items, VCR, TV, answering machine and finally your watch.

Michael's depression over Billy didn't last long.

'Hi! How are you?' asked Michael, greeting a customer.

'Fine thanks, and you?' asked the browser as a matter of form.

'Well, if you must know . . .' Michael proceeded to tell the stranger his life story.

'I'm really a domestic type. How about you?' Michael finished.

'I've just returned from Stockholm,' said the customer.

'How's Stockholm these days?' Michael asked, although he had never left the eastern seaboard of the United States.

Another customer asked Michael if the Cecil Beaton books were for sale. 'Everything is for sale, even some of us – for a price.'

* * *

After a few weeks the frenetic pace of New York life was beginning to take over; in addition to my doing overtime at Paul Smith, the early hours of the morning were taken up by a cleaning job and on my day off I was working as an assistant to Barney, a picture restorer. However, there was still time for dates with JAPS – Jewish American Princesses, WASPS – White Anglo-Saxon Protestants, SINKS – Single Income No Kids, and Euro-Trash. Quite often the only time to call a girlfriend for a date was during the shop's lunch break. Ginny only allowed us short calls, but it wasn't always easy to disengage from a phone conversation. Julia, who lived on the Upper East Side of Manhattan, spent the better part of ten minutes telling me about her impact aerobics: 'My biceps need all the *overload* they can get. I bring my body to fatigue. My muscles *burn* and I cry from exhaustion . . .' but it kept her trim. Her biggest problem in life seemed to be the $800 lace curtains that had shrunk two inches. When I hung up, the rest of Paul Smith could be heard saying goodbye to her on the phone – they had been listening to us on the public address system Speak-a-Phone and the conversation had been heard throughout the shop.

Ginny explained to Pam and me that holding down two jobs was no excuse for arriving late. One morning to save time I hopped into a cab. The driver was listening to a Paul McCartney song on the radio. During one of the song's choruses the driver turned to me and asked if I understood the words. No, I couldn't make head or tail of it. As far as I could tell the choruses were simply hummed to match the tune. The driver translated: 'I'll shit all over you . . . you mother fuckers.' He read my bewilderment in his rearview mirror. 'Ah,' he explained, 'you may wonder how I know. Well, I'm from the planet Mars too. There are many of us here in New York and we take on many disguises.'

He was right. Several days later, while I was going home on the subway, a man entered my carriage between stations. He was dressed in silver foil, wore twin antennae on his head and was playing the theme tune to *The Twilight Zone* on his saxophone. He interrupted his tune to tell his incredible story: 'You might not believe this, but I am from Mars and my spaceship has crashed. No one will accept my Martian money so please give me some spare change.'

The woman next to me hadn't given the Martian a second look. She, like many others, remained engrossed in her reading material. I looked over her shoulder; she was reading a worn paperback: '*In Julie's case the initial consideration of her therapist was to control and in time eliminate her colourful psychotic symptoms.*'

It was through my Samoan friend Lelei Le Laulu that I met Margaret, who was tall with hair somewhere between the last flame of sunset and gold. She had been born into a White Anglo-Saxon Protestant family but had converted to Buddhism. Her apartment was furnished in Laura Ashley 1920s English with one difference: in the corner of her living room was an ornate Japanese shrine to Buddha with small bowls of food placed in front as offerings. Margaret was unemployed and spent two hours each morning kneeling before her shrine, chanting for a job. She nagged me all summer to attend one of her Buddhist meetings, explaining that she had to bring a new person to each seance; if she didn't it would bring her bad karma. But as I was to discover when I eventually agreed to attend a session, this was Buddhism USA. The congregation cheered, clapped and chanted for material wealth, large incomes and financial prosperity. The beautiful congregation of actors, models, fashion designers, art critics and accountants gave testimony to the power of the mantra 'Nam Myoho Renge Kyo' which had been handed to me on a visiting card as I entered the apartment where a former actress had converted a large living room into a temple.

After twenty minutes of chanting from their holy book several members of the congregation stood to give testimony on how Gonyo, which was explained to me as the motor or the assiduous practice of chanting, had entered their lives; the mantra or chant was the gasoline for the motor. Jackie Munroe, an aspiring director, had been chanting for seven years: 'I want to bring into *focus* what I want to change and happen – I've made a lot of money, I'm very successful, but I want a challenge, I'm on hold for something. But having become a Buddhist and since *chanting* I've been asked to make a video.' The congregation roared their approval and applauded her success.

Another member, Herbie Jacobowitz, told us: 'I chanted to be the best in my job, to be my own boss, have my own practice, but I had a lot of bad karma. I kept calling for guidance and chanting to make lots of money – my Daimoku [reciting out loud] was really powerful and I now run my own very successful practice.'

On the way out of the apartment the Hancho or leader told me that, 'Just one person chanting "Nam Myoho Renge Kyo" can change the destiny of this country. If you slack even a bit the demons will take over. It's not brain-controlling, it's not a cookie cruncher, but the mirror of life.'

The following weekend Margaret was to attend a Simulcast (simultaneous broadcast) when their Japanese spiritual leader would talk 'live' from Los Angeles to his many followers across the United States. Two years later, Margaret was still trying to convert me to Buddhism; she told me she had irrefutable proof of the power of chanting: 'During the San Francisco earthquake all our San Francisco members were protected and their houses were un-damaged by the quake.'

The closest I got to returning to painting was when I worked with Barney on restoring valuable works by twentieth-century masters. Having just restored a large abstract painting by Clifford Still we were somewhat miffed by a passer-by's comment that the painting looked like 'chocolate ice-cream splashed on the Spanish flag'. But then a tour of the Metropolitan Museum one Sunday with a friend revealed an altogether more accessible view of art history. In the fifth century BC Attic pottery she saw 'little dicks'. The room of Dutch masters was proof that 'Van Dyck must have been gay', and in the Met's room of remarkable Roman statues my companion stood in awe. 'Look at those bodies!' she marvelled. 'When I was in my drug period, I liked medieval painting,' she added matter-of-factly. Many culture vultures passed by the museum's original works of art to sit in a room where they could look at reproductions of the originals in a catalogue. 'The originals are so big and untidy,' one student complained. Compared with the television, magazine, not to say shopping-bag, table-mat and playing-card formats of the paintings they were used to, the originals appeared crude. In these the 'nasty pimples' – the artist's unique brushstroke and texture that they found so distracting – had been eliminated in one stroke.

Whilst many people still mock the American abstract

expressionist Jackson Pollock, his drip paintings have found new life printed on jeans worn by the young and trendy. The sliced canvases of Lucio Fontana have been synthesized into expensive designer-ripped jeans. The ragged, hip look could be achieved by taking a knife to any pair of jeans but you had to pay a designer to know where to rip for the best look. Art dealers were marketing graffiti, art appropriating life – or is it the other way around? In vogue were the graffiti-faced subway stations, walls, trains, paintings, drawings, watches, towels, T-shirts, pencils and pants. Art and money, commerce and marketing were inextricably linked together in a secular society whose social status or mark of distinction and existence was financial and self-centred. Since everyone focused on the visible, many people believed they could buy a new identity with a new set of clothes, and ironically, people from the safe, affluent neighbourhoods bought cast-off clothes from those who spent a week's salary to buy a pair of Azzedine Alaia shoes on credit.

I had many excuses for not returning to my art; there was no room at my aunt's, who objected to my long hair tied into a braided ponytail. This meant I had to creep into her apartment via the back door so her bridge partners wouldn't see me. As for finances: I could hardly complain when I spent half a week's salary on drinks at a trendy nightclub – I had no one to blame but myself.

It was a chance encounter that led me back into the past – my travels in Afghanistan – and to question my future. Lelei, who was working at the United Nations as editor of *Secretariat News*, told me that a representative of the Afghan mujahedeen was in town. As luck would have it the mujahedeen representative was Professor Rabbani, leader of the Jamiat-i-Islami of Afghanistan, the group with whom I had travelled clandestinely in Afghanistan in 1984. I went to meet him at the Roosevelt Hotel on Madison Avenue. As I entered the suite I was transported back to his country. Two rooms were packed with more than thirty or forty Afghans all dressed in the traditional dress of shalwar camise and Chitrali hat. A pile of shoes stood heaped by the door. Everyone stood up to greet me with salaams. I was beckoned to take a seat in a chair. I felt honoured, but also embarrassed and amused at the same time, for as I looked around the room the Afghans had moved into every available space; they sat cross-legged on the double bed, on the floor, on the chairs and radiator covers. Each time a newcomer entered, we all half rose to greet him with little murmured enquiries before sitting down to collect ourselves again and resuming our conversation. In a single stroke the fourteenth-floor room of a Manhattan hotel had been turned into a small corner of Afghanistan. What little Dari I had learnt was almost forgotten, but several spoke English. I immediately asked for news of my friends: Abdullahjon, the commander of Hauze Karbas, a village I had stayed in, had died as the result of a mine explosion. I thought back to the ferocious battles that had raged around Herat. Ismail Khan, the local Jamiat supreme commander, was still alive, but the battle was by no means over. When was I planning to return? they asked. It was a painful question, one to which I did not know the answer. My initial embarrassment over etiquette was now subsumed by the paucity of my present pathetic city life.

As I walked home I realized that I had lost direction: I was coasting. I was torn between the unchallenging, undemanding life I was leading with the comforts of a steady job and the carefree but precarious life of a nomad. I missed the space, adventure, distance, history and danger of travelling into remote and inaccessible areas of the world, cut off by cultural proscription, geography and war. But the naked force and the art and joy of living that I had felt in distant lands were also rooted in New York, a stimulating, dynamic city for its multi-layered and multi-cultured components, a city that was both challenging and needed to be challenged, its dynamic and eclectic culture walking a tightrope between enlightenment and disintegration.

The destitution and degradation I had witnessed in developing countries was for many here a daily reality. A sign held by a beggar on the subway read: 'I have AIDS, my wife has left me, my kids have deserted me, I am hungry and homeless.' Not a single day passed when the newspaper didn't feature a grisly tale of horrific murder: a thirteen-year-old girl beaten to death by her mother's boyfriend; a tramp knifed in the subway in a fight over a turkey leg; three teenagers who methodically set fire to a homeless couple. When at first the rubbing alcohol wouldn't ignite the couple, they went to a local service station for gasoline.

In the United States one person dies from gunshot wounds every sixteen minutes. More poignantly, more people die from gunshot wounds and are murdered each year in New York City than Soviet soldiers were killed annually in their war with Afghanistan. (Soviet records admit that 15,000 Soviet soldiers died during the ten years of the Afghan war.) I discovered later whilst on a lecture tour in Florida that I could buy an AK-47 semi-automatic assault rifle for less money in West Palm Beach than I could in either war-torn Afghanistan or Pakistan, and what's more, I could pay by credit card. In some New York neighbourhoods life expectancy rates are actually lower than in developing countries. One report shows that black men in Harlem have less chance of living to fifty than the inhabitants of Bangladesh.

I didn't feel my painting could address these problems. I wanted to travel again, and I hoped that my photography could see through what is perceived as exotic and focus on the harsh daily realities of the less fortunate. I resolved to try and find work that would allow me to travel to those parts of the world where people were caught up in civil strife, wars and persecution.

Ginny asked if I would stay until after Paul Smith's visit from London – there would be a lot of extra work as Paul's US retailers would be visiting to see next year's collection.

Margaret was going through a crisis; she had been visited by a mouse in the night. Worse was to come. She was forced to call in the exterminator – she suggested he stay for three days to make sure the coast was clear. He couldn't, and so as an extra measure she barricaded herself into her bedroom. To her horror, the mouse, unable to gain entry to her bedroom, devoured the little bowls of food she had placed beneath her shrine as offerings to Buddha.

On the day Paul Smith was meant to arrive in New York, Michael was serving a couple who had remarked on the beautiful antique ties.

'Have you ever smelt the aroma from a cabinet of new ties?' Michael asked solicitously.

'No, we haven't,' the pair replied.

'I get a real *rush* – a "hit" – off them every morning when I stick my head into the cabinet,' Michael explained, and suggested they try it.

The two customers got down on their knees, placed their heads in the cabinet and took deep breaths.

'What are they doing?' asked a tall, smartly-dressed gentleman who had just entered the shop.

Michael described the buzz. 'Would you like to try?' Whilst the polished gentleman waited his turn he asked Michael his name.

'Hi! I'm Michael, what's your name?'

'Paul – Paul Smith.'

Michael was promoted. Al quit his job. Margaret's bad karma changed through chanting and she found work, and a club called Mars was opened in a former meat-packing plant where Martians could find high energy, vibration and non-rational behaviour. I returned to Europe.

It was nearly a year before I finally got my chance. In the late summer of 1988 news had reached the West of Iraqi chemical attacks on the Kurdish peoples living in northern Iraq and I was to leave immediately on a major photographic assignment for the *Sunday Telegraph*.

3

WHERE'S THE OUTRAGE?

> When the Shah of Iran asked in 1972 for secret American military aid to be given to the Kurdish rebels in Iraq, Kissinger agreed over the opposition of the CIA station in Tehran. When the Shah later embarked on a policy of reconciliation with Iraq the Kurds were abruptly cut off; at least 35,000 were killed and more than 200,000 refugees were created.
>
> William Shawcross, *Sideshow*

> Both Iran and the US hope to benefit from an unresolvable situation in which Iraq is intrinsically weakened by the Kurds' refusal to give up their semi-autonomy. Neither Iran nor the US would like to see the situation resolved one way or the other.
>
> CIA memorandum, 1974

> Kurds have no friends.
>
> A favourite Kurdish saying

Kurdistan, September 1988

Losing patience, Trisha screamed, 'This is not a Mickey Mouse operation!' I was on the phone trying to explain the delay to my photo agent. It had been impossible to catch a scheduled flight from

Heathrow to Istanbul – the air traffic control computer at West Drayton had gone down. I was now at Gatwick trying to hitch a lift to Turkey on a charter flight. In the background a group of drunken passengers on a delayed flight to Ibiza were chanting inappropriately, ''Ere we go, 'ere we go, 'ere we go!'

It was nearly midnight and my chances of reaching Turkey were fading fast. My hopes rested on a student flight to Istanbul. Minutes before take-off, with the 'last call' light flashing, a flight supervisor told me I could board the plane; there was one spare seat at the back.

I sat in the confined space of the chartered jet with my knees tucked under my chin, sandwiched between two students. One of them, Miriam, had just graduated from the French Lycée in London and was going to Istanbul to visit her family. The other, like most of the passengers on the flight, was going on holiday for the sun and sand of the Aegean and Mediterranean.

I was heading for the inhospitable mountains between Iraq, Iran and Turkey where tens of thousands of Iraqi Kurds were fleeing for their lives from Iraqi chemical attacks. Trisha had called me and asked if I was prepared to go to Turkey to photograph the Kurdish refugees. I didn't hesitate. I packed a small bag with a change of clothes and waterproof poncho and left for the picture agency to pick up an advance and some film.

As the plane reached its cruising altitude I checked that I hadn't forgotten anything – pencils, masking tape, notepad?

I opened the notepad.

'Do you speak Turkish?' I asked Miriam.

'Yes, but it's a little rusty,' she explained.

I reeled off a list for her to translate that said much about where I hoped to go and what I expected to see – refugees, hospitals, tents, medicines, casualties, family . . . Meanwhile several students were fingering their Turkish survival kits: guides on how, in Turkish, to get to the beach, the cheapest *pension* and the bus station.

On arrival in Istanbul I hoped to transfer to a flight to the eastern part of Turkey but it would be a long wait. No flights were scheduled to leave until the afternoon, and the nearest airport to my eventual destination was still a further twelve hours by bus, and then some. I seemed to be getting further and further from my goal.

Miriam suggested I join her on the students' coach into town; she didn't want to wake her family, it was too late but equally too early to telephone.

The coach driver played Frank Sinatra; we glimpsed various Ottoman mosques through the darkness and the students were dropped at different hostels. Beneath the Topkapi and Haghia Sophia, Miriam and I sat at a table in old Stamboul. There was no one to serve coffee or *chai*, but within a matter of hours the sleeping city rose to a deafening roar, drowning out all sounds of the birdsong that had serenaded us as the golden dawn broke over the Bosporus.

I spent the morning in the Iranian consulate in a bid to get a visa to enter Iran to cover the Kurdish plight from the Iranian side. The Iranians weren't always helpful to the Kurdish population – their own, Iraq's or Turkey's – at the best of times. However, in a moment of solidarity, wrenching pictures of dead bodies with horrific burns had been pinned to the consulate's walls. These were the result of an Iraqi chemical attack on Halabja which had annihilated the village's 4,000 inhabitants, who suffocated to death.

I left the consulate empty-handed; Tehran wouldn't authorize a visa. I had waited at the consulate until the last possible minute before my flight to Adana in southern Turkey in the vain hope that it might reconsider its decision.

In telephone conversations, the Turkish authorities hadn't been much more helpful than the Iranians. They too considered the Kurds inferior, banning their language and their music and even outlawing Kurdish names. To sing a Kurdish song could bring a jail sentence. My best bet was simply to head for the most easterly part of the country where the refugees were most likely to enter Turkey. My only tip had been that some of the casualties were being taken to a hospital in Cizre some twenty miles from the border with Iraq.

Waiting for my bus at Adana I spoke to a Turkish schoolteacher who was keen to practise his English on me. Beneath his contempt for the Kurds was a vein of distrust and fear. 'They're so dirty, they have too many children, they're underdeveloped and indifferent to the civilizing things in life.' He couldn't understand why I was interested in their plight, although he admitted that the chemical attacks on the Iraqi Kurds were 'unfortunate'. I concluded that to the Turks the Kurds were the bringers of pollution and ill-fortune.

From Adana I travelled through the night and the best part of the morning by bus to Cizre. The dramatic scenery of soft rolling barren hills like worn velvet, plains to the south and mountains to the north, bespoke a harsh, impoverished existence. Here and there, choking dust tracks led off the main road to small mud-walled settlements scraping by on subsistence living. When the bus stopped in towns we were besieged by eager children working as street vendors. I shopped well from my bus seat and, likewise, for the locals the bus stop is a lifeline.

It was with a mixture of anticipation and trepidation that I arrived at Cizre: the thrill I always experience on arriving in a new town tempered by the horror of what I might find there. As we approached the town I was greeted by a scene from biblical times: men in the fields with their flocks, women down by the river washing clothes. The town was half asleep in the approaching midday heat. There were a few market stalls in a wide, littered and dusty street where men dressed in baggy trousers sat amongst their produce. Within minutes of the bus disgorging its passengers, I was alone at the bus station. I walked into the main road and asked directions to the hospital. Eventually, I was taken there on the back of a horse-drawn cart.

The resident doctor, a Turk from Ankara, was one of only a handful of Turks in the town. Yes, he had heard of casualties from the chemical attacks but he hadn't seen any. It remained a mystery as to where the victims were being taken. The doctor had nothing to hide; he showed me around the grim and dilapidated wards and invited me to take lunch with him in the lower ground-floor canteen, where our view was restricted to the hoofs of cows as they rubbed themselves against the hospital's outer walls.

After lunch the doctor escorted me to the edge of town and directed me towards the refugee camp at Silopi, only a few miles from the border with Iraq. Silopi, like Cizre, is on the main highway to Iraq where daily hundreds upon hundreds of oil tankers trundle back and forth carrying precious Iraqi oil to Turkey and its Mediterranean ports for export. I hitched a lift on one such tanker. No sooner had I told the driver I was from England than he proceeded to talk football:

'Gary Lineker – good footballer, Shilton, Anderson, Robson . . .' The Turkish truck driver knew the whole England team by heart.

We passed Silopi and were closing in on the border with Iraq when the refugee camp came into sight. The driver put me down 500 metres from it; he didn't want to be seen dropping me too close.

It had been a wise precaution. The camp, normally a rest stop for pilgrims *en route* to Mecca, had been transformed into something of a military base with the army at one end and the refugees at the other. Two guards in military fatigues blocked my entrance. A senior officer was summoned. He checked my credentials: my passport and a very battered fake press card. I signed my name in a registrar's book and then the officer escorted me across the camp to a handful of Turkish relief workers who sat in the shade of an outhouse, drinking *chai* and looking bored. They didn't want to be photographed. The military officer quickly tired of me and returned to the temporary barracks. I walked across to the infirmary where a doctor and two nurses were besieged by a tide of exhausted and wretched refugees. Women and children were asleep on the floor, mothers were nursing their babies. The makeshift infirmary's small rooms and hall echoed to the sounds of coughing and cries. The small team of medical workers were processing the refugees in conveyor-belt fashion with vaccinations. With 16,000 refugees already packed into the camp without proper hygiene facilities, contagious diseases and diarrhoea were a real danger.

These people had fled their valleys and villages in panic. Families had become separated; wives had lost their husbands; children had lost their parents. Uncertainty shrouded their missing brothers', sisters' and husbands' fate.

They had no vehicles to help them in their escape and their livestock had either perished or been left behind. They had trekked for several days across 2,200-metre (7,500-foot) mountains: shoeless grandmothers, old peasants haggard and bent double from years of toiling in the fields, and children as young as five carrying babies strapped to their backs. Terrorized and chased from their country, they entered the unknown with nothing but the clothes they wore. Surrendering to the Turkish authorities, they were promptly shepherded into refugee camps. Some considered themselves lucky; the Iraqi army had now created a *cordon sanitaire* along the border: anyone attempting to cross would be shot on sight. Those Kurds who lived too far from the border remained trapped inside Iraq with no means of escape.

The Kurds are a non-Arab Muslim people. Over twenty million of them are spread through Turkey, Iran, Iraq, Syria and the Soviet Union. Most had been shepherds raising sheep and goats. They had lived in the mountains as far back as their communal history could be recounted, although the moments they had lived in peace were admittedly rare. Life under Arab, Turkish and Iranian rule had never been easy. Following the collapse of the Ottoman Empire after World War I, the Treaty of Sèvres in 1920 promised them an independent state, but this was never ratified. Instead Britain annexed the oil-rich Kurdish region of Mosul to Iraq, then a British mandate. The Kurds had lost many campaigns for autonomy and are treated with hostility by most of their host governments, who have prohibited the teaching of their language, razed their villages, denied many of them citizenship and forcibly deported others. During the course of the twentieth century, the world's largest stateless minority has on several occasions been betrayed and neglected by foreign governments. In recent years Syria, Iran and Turkey have given military aid to Iraqi Kurds. Syria has also supplied military aid to Turkish Kurds, as has Iraq which has also given military assistance to Iranian Kurds. In each case the assistance to rebellious Kurds has only been enough to create a nuisance, never enough to enable them to break loose and become independent.

In the last few years, since the beginning of the Iran–Iraq Gulf War, they had been chased, persecuted, decimated, forcibly deported, expelled and exterminated on political, racial and religious grounds by the Baghdad regime. Some had correctly predicted that, when the war between Iran and Iraq ended, Iraq would set the might of its armed forces on its irrepressible Kurdish population.

Nothing, however, had prepared them for the venom of the slaughter that was to take place. The refugees recounted how the first sign had been the smell of the acrid gas, even before they heard the jets and helicopters and the explosions releasing their deadly toxic charge. I was given an account by a woman who had watched her father die as he stood by a stream with his grazing flock. Others recounted how they had fled up the mountainsides and watched the onslaught of phosphorus bombs. Civilians had been deliberately targeted. The fields and villages were strewn with corpses. Two women told me they had watched their children killed by strafing as they tried to join them on the mountainside. No one knew how many had been killed in the attacks.

Here in the clinic were the agonized cries of the survivors, and the grief and trauma of having been brutally uprooted from their homes and valleys for reasons beyond their understanding. Bewilderment and incomprehension surrounded the events that led them to flee their birthplace and homelands. Very few had ever left their tight-knit communities – some had been to Baghdad, slightly more had been to the Kurdish and oil-rich city of Kirkuk.

Access to their lands had been difficult at the best of times. The steep and narrow valleys had always given them a certain degree of protection and enabled them to continue a way of life unhindered by central authority. The aerial bombardment had, however, irrevocably altered the equilibrium which had been in place for centuries. A people who had never been subdued by land forces and had up to this day maintained a formidable guerrilla resistance that had held the invaders at bay, suddenly found that the odds were changed.

As I walked into the main area of the camp, I found a vast amalgam of tents and shelters improvised from blankets, carpets, clothes and strips of material and sections of plastic held together to form crude protection against the elements. Many slept in the open. The tired and frightened refugees were grouped together in pathetic bundles of exhaustion, often fast asleep, huddled together in domino patterns. Each represented the misery of a broken family, an abandoned home, a flight into the unknown, pain, despair and destitution.

A curious thing happened as I entered this part of the camp: the tranquillity was abruptly shattered. News of my arrival had travelled quickly through the camp and a massive, heckling crowd came storming towards me. My camera captured the mob as it approached and finally engulfed me. The children were in the vanguard, shouting and chanting battle cries; they waved their arms and clenched their fists, their wild blue eyes unfocused with frustration, anguish and rage. I continued to photograph the sea of faces. People were pushing, shoving and jostling, and I was finding it difficult to stay on my feet. The grown-ups tried to offer me some protection from the crowd, but were themselves jostling and shoving to get to the front. Emotions were running high, the deafening screams now at a startling pitch. Several men created a small distance between me and the seething mass, but the distance kept breaking down as the mass pushed forward. Whichever way I moved, the crowd moved with me; there was a serious risk of tents and shelters being trampled underfoot. The women and smaller children sat impassively throughout the disturbance. I decided to put as much distance as possible between myself and the main area of the camp in the hope of losing the crowd, and partially succeeded by reaching a mound at the far end.

My feeling of relief was momentary. Quite suddenly the sound of semi-automatic gunfire reverberated all around. Terror and panic swept through the camp. Old men stood bewildered and lost, women and children were screaming and crying hysterically. Clutching my cameras, I ran towards the Turkish soldiers who were indiscriminately shooting the defenceless refugees. There was no escape.

The refugees were dragging the dead, dying and injured away from the barracks and back into the camp. In the background above their heads I could see the soldiers lined up, holding their guns ready to shoot again. Sprawled on the ground in front of me was a man whose head had been partially blown away. His friend picked him up and cradled him, looking at me despairingly, his face pleading and full of anguish. I photographed. There was nothing I could do. The man was dead.

Another man lay injured not far away, surrounded by enraged men. Some of the children had caught sight of his horrific wounds. A young girl screamed uncontrollably, she *screamed* and *screamed* and *screamed*.

There was a steady train of injured; a man was swept along the ground on a blanket, blood gushing from a wound. I was taken to a tent where a man had a bullet wound in his stomach. He lay on an improvised bed; as he breathed, part of his intestine moved through the wound. I felt sick. I also feared for my own safety; the soldiers knew I was in the camp and they wouldn't relish a journalist broadcasting the barbaric treatment they had meted out to the refugees.

A Kurdish man grabbed me by the arm and led me back through the camp. I hid amongst the Kurds and was moved from tent to tent. Children were posted throughout the camp to warn me of approaching soldiers. I thought of escaping, but by the time I had devised a plan to get over the compound wall Turkish commandos had been brought in and we were surrounded. I set about hiding my film, crucial evidence of their fatal aggression.

I thought desperately about the various possibilities of hiding the film and decided to dismantle my telephoto lens and hide the films in the lens casing. I was sweating profusely and had the greatest difficulty with the miniature screws. The sweat poured from me, clouding my vision and making it all but impossible to work with my hands. It was a ridiculous choice anyway; you could see the film inside the lens. As I searched for an alternative hiding place my publishers' words came back to me: 'Be careful, don't get into any trouble.' I didn't want to die! I thought how often I had said that to myself and also, after each dangerous journey, 'That was the last.' Yet here I was again. But then I thought how lucky I had been. I considered the humility of these extraordinary people and the dignity they had maintained under such inhumane and trying circumstances, compared to which my plight seemed insignificant. And so with renewed effort I searched for a way to hide my film.

I thought back to customs and airport security checks. What had they considered the most and least obvious hiding places? I looked through my camera bag and remembered that they had checked the unwrapped cartridges of film but not the forty rolls of unexposed film which remained intact, still untouched in their original boxes and thin cellophane sleeves at the bottom of the bag. I set about carefully opening the cellophane sleeves and replaced the virgin rolls of film with exposed rolls. Now I needed to reseal the boxes and the cellophane. I explained to the woman in the tent that I needed some glue. I tried everything to make her understand 'glue', but to no avail. However, as I worked with the boxes of film, the woman, her two children and the man who had brought me to the tent became fascinated by my attempts. With no glue I decided to use my masking tape to close the boxes. I began by folding the tape over onto itself, making it double-sided. The woman immediately stopped me proceeding any further. She left the tent and minutes later returned with a tiny roll of Sellotape. Now everyone was engaged in the spirit of the task. 'Glue' was concocted from sugar and water, and the job was completed. The cellophane didn't look perfect; there was a small tear down one side, but it did appear as though it had never been opened, which was the desired effect.

Before surrendering to the authorities I walked around the camp, taking in all I had seen. I was escorted by several men in turbans and the traditional brown overalls and distinctive waistbands of the Kurdish resistance fighters, the peshmerga, which means literally and, after the day's events all too prophetically, those who face death. Their despondency was total. As they saw it, their struggle for self-determination or independence was over; with no friends and no defence against chemical weapons they felt crushed. Now their immediate concern was that the Turkish troops should refrain from further indiscriminate shooting. They had massed in the open clearing to protest against the arrival of two Iraqi agents in the camp; the soldiers' answer to the demonstration had been to open fire on the protesters. Once again they felt embittered and forced into submission by a brutally hostile force. Their future was bleak, their choice stark: they could return to Iraq; Saddam Hussein had appealed to them to come home and promised an amnesty whilst he continued to strafe lines of fugitives and bomb and shell their villages, or they could accept Turkish hospitality and remain at the mercy of the Turkish army. They pleaded for international help which would never arrive.

The peshmerga took me to a man injured in the chemical attacks. As I entered the tent a young man propped him up.

'Look at his eyes,' said the young man, who spoke some English. The whites of the victim's eyes were no longer visible, they were completely bloodshot. I had no way of knowing what had caused this.

'Why is he here?' I asked.

'We are keeping him here because when we first arrived they

took all the injured people away and they won't tell us where they have been taken.'

'What about the men injured in today's shooting?'

'We had no choice but to ask the Turkish authorities to help, otherwise the men would most certainly die.'

I was curious as to where he had learnt his English. 'I speak French as well; I studied tourism in Baghdad.' He looked up at the group of gaunt, strong, unshaven faces lost in the uncertainties of exile.

We passed young children, some still crying inconsolably for their lost parents; other children cried because they heard others cry. A twelve-year-old girl sat alone in a tent; hopelessly vulnerable, she looked forlorn and melancholic, a statue of robbed innocence. Some mothers began to cook bread, their dinner, on hot plates resting on stones. The men had agreed to go on hunger strike to protest against their treatment and the massacre.

I took some last pictures in the fading light, but neither my mind nor my heart was in it. I was thinking about what the authorities would do to me. Several rows of tents before the open ground and the barracks, the peshmerga and a group of children bade me farewell and wished me luck.

As I crossed the open ground, two uniformed soldiers came forward and arrested me. They took me to a clearing next to the barracks. One of them took my camera bag away and I was given a seat before being questioned by five men in civilian clothes, all of whom were armed. They weren't soldiers. They were almost certainly the much-hated special Interior Ministry police force, the Ozel Tim, formed to fight the Turkish PKK insurgency.

'*Sprechen Sie Deutsch?*' one of them asked. A tall brutish man kept his sub-machine-gun trained on me.

'No.'

'*Parlez-vous français?*'

'*Oui.*' They questioned me in French.

'What are you doing here?'

'I came to take pictures,' I explained.

'Who do you work for?' This was a question I knew was going to come up. I worried about the fake press card I had presented to the officer when I entered the camp. I told them I worked freelance for a photographic agency. My interrogator was unimpressed.

'What pictures did you take?'

'The tents, families, children, the infirmary.'

'Nothing else?'

'No.' My interrogator didn't sound convinced.

'What did you see in the camp?' he asked.

I tried to give what sounded like an honest but naïve account. 'At one point there was a commotion, I heard some bangs, I was at the far end of the camp. Later, I saw a man with a stomach wound.'

'Did you take any pictures of him?'

'No,' I lied.

The questioning stopped. They went through my camera bag and took all the opened rolls of film, but they left the two packages of 'unused' film in the bag. There was a long silence punctuated by groups of soldiers passing to and fro in quick marches. Close by, five or six Kurdish men were standing in a shallow open pit guarded by some soldiers. I sat gloomily as the night chill began to cut through me like a knife. The tall man pointing his gun at me ordered me to stand against the barracks wall. I braced myself. After what seemed an eternity I began to shiver under the eerie glow of stadium lights. My heart was pounding wildly; I was terrified. As I was being searched a military officer joined the group. He looked at me contemptuously and scowled what sounded like an order to the man questioning me.

'What did he say?' I asked.

'He said you should be shot in the interests of national security.'

I blurted out, 'What about my companion?'

'What companion?' my interrogator demanded.

'The one I arrived with.'

I made up a story to persuade them to believe I wasn't on my own. I had to establish that it was known I had come to the Silopi camp and that if I disappeared people would come asking all sorts of difficult questions.

I invented a name for my non-existent companion and embellished the cover story as I went along. 'Paul Davison, he works for an American newspaper . . . He dropped me near the refugee camp . . . We agreed to meet later.'

Abruptly a sense of urgency overtook my inquisitors. They wanted all the details: my companion's age, his nationality, the type of vehicle he was driving and where and what time we had agreed to meet.

We were going through the details when all of a sudden a flurry of activity transformed the camp and halted the questioning. The soldiers started to line up in formation and my five interrogators stood to attention. A helicopter and a cavalcade of black limousines and military jeeps brought the province's governor and military commander to the camp. The governor and commander made a cursory inspection of the soldiers, conferred with several officers and left as suddenly and in the same sweeping cavalcade as they had come. I had tried to appeal to the governor, one of the interrogators trying unsuccessfully to stop me: nonetheless, my pleas to be released fell on deaf ears.

The questioning resumed. They wanted to meet Paul. 'At what time are you going to meet your friend?'

It was now around eight o'clock. I told the Ozel Tim that we had agreed to meet at about six o'clock.

'Where?'

'At the bus station in Cizre.'

In the distance, as we walked to a car, I could see a hundred or more Kurdish civilians sitting on the ground in rows, their hands on their heads; they were being herded silently into two open trucks.

I sat in the back of the car sandwiched between two of the men. One man in the front left his submachine gun resting on the hand brake. On the outskirts of Cizre we were stopped at a roadblock. The driver wound down his window, conferred with the soldiers and we were waved through.

The bus station was deserted. 'There's no one here,' they remarked angrily. 'Where is he?'

'I don't know,' I said weakly.

'Why isn't he here?'

'I was meant to meet him three hours ago. He probably gave up waiting and is wondering what has happened to me.'

'Where do you think he went?'

'Our plan was to head for Hakkari or Diyarbakir; we hadn't decided. Maybe he checked into a hotel for the night,' I said helpfully.

'Which one?' they asked.

'I don't know, we hadn't planned on staying here.' They checked all the hotels. I didn't think there would be many hotels in the small town of Cizre, but surprisingly there were a handful, and they were determined to find him. I sat back in the car – I was going to enjoy this charade chasing a ghost for as long as I could.

At each hotel three of my gaolers entered the reception area clutching their guns. One remained in the car guarding me. As they checked the hotel registers they grew increasingly impatient. At one hotel they kicked the young receptionist out into the street.

When they had finished we drove back along the road towards Silopi. At one of the first dust tracks beyond Cizre they pulled off the main road and headed towards the hills. My heart began to beat faster. They stopped the car and made me get out. One of them pulled me around to the back of the car and placed a gun to my head. The only light was from the car's headlights.

'You say you are a photographer.'

'Yes.'

'Who is this American friend of yours?'

'Paul Davison, he's a journalist.'

He paused. 'Apart from your American friend, who else knows you are here?'

It was a menacing question. My heart began to pound again. Amongst themselves I heard them talk about the PKK – the Kurdish peshmerga. Out here the Ozel Tim could do anything they wanted. I realized they could easily put a bullet through my head and dump me in the mountains, and if I was ever found they could blame the Kurds. Foreigners had been kidnapped and shot by Kurdish separatists elsewhere, and the United States Department of State has for many years issued a caveat advising travellers not to leave the main highways in remote rural areas of Turkey or generally to drive at night.

'Does your embassy know you are here?'

They didn't, nor did anyone actually know I had gone to Cizre, but I wanted the Ozel Tim to believe that there was quite a list of people.

'There's my picture editor at the photographic agency, the newspaper that sent me on this assignment, my family – in fact they will already be worried because I telephone them every evening and they'll wonder why I haven't called.' I suggested they let me telephone them so that they wouldn't worry about me. They didn't answer.

One of the men opened the boot of the car and pulled out my camera bag. Were they going to leave me here? He walked with the bag towards the light and began to rummage through the contents. They had already confiscated all my loose film, but the rewrapped film was still in the camera bag.

Holding all the unwrapped film in their hands, they asked me again, 'Is this all the film you took?'

'Yes,' I replied.

'What about these?' One of them returned to my camera bag and began to unpack it.

'What are you talking about?' I swallowed hard.

He reached into the bag and pulled out the cameras. 'Is there any film inside?'

'Inside?'

'The cameras.'

It was an obvious place but one they had overlooked. They opened the cameras and pulled the rolls of film from them.

I was driven to a military barracks where an army officer took charge of me. The Ozel Tim seemed angered that they had to release me into the army's custody.

I had no idea what time it was. The major took me through a garden to a veranda where the province's military commander, the governor and various high-ranking officers had gathered. There was plenty of food and drink and I was told to eat. I had only eaten a small lunch in the past two days, but I wasn't hungry, I had no appetite. The officials sat around the table hardly speaking except to ask me questions. Who was I working for? What had I seen? Had I taken any pictures? I was to spend eighteen hours under repeated interrogation. I stuck to my story that I had seen only a single wounded man. I said I hadn't taken any pictures of him; besides, the Ozel Tim had taken all my film from me. I also said I was worried about my friend who had driven me to Cizre. Did they have any news of him? I asked to call my family or my editor or the newspaper – they knew I was here and would be worried if I didn't call. I asked the governor what they were going to do with me. Solemnly he said, 'We haven't decided.'

I spent the night incarcerated in another barracks. Whilst I was being driven there in a jeep, an argument broke out between two officers. 'What's your name?' one of the officers had asked me. 'Nick – and yours?' I answered politely. When the officer told me his name his companion severely reprimanded him for doing so. Such petty behaviour didn't give me cause for the slightest optimism. Once locked into a room I dared not sleep.

I was released the following day. No explanation was given and I considered it prudent not to ask for one. The officials returned my film, which they had processed, but the developed film was cloudy and failed to reveal any images, which must have surprised them. They even arranged a seat for me on the bus out of Silopi to Ankara. I thought I was free but, having been driven into Silopi, I was told not to leave the bus company's ticket office. Outside, across the street, were two of the Ozel Tim who had interrogated me; they were talking to three men I hadn't seen before. A sickening feeling returned to my stomach. The army had been positively pleasant compared to the Ozel Tim. I sat in my allocated seat on the bus only to discover I was being followed by one of the men who had been talking with the Ozel Tim. He sat one row behind me across the aisle. I could see the butt of a revolver sticking out from the bottom of his shirt.

As the bus pulled out of Silopi I remained nervous. They had said I could go, but was this some kind of trap? I turned around and looked at the man who was following me. I searched for clues and played a hundred and one scenarios over in my mind. I was overcome by tiredness but was fighting to stay alert. I kept thinking they might try to shoot me and dump my body somewhere. I tried to convince myself that there were too many witnesses. They would have to get me off the bus and to do so we would have to stop in the middle of nowhere. As we travelled across the bleak stretches of barren hills along the border with Syria, what I feared most was the noise of the engine decelerating. Several times we slowed to a crawl and I wondered each time whether it was the moment I had been anticipating. When the bus began to decelerate in jerky movements and I could see the driver pumping the brake, I began to panic and the adrenalin started to flow. Was this the moment I had steeled myself for?

The bus came to a stop close to a car that had been flattened in a crash. I was drenched in sweat and as I stared out of the window I thought how clever and convenient it would be to make my disappearance look like a road accident.

After a long delay, we reboarded the bus. I didn't return to my allocated seat; instead I went to the back where the man who was following me couldn't see me. No sooner had the bus driver moved into gear than my guard leapt from his seat screaming at him to stop. 'Where's the foreigner?' he shouted. I peered up from behind the back seats; the relief driver next to me was highly amused by my simple ruse, and I asked him where we would be stopping *en route* to Ankara. He told me Mardin, Kiziltepe, Gaziantep and Adana in the early hours of the morning. 'Are there any buses from Adana to Alanya and Antalya?' I asked.

He laughed, 'From Adana there are buses to everywhere.' I hoped to use the Adana airport as a quick gateway to Istanbul, and the information was just what I wanted to hear. A false trail would allow me a few extra hours in which to seek help.

When we reached Adana, I disembarked like most of the passengers, but then reboarded and disembarked several times, as is quite normal during lengthy stops. At one point, choosing my moment carefully, I disembarked with my bags and asked a rival bus company to hold them for me. The bus from Silopi blew its horn signalling our departure for Ankara. I had other ideas. I reboarded and walked past my original seat in front of the man following me so that he could see I was on the bus. I then made a show of retiring to the back of the bus, but just before we pulled away from the parking bay I left the vehicle by its back door praying that my 'shadow' wouldn't notice, ran to collect my bags and headed for the airport.

It was a nerve-racking wait. The first plane departure from Adana wasn't until eight o'clock. I had two hours to kill, so I bought a ticket for that first flight and joined some American soldiers. To calm my nerves, I asked, 'Where are you guys headed?'

'Get us some ass,' said the air force engineer. From what I gathered, their base to the south of Adana was a backwater in a sea of abstinence.

I reached Ankara and called the British embassy to tell them what had happened but, more importantly, that I was leaving Istanbul the same afternoon and wanted them to check that I had got on the plane. I called Trisha to put her in the picture and to expect me back that evening.

In London, mentally and physically exhausted, I had the film processed immediately. The images of the dead and dying civilians were all too graphic. The editor of the newspaper that had sent me on the assignment explained that their readers didn't want to have their breakfasts ruined. Two other national newspapers bought the pictures, but neither was prepared to carry them.

Back in New York, the picture editor of a leading magazine looked at the photograph of a refugee clutching his dying friend who had been shot in the head. 'It's a pity that the man's head isn't turned a bit more away from the camera,' he said.

Nearly three years later, some of these Kurdish refugees were still languishing in Turkey, interned in temporary settlements and forgotten by all.

4

BOOK TOUR

Almost everything we do is determined
by whether we think it will get on the
network news shows in the evening.

Larry Speakes, President Ronald Reagan's
chief White House spokesman

1988–January 1989

The launch of my first book, *Danziger's Travels*, had involved me in a
whirlwind publicity tour, travelling between Britain and the
eastern seaboard and west coast of the United States like a human
yo-yo. My callers on live phone-ins included irate right-wing
British, who jammed the BBC switchboard, and American communists. I gave lectures in packed libraries and arts centres and sat
at empty tables like a beached whale biting my lips waiting for
customers during book signing sessions. Fitted into the tight
schedule was an invitation to a reception at Kensington Palace at
which Prince Charles told the guests how as a child he had watched
Sir Winston Churchill fish for the Loch Ness Monster.

Now, in the new year of 1989, the tour almost over, I felt deflated.
It seemed a million light years ago that I had wondered who could
possibly be interested in my clandestine journey across much of
Asia disguised as an itinerant Muslim in turban and robes. I
remember going to my first local BBC talk show and how I had
begun to panic as I watched the studio clock count down each
second towards zero hour. What would the talk show host ask me?
How would I answer his questions? This is the easy part, I
reassured myself. The journey through unknown territory had
been the hard part, or so I mistakenly thought. After all, there was
no one to ambush me here in the security of the studio, and if I
stumbled the presenter would come to my rescue.

At exactly five minutes past the hour the green light blinked to red. The host switched mood to animated affability – we were on the air.

'Today's weather for the local area will be cold to begin with, followed by intermittent showers and sunny spells during the day with the possibility of drizzle later on . . . With me today in the studio is a young man . . .' The interviewer's finger began to trace the route of my journey across the map of the opened book, past the Ayatollah's Iran, across mujahedeen-held Afghanistan and over the closed areas of China and Tibet, until then unseen by foreigners since the Chinese revolution in 1949. His finger came to rest somewhere in South East Asia. 'Singapore, tell me about Singapore.'

I was caught off-guard. I hadn't expected to answer questions on Singapore. I remembered the counselling words of the publishers' publicity department: 'Don't expect everyone to have read your book.' What could I tell him about Singapore? I had spent one evening there amongst transvestites and prostitutes with the crew of the ship on which I was returning home. I protested gently, explaining how I had travelled by foot, camel and donkey cart along the ancient silk routes through Turkey, Iran, Afghanistan, Pakistan and China. 'Yes, but I'm interested in Singapore,' he persisted, 'I'm stopping there *en route* to Australia for my holidays.'

He did eventually get around to talking about Afghanistan: 'Tell me, Nick, how do the prices of Afghan carpets here compare with those in Afghanistan?'

This was not an auspicious beginning to a book tour and worse was to follow. As the interview drew to a close my host came to the book's photographs. He found the pictures had been printed upside down, an embarrassing moment for me even if I couldn't see my audience. Searching for an explanation I told him he had the cover the wrong way up, but indeed the photographs had been bound into the book upside down, one of only two copies found to have been misbound.

Just before appearing on a Washington cable channel, the host apologized to me for not having had time to read the book, 'but the plumber came to fix my washing machine this morning.' I should have considered myself lucky; her co-host would have refused to interview me because of my long hair, which for him was synonymous with left-wing radicals. 'He doesn't interview communists,' I was told.

But for every presenter who hadn't read the book there was one who had done his or her homework thoroughly. And amongst those that hadn't there were always surprises. In Seattle, after visiting the Pike Market where a cornucopia of fresh fish was on display and an art gallery's street sign read FRESH WATERCOLORS DAILY, my escort took me to a radio station where the presenter had either been taken ill or had simply forgotten to show up for the pre-recorded interview. I sat glumly with my escort in an anteroom in a corner of the warehouse that housed the studio while the sound engineer attempted to track down the presenter. His efforts were in vain. With no one else in the studio the engineer, taking matters into his own hands, decided to conduct the interview himself and made a startling show of it. He referred to China as the Far West, which if you lived in Seattle, it was.

As the tour built up steam so more people became interested in booking me for their shows. Authors, like actors, are commodities that can in some cases increase the ratings of a show. Conversely the reviewers, DJs and TV hosts appear almost godlike in their ability to make or break your work. Some demand exclusivity – either you appear on their show first or not at all.

My American publishers' publicity department gave me split-second schedules; one couldn't be late for live shows. Normally they would send an escort to make sure you didn't miss appointments, but until I reached the west coast of the United States I managed to persuade them that I didn't need one. If I could find my way to China, I reasoned, I could find my way to the studios. I was astonished by the prices hotels charged for meals. I called my publishers to confirm that I could charge these to their account. 'Order champagne,' I was told. I invited some friends to a hotel bar. After a couple of drinks James suggested we go for an Ethiopian meal. James was one of Washington's most gifted correspondents; he was also a workaholic who remained contact-able twenty-four hours a day through his pager, not one that bleeps in the middle of an important meeting but one tucked into his pocket that vibrates when he is being paged, thus putting a new slant on Mae West: 'Is that a pager in your pocket, or are you just glad to see me?'

Of course the premise that I could find my way to the studios ignored the fact that I could still get into a lot of trouble. The American leg of the tour was a sort of 'visit Beirut, USA-style'. An undeclared war was being waged across the States, a civil war that kills and maims, without campaigns, battles or enemies, in the neighbourhoods, in the streets, in supermarkets, on the buses and subways, in vacant lots and derelict buildings. The bullets were drug-induced and the battlefront everywhere. A tour through Washington, not only the nation's seat of government but also known as the murder capital of the United States, revealed dozens of drive-by open-air crack markets. You didn't have to go down 'T' street and on past the Nubian Islamic Hebrews' headquarters to discover the rampant destitution of the city. Outside the seat of the richest, most powerful government in the world, along an esplanade of some of the finest museums of the most envied nation, the homeless slept over belching steam vents. Beside the White House in a small park the homeless survived curled up in cardboard boxes. Law enforcement officers had introduced startling new methods to combat 'street sweepers' – modern tommy guns with shotgun shells. When DEA and FBI agents raided 'crack houses' they carried semi-automatic handguns and wore bullet-proof vests. It had even been suggested that the Washington police should borrow a helicopter gunship from the National Guard.

Within the studio, presenters as a matter of form tried to put their guests at ease.

'What goes 10, 9, 8, 7, 6, 5, 4, 3, 2, 1?' asked one presenter before Vivaldi's *Four Seasons* came to an end and the 'real' questions began.

'What?'

'Bo Derek ageing!'

Some presenters were more abrasive. As the lights dimmed for the commercial break during one nationally televised late-night chat show, I took a polite interest in the presenter's work. The host listened but remained rigid as a waxwork while the make-up artist worked furiously to restore his looks; the quixotic smile and black eyebrows had melted under the strong studio lights.

'Do you present the programme regularly?' I asked.

'No!' he replied indignantly. With stony contempt he added, 'What do you think I do? I'm filling in for someone else? I normally drive a taxi?' I had merely asked the question in the belief that two hours every night of the week was a heavy burden for one presenter alone.

As the chat show returned after the break, Charlie, the presenter, stared soulfully into the camera. He told the country's insomniacs, 'Nick just asked me if I usually present the show! "No," I told him, "I'm normally a taxi driver!" ' As I faced the camera I turned beetroot with embarrassment.

Later, as the programme drew to a close, the floor manager signalled that we had a minute left. By the time Charlie had wrapped up, the floor manager was counting down the last ten seconds. Grasping the moment, I interjected: 'Thank you Charlie, I thought you did great for a taxi driver.' And on that note the stage manager waved his hands; the show's credits rolled.

When I was in Miami I got a call from a rival network.

'Hi! This is Joan, I'm calling from New York. We'd like you on our prime time show tomorrow night. We want five bullets – five sexy snaps.'

Iran's Ayatollah was considered sexy. I had three and a half minutes to recount an eighteen-month adventure of a lifetime. They would fly me to New York, collect me in a limousine, take me to dinner, put me up in a hotel, take me to the airport, fly me back to Miami and all I had to do was talk in sound bytes.

Joan and I went through the host's five questions. They were marked up on cue cards. 1. WHY DO YOU DO THIS? 2. WHAT IS THE GREATEST ADVENTURE YOU'VE EVER HAD? 3. HAS YOUR LIFE EVER BEEN IN DANGER? 4. ROMANCE ONLY A NATURAL THING A MAN TRAVELLING ALONE. 5. WHAT HAVE YOU LEARNED FROM ALL YOUR TRAVELS/WHAT WAS THE MOST MOVING MOMENT? The host didn't like the last question; he replaced it with: 5. I UNDERSTAND YOU WERE IN TIBET. But Joan explained, 'We might never get to question 5, so let's tie in answers 4 and 5. You've got 2 minutes and 27 seconds in which to give your answers. Remember, think TV, think bytes . . .'

Wrapping up the previous item, the presenter meaninglessly

told his audience, 'Jeff Daniels is an actor in perspective.' The studio guests played musical chairs to a commercial for the Worldwide College of Auctioneers of Idaho, and I took my seat next to Eugene from Illinois, a guest from the National Association for the Advancement of Time.

From taxi drivers I learnt a lot about Middle East politics and African revolutions. In the District of Columbia my first taxi driver was an exiled Iranian engineer and a member of the Iranian Tudeh party. In another taxi on the way to a party to celebrate the future opening of the African National Congress's Washington office I discussed the Nigerian civil war with the driver who was himself from Oweri in Nigeria. 'Didn't the federal troops take Oweri in November 1967?' – 'They took Nsukka near Mamfe before they took Oweri.' One encounter proved more astonishing than the others. On the way to the American University campus for a phone-in on WAMU (American University Radio) I had mistaken the Iraqi taxi driver for an Iranian. I apologized; there was no greater error to be made when it came to nationalities. In turn, he requalified himself – 'Actually I'm an Iraqi Kurd.' The encounter was not unusual in a country where your taxi driver is more likely to come from Haiti, the Ukraine or Syria than from North America. I was keen to tell the Kurdish taxi driver of my recent visit to Kurdistan, except before I had time to complete the next sentence – 'Two weeks ago, I was in . . .' – Hajir cut me off. He turned towards me so that I could clearly see his gaunt features and handsome moustache in the rearview mirror. 'You're the British journalist who witnessed the massacre of Kurdish refugees.'

I was at once flabbergasted and speechless. How could he have possibly known? The news had yet to receive any mention in the Western press and only later did Amnesty International publish a picture of the refugee camp. The Washington Kurdish community was a tight-knit circle of about seventy Kurds, who knew everything. Hajir's own family were being held in a camp in Diyarbakir. He had travelled there, but the authorities had prevented him from entering the camp and the only means of communicating with them had been across a barrier that separated him from his relatives.

I was in my element on the Mike Cuthbert show on the American University radio station in front of a console of flashing lights. Phone-ins are popular with the lonely, spinsters, political activists and those with sexual problems who are too embarrassed to go to their doctor. I took my first call from Mohammed. 'There is nothing wrong with dried raw yak meat,' Mohammed assured me. I was intrigued.

'Mohammed, how have you come to this conclusion?' I asked.

'I have tested dried raw yak meat in the laboratory and I found no bacteria.'

The next caller was Sue – a regular and a supporter of left-wing revolutionary movements from Angola to Zanzibar. 'The Soviets are doing their internationalist duty in trying to crush the oligarchic, feudalist and reactionary forces in Afghanistan. They have never bombed civilian targets during the course of their duty; this is a myth built up by the imperialist, reactionary Western media.'

Steve from California was seeking more practical advice. 'I'm tall, I have blue eyes and blond hair. Do you think this would exclude me from travelling to Pakistan and Afghanistan?' Not any more than it would stop me from travelling to California on the following morning's flight to Los Angeles.

'SURF OR DIE' read the graffiti at LAX, Los Angeles's International Airport. I had flown in over a huge and sprawling city interconnected by rivers of moving steel and chrome. Below us cars glittered and swimming pools gleamed, reflecting the sun like a thousand lakes. Sheri had been sent by my publishers to meet me.

'Hi! I'm Sheri.' She was blonde, sun-tanned and beautiful but she wasn't from California. Rumour had it she was a space cadet and they weren't referring to the training corps. She had the sweet singsong voice of the South; words hung seductively on the tip of her tongue. Sheri managed to combine her regular work at the publishers with a part-time course on the record industry as well as following her ambition to become a singer. As I was soon to discover, waitresses weren't waitresses in Los Angeles but aspiring actresses; lifeguards weren't lifeguards but hopeful silver-screen-bound Arnold Schwarzeneggers. They say Beverly Hills has more

Rolls-Royces per square mile than any other place on earth. Maybe, but there are also more Bo Dereks waiting to be discovered.

Sheri was a New Age thinker. She told me, 'You create your own reality.' Reality here was tailbacks – six lanes of bumper-to-bumper freeway traffic and a hectic schedule of interviews. First stop was radio KIEV. We parked in a parking structure – a multi-storey car park, with a four-lane ramp that would have put any European autobahn to shame. Radio KIEV was situated in a shopping mall. The studio was a fishtank amongst storefronts. I sat with my radio host behind a huge sheet of glass outside which a group of shoppers had gathered on benches to observe us as the interview was broadcast across the city and piped into the shopping mall.

I was invited to dinner at a Beverly Hills mansion. The steps to the house were cracked by an earthquake. The parking area looked like a car showroom, the cars as shiny as the gold taps in their owners' bathrooms. The guests included the wife of a bestselling author, who wore 18-carat gold dagger-like fingernails. And there was Claudia. Claudia was petite with long black curly hair and an athletic body. She was from California. She asked me where I was from.

'England.'

'I've just been to Austria. It's so backward. The Austrians seem to enjoy denying themselves. I'm trying to get at what is *real*, they [the Austrians] are doing just the opposite.'

'Oh?' I said with interest.

'I'm a person of such directness.' There was a pause, I didn't know how to answer that one.

'I'm thinking of moving my money to Germany,' she said.

A young man called us to the dinner table. He claimed to be Terence Stamp's agent but looked barely old enough to have a driving licence.

It was the cook's day off so the food was zapped and nuked in the microwave. We had lobster for starters and pseudo-browned lasagne for the main course. Everyone pushed their food around their plates in a demonstration that they were eating but couldn't because of the calories.

Dinner conversation was intense. The attractions of valium and ice were discussed – not the variety of ice that comes in cubes and melts but crystallized methamphetamine, better known as speed. A joke on LA smog was doing the rounds: 'For a couple of pieces of crack, I'll let you have a snort from this jar of fresh air,' said the eighteen-year-old who claimed to have given up doing drugs, which he had started at the age of thirteen.

In another corner two women, a producer and a director, were discussing future projects. Using last names was out. 'George [Lucas] and Steven [Spielberg] are very close. Steven is a real human being. I can do it better than Steve, but Steven and George have got a relationship going. George made *Star Wars* for $18 million – I could have done it cheaper, but . . .' In Hollywood, it seemed you only wished someone well if they were terminally ill.

After dinner I went to the bathroom. I found a tube of self-tanning milk. The label read: 'This superb product works magic in 2–3 hours to achieve a natural, golden halo of color, a fresh "just back from the holidays" look.' There was also an atomizer of skin-firming concentrate, an anti-slackening treatment to help regain firm facial features and an eye contour balm for a youthful appearance. All of them were for men.

The house was immaculate, everything arranged as if each item were displayed in a museum or a clinic. The hostess had commissioned an artist to paint her in the fashion of Andy Warhol's portraits of the Rich or Famous in her favourite colours. Six such portraits hung in a block. I was beginning to wonder whether anything was real: the Armani suits, the Gucci shoes, the Rolex watches, the people.

The only thing missing was a video of a log fire I had seen for sale in New York; they came in 60- , 120- and 180-minute versions.

Later, one of the guests saw me contemplating a neon sculpture. 'Neon,' he informed me, 'is one of my favourite gases.'

The next day I travelled north to Seattle and then south to San Francisco. I began to stagger from one studio to the next, although I never fell asleep in the host's lap. I presumed most hosts were accustomed to interviewing semi-conscious book tour victims. Each hotel I stayed in seemed a clone of the previous one with a ritualistic similarity: the subtle but annoying air-conditioning buzz, the clinical sweetness of the bathroom and, on the pillow of the

turned-down bed, a chocolate placed on a card that read PLEASANT
DREAMS. But I do remember the Portman Hotel in San Francisco. I
was greeted by the assistant manager, Pedro Maria Barranchea
Apostol. In turn he handed me over to Kim Sun, my personal valet,
who gave me a lengthy orientation course and served chrysan-
themum tea. He would gladly arrange for the repair of clothing or
other possessions and would be happy to explain the three jogging
routes close to the hotel. I settled for having my shoes polished. I
was accustomed to a telephone in the bathroom but from my bath
in the Portman I could watch a television set, listen to the radio and
make a telephone call. I called Japhet, my brother's closest friend.
Japhet was only twenty-seven, but he was in charge of a production
company called Big Pictures, described as 'not a small part of
Colossal Pictures'. We had a power breakfast to discuss some ideas
before Bridgit, an ex-airline stewardess, whisked me off to the local
radio stations.

The first two were located in Berkeley across the Bay. One was
situated in a bunker-like structure in the middle of a swamp. The
other was close to Berkeley's People's Park, a hangover from the
sixties. We climbed a set of rickety wooden stairs to a tumbledown
first-floor studio. The station was still a bastion of People Power.
Ever curious, I asked a man sitting next to me in the hall what he
did. 'I just kinda hang out,' he told me. I was shown to the studio. A
sticker on the door said, 'SUPPORT THE CONTRAS – BUY COCAINE FROM
A REPUBLICAN'. The studio was draped in wall-to-ceiling paisley
saris. It was a live phone-in but the studio door was left ajar. In the
hall a mother took to breast-feeding her baby. After the news a
caller said he planned to disrupt a meeting at which a former
Secretary of State was to give a speech. Another caller invited
listeners to demonstrate between 1st and 2nd Avenue against US
policy in Central America. 'Our Central America is Kansas not
Nicaragua,' he said. When my turn came the DJ gave me a clenched
'power to the people' fist or the 'right on' hand sign for every
answer that indicated solidarity with the people.

After a morning of interviews Bridgit asked me where I would
like to have lunch. I knew this great little restaurant in the Mission.
She thought I meant Mission Street, a misunderstanding not so
different from my address in London's Blenheim Gardens being

mistaken for the stately home rather than the street in Brixton I had recently moved to. I explained I wanted to eat Mexican food.

'I know this lovely Mexican restaurant near Market Street,' she said.

Once again I said I meant Mission the district, not the street. She reached for her guide book. 'There's a lovely four-star Mexican restaurant near the Portman.' When she realized I was serious she began to panic; she had never been into the Mission. I reassured her. She asked me if it was beyond 15th Street. A little. By the time we had reached 17th Street she was in virgin territory. We had both become illiterate; everything was in Spanish except for the street signs. She had also become a nervous wreck, cursing her luck. 'I should have known from your book this was the kind of place you'd want to go to!'

We parked her car on 26th Street. I advised her to lock it.

'I know,' she yelled. 'You needn't remind me!'

I took her to the restaurant; well, it wasn't actually a restaurant but a cantina. We queued for tacos and burritos, sat down and feasted. She began to relax.

At the end of the day she dropped me at the airport. A mixture of relief and joy crossed her face. She had survived the ordeal, but there was a minor problem. 'The publishers will never believe I took you to lunch; the check came to less than twelve dollars. Most authors want to eat at Fisherman's Wharf – it's nearly fifty dollars a head.' I kissed her goodbye and looked forward to spending the weekend back in LA.

I called Sheri at my publishers' press office from the airport. 'Hi, Sheri.'

'Nick, I was just about to call you to see if you had arrived.'

'Telepathy!'

'No, synchronicity.'

'Synchronicity?'

'Synchronicity is quite different,' she explained. 'It's the simultaneous occurrence of two meaningful but not causally connected events.'

'How about dinner?'

'I can't, I'm having problems with my man. He hasn't done the washing up for over a year and a half. I need to *deal* with it.'

* * *

I had dinner with Claudia. Claudia took me to Rodeo Drive and then to see her nanny who lived in Central Los Angeles. Claudia drove an open-top jeep. Wasn't she worried about driving on the freeway? – there had been a spate of random shootings, or ventilated heads as a bullet through the head was called. Over the music of a group called Bad Brains and another called Dead Milkman, she screamed, 'When I'm about to change lanes, I'll tell you to keep your head down!' On the console of her jeep she had a little gadget called Revenger; at the flick of a switch you got the sound of a death ray, machine-gun or grenade launcher. I was in safe hands.

As far as I could see the only thing that Central Los Angeles had in common with Beverly Hills was the use of mind-bending drugs. On Rodeo Drive, the spiritual heart of Beverly Hills, you could buy a plain wool suit with 14-carat gold pinstriping for $6,000, a pair of crocodile shoes for $1,700, a mink-lined denim jacket (originally designed for Ronald Reagan) for $7,500 or a leather jacket at $25,000 and a wristwatch for $125,000. One jewellery shop claimed the average couple buying a wedding ring would spend the equivalent of the price of a suburban apartment on jewellery. Claudia told me it was easier to find a psychiatrist than a gas station and beauty shops outnumbered booksellers by 500 to eight. She said Bedford Drive was so crowded with psychiatrists that it was known as 'Couch Canyon'. As for the garbage, it was carted to a central collection point where it was sprinkled with a granulated banana perfume before being taken to a landfill. That's if the sanitation board could get to it before some smart entrepreneur hoping to market the garbage of the local stars.

If Beverly Hills was movieland fantasy, Central Los Angeles was most definitely hard reality. Violence was endemic and far worse than in some of the rubbish-tip *barrios* and *favelas* I had visited in the slums of Peru and Brazil, and I imagined the living conditions were not dissimilar to those in some of South Africa's townships. Claudia's eighty-three-year-old former nanny was a great-grandmother. She lived amongst the stench of abandoned bungalows. She had been in this neighbourhood for over forty years; it had changed from Black to Hispanic and a recent influx of Asians was once again changing the character of her street. The neighbouring house was colonized by crack dealers. A young boy farther up the street had just bought a new Jaguar, but he wasn't old enough to drive. She didn't dare call the police for fear of reprisals. Her windows were fitted with security grilles but that wouldn't prevent her house from being firebombed. She looked after her great-grandchildren and her house was often home for her daughters and granddaughters. She no longer dared walk in the parks where the gangs fought each other with guns and there was always the danger of drive-by shootings with Kalashnikovs and Uzis, but that didn't prevent her from organizing her local church to take meals to the elderly. She never ventured out at night; sometimes she woke suddenly to the hollow ring of gunfire. I didn't know what to say to this fiercely proud lady who had struggled all her life to provide for herself and her family, but who was now hemmed in on all sides by drugs and decay.

The next day I decided to go on a tour of Beverly Hills and Hollywood. I have always shunned tours, they remind me of school, but this was a tour with a difference. The brochure promised: 'A Lively Look at the Deathstyles of the Rich and Famous. Grave Line Tours takes you back through time to the tawdry, twisted, titillating tales of Tinseltown like no other tour service dares! You'll see Hollywood's Babylon at its most unflattering angle – the sizzling scandals, jilted romances, real murder scenes, hottest suicide spots, hospitals of horizontal dismissals and the churches of famous funerals! You'll see the last-breath locations from Gary Cooper to Peter Lorre, Groucho Marx and many more. You'll be escorted to an exciting array of exotic locales such as the street where "Fred Mertz" dropped dead, the home where the Tin Woodsman's heart stopped ticking and the apartment building where God told Mae West to come up and see *Him*! The Grave Line Tour will show you the house where "Superman" was felled – not by Kryptonite, but by his own "speeding bullet"! And much more for $30 a body.'

Six passengers and myself, sorry, six 'mourners' and myself, piled into the back of a 22-foot-long Cadillac hearse. Greg Smith, our tall, lean, amiable tour director or director of undertakings for the 2½-hour, eighty-site death trail, was dressed in undertaker's robes: black tails and grey trousers with black pinstripes. A fellow mourner arrived dressed all in black wearing a badge in the shape of a skull and a necklace hung with a crucifix. She had long black hair and looked like Morticia in the television series *The Addams Family*. I asked her what had possessed her to come on the tour. 'My boyfriend gave me a ticket for my twenty-seventh birthday present.'

As we pulled into Hollywood Boulevard next to Graumann's Chinese Theatre a family ran into the street and thumped desperately on the hearse's tinted windows – they wanted to join the tour, but the Tomb Buggy, as the hearse was affectionately known, was full. Our tour director greeted us with 'Dearly Beloved'. In the background the hearse echoed to Chopin's Funeral March. Bette Davis's recorded voice interrupted, 'Fasten your seat belts. It's going to be a bumpy night.'

First stop was the seedy motel where Janis Joplin overdosed on heroin. We passed Château Marmont, a concrete imitation French château where John Belushi met a similar fate from too much 'tooting and shooting'. The room where he overdosed was usually booked a month ahead. We saw where Roman Polanski was arrested; we traced the route Montgomery Clift took the night he lost control of his car and slammed into a telephone pole; we passed the Beverly Hills Hotel where Peter Finch 'checked out for good' – he keeled over in the lobby and died from a heart attack – and we visited the site of the restaurant where James Dean ate his last supper. We learnt that Peter Lorre died half an hour before he was due in divorce court, that Humphrey Bogart and Princess Diana are sixth cousins and that Jayne Mansfield (40–24–26), 'the not so dumb blonde', had an IQ of 163. As the hearse glided past the empty lot that had once been the apartment house of the Wizard of Oz's Auntie Em (Clara Blandick) we learnt that in her eightieth year she attended church on Palm Sunday. When she returned home she penned a note: 'I am now about to make the great adventure . . . I pray the Lord my soul to take, Amen.' She then pulled a plastic bag over her head and suffocated herself. Our tour director credited Auntie Em with being 'LA's first bag lady'.

We stopped outside Elizabeth Taylor's home which once belonged to Frank Sinatra and was where his son was dropped off after his kidnapping. We cruised past Ronald and Nancy Reagan's

$2½-million retirement home (neighbours to the Beverly Hill-billies). The original address was 666 St Cloud Street, but because 666 is the number of the Antichrist the Reagans petitioned the council to change the number to 668, possibly on the advice of Nancy Reagan's astrologer.

At the end of the tour Greg gave his guests a parting gift –detailed maps of the local cemeteries with the graves of celebrities marked out on each one. As he put it, 'You'll actually be able to get within six feet of your favourite stars.' Alternatively, for $25 you could order photocopies of celebrity death certificates. The most popular on his list were the Three Stooges followed closely by Marilyn Monroe and Eleanor Powell.

I was curious to know more about Greg Smith and his necromancy. He invited me back to his Hollywood apartment-cum-office. Behind him was a map of Los Angeles marked with different-coloured spots: red for murders, yellow for suicides, orange for scenes of death, blue for points of interest and cemeteries marked with a highlighter. Greg had become obsessed with death whilst at school; he wanted to become either a monkey trainer or a mortician. He decided on the latter and studied mortuary management at the Cypress College of Mortuary Science, 'the Harvard of funeral schools', he called it. But he dropped out. 'There's a misconception that funeral directors are rich, but most are owned by nameless corporations.' He worked as a house painter, a waiter, with the retarded and as a paramedic before he came up with the idea of Grave Line Tours.

'Isn't it a little morbid?' I asked.

'Hell no, getting dressed in a suit and tie and going to a nine-to-five job would be morbid.'

Was Greg afraid of death? 'You're here for seventy years to give and bless people, seek wisdom, mature and connect with people. I'm sometimes afraid of living; after all, you're lucky to live for eighty to ninety years and you're dead for billions. I don't know why everyone is so hung up on dying. I can hardly wait to die.'

And the future? 'I want to open a shop to sell photocopies of celebrity death certificates, T-shirts, mugs and other memorabilia such as ashtrays with Yul Brynner's picture on the bottom and matchstick boxes with a picture of people who burned up on the cover.'

'Is Grave Line Tours successful?'

'We're booked solid every day. People want to know and see what happened to the stars. The only certain things are death and taxes, and nobody wants to see where the stars paid their taxes. It's a way of making a buck.'

Sheri had offered to collect me at the end of the tour. I asked her how things were going with her boyfriend: had he done the washing-up? He had. He had piled the washing-up into a supermarket trolley, wheeled it into the garden and took the garden hose to it. She was going to ask him to move out.

She told me a little about her family. Her mother was involved with US–Central American solidarity groups. Her grandfather had once been a farmer, but one day as he worked in the fields he saw a vision in the clouds. It read 'PC'. Understanding the letters to mean Praise Christ he abandoned farming and became a preacher. Many years later, as he approached retirement, his family were by no means well-off, and so he had begun to question not only the wisdom of his decision to have left the fields for the pulpit, but God's message. He now considered the possibility that 'PC' might not have stood for Praise Christ after all, but Plant Corn.

Sheri drove me to the ocean along Sunset. We took a detour through Beverly Hills and Bel-Air; we could see the makings of a house being built by Aaron Spelling, the television and film producer, a $30–50-million, 40,000-square-foot cottage, a hillside French château with over twenty bedrooms equipped with two gymnasiums, a tennis court, a two-lane bowling alley and a disco. Amongst the imitation Tudor houses, Spanish colonial, thirties International-style steel and glass boxes and a Hansel and Gretel cottage, there was a Moroccan palace with five domes, an art gallery, ten baths and, although the owner would have liked large reflecting pools like those at the Taj Mahal, something a little smaller in the way of a private pool. There were homes with recording studios, tanning parlours, servants' quarters and double kitchens (one for catering). Outside were polo fields, putting greens, petting zoos, heliports, waterfalls and a miniature railroad. The cheapest home in Beverly Hills cost over half a million dollars, for a house with one bathroom. Los Angeles could also boast a toy hospital, a pet limousine service, an animal psychiatrist and, of course, a pet cemetery – Pet Haven where some 1,500 visitors a year make the pilgrimage to visit interred boa constrictors, monkeys, goats, goldfish and turtles.

I took the shuttle minibus to the airport. There were three of us in all, the driver, another passenger and myself. The young driver gave us a rambling speech about the Antichrist, '. . . although each of Ronald Wilson Reagan's names contains six letters, 666, I'm sure our President is not the Antichrist.' As we took the ramp to the San Diego freeway he added, 'I'm a humanist: I believe in mass transit, clean air and biodegradable products.' John T. Perkins III, my fellow passenger, was in his early seventies. He was also a member of the Society of Separationists (Incorporated). He gave the driver and me the first issue of the *Truth Seeker Newsletter* which contained a charter from the AAAA – The American Association for the Advancement of Atheism. John told us that the AAAA were demanding the taxation of church properties, the abolition of oaths in courts and at inaugurations, the repeal of anti-revolution, anti-birth control and censorship laws and the erasure of superstitious inscriptions.

I asked John what he meant by the erasure of superstitious inscriptions. 'The removal of "In God We Trust" from our coins and banknotes as well as the removal of the church flag from above our national flag on battleships,' he said.

John bade me farewell at the Pan Am terminal. He quoted from the newsletter: 'Read it and weep. Then you can get angry enough to try to do something about it!' I suspected this wasn't the kind of literature that would help me win friends in Belfast, my next stop.

I arrived at Heathrow after twelve flights in as many days, and still had to catch another to Northern Ireland. First I would have to clear immigration and customs. My body had landed, but my head felt as though I had left it at 31,000 feet. One of Her Majesty's young customs officers beckoned me to a table at the side of the customs hall. She eyed me suspiciously:

'Do you have any drugs?' she asked.

'No.'

'Have you ever smoked dope?'

'Have you?'

'I ask the questions here!' She looked at my passport with its bewildering array of immigration stamps – Syria, Iran, a safe-conduct pass from an Afghan mujahedeen leader.

'Where are you going?'

'Belfast.'

'Holiday?'

'Not exactly.'

'Business?'

'Well, sort of.' She thought about it for a moment and then dismissed me.

I stayed at the Europa Hotel, reputed to be the most bombed hotel in the world. Tall reinforced security grilles surrounded the hotel and a barrier to the car park was manned twenty-four hours a day. All vehicles and guests were thoroughly searched before being allowed into the small hotel compound. Once inside I didn't experience fear or trepidation. But the city, like so many other places in the world, was a tale of two cities: the one of middle-class suburbs relatively untouched by the violence, and the other the working-class areas where urban deprivation and unemployment went hand in hand with prejudice and resentment. Nothing could be taken at face value. A fireman who said he didn't have any prejudices later told me that the Ulster Protestants were like the Afrikaners and the Jews – a chosen people. His parting gift to me was an Ulster badge. It was unsettling to see British soldiers marching at a measured distance from one another up through the Shankhill in full battledress. One of them stopped briefly and aimed his SA-80 at a mother pushing her baby in a pram. Belfast city centre looked like many rejuvenated British city centres striving for an image of modernity, only here a soldier adjusted the sights of his semi-automatic. Above him a sign for the Prudential blew in the wind.

Most symptomatic of the horrors of a society split apart by sectarianism was the inability of many to choose certain types of work, or indeed find work or talk freely without fear of reprisals. Freedom of choice was limited to certain professionals who could always choose to leave Northern Ireland and go to England; many of them had their children at English schools.

It was a question of 'real estate', as they would say in America, of boundaries and territory, and the barriers weren't coming down in Northern Ireland; they were still being built. In Belfast, the ugly purpose-built concrete and brick walls that separate communities down the middle of streets are called Peace Walls.

Depending on which side of the wall you lived the forces of law and order were the forces of either freedom or oppression. Bombings, arson attacks, extortion and killings were announced by the media with the numbing regularity of weather forecasts. The armed protagonists' killings were signed with three- or four-letter acronyms: IPLO, UDF, IRA, UVF, SAS, RUC, all the hallmarks of tribal allegiances, the struggle for righteousness, supremacy and *justice*. Northern Ireland was Lebanon, Guatemala and South Africa with only one difference: everyone spoke English.

In a different setting it might have been easier to have enjoyed an evening at Stormont Castle. Security was tight; the castle was ringed with armed RUC units and I presumed the grounds were also protected against infiltrators. However, far from what I had considered to be the norms of diplomatic protocol, conversation was open and often hilariously amusing. Safe subjects, permissible levels of response, correct voice and laughter levels were all forgotten in a wave of natural merriment.

There was a Member of Parliament, the grandson of a famous politician, who told me about Egypt and the 'Sewage Canal'. And there was the wife of an elderly gentleman about to embark on a trip to Tibet with her husband. She told me how she had warned him not to die on her in Tibet for his own sake: 'I have insisted he must live. I have told him if he doesn't the Tibetans will feed him to the vultures as is their custom.' She turned to see if he was all right. He was standing on the opposite side of the vast reception room. 'For heaven's sake, he ought to know what they do. He was in intelligence.'

Dinner was sumptuous. However, I was confused by the rows of knives and forks, each set for a different course, and different glasses for the wines, mineral water and liqueurs. I took small polite bites of the salmon rather than the quick, hearty chunks of food I normally gobble down. I watched to see if anyone would help themselves to seconds; there were still leftovers, but I didn't dare ask for a third helping.

After dinner we retired to one of the many large reception rooms. Entertainment was provided by the assembled guests, and our host, the Secretary of State for Northern Ireland. A vicar's wife played the piano whilst an entourage sang songs by Noël Coward, Frank Sinatra and Julie London. However, it was the Secretary of State who, without any question, stole the show with an excellent impression of Louis Armstrong singing 'Old Methuselah'.

The guests all left at the same time. As we walked to the parked cars, morning dew had already begun to settle on the lawns. Everyone bade each other farewell and goodnight. Car doors clunked shut in irregular patterns. Lights were switched on and engines whirred into action. As one guest's car drew away it was followed by a dark blue saloon that had been parked near a police jeep. On every country road there was the possibility of ambush. They were going home with an armed escort.

I returned to New York to audition for a corporate show and then flew on to Palm Beach to give a lecture. My agent had warned me that my audience would consist of a 'very charming' but 'very old' group. On the plane to Florida I had read that an astonishing 22,268 Florida motorists were aged ninety or more. And Mrs Lockham, my host, was having a problem finding me a suitable dinner partner – the minimum age requirement for the junior club was fifty.

Before appearing at the arts club, the director took me to one side. He told me I wasn't to take it personally if some of the audience fell asleep during the talk and he apologized for the likelihood of members entering and leaving the auditorium during the lecture – 'Some have weak bladders.'

Mrs Lockham did eventually find me a young dinner partner. 'It has been difficult; there are not a lot of young people here,' she explained, 'but I've found a simply delightful girl called Francesca. You'll just love her. She has a healthy trust fund, her liquid assets are husbanded and the family retains an investment counsellor. They have houses in Dublin, London, Palm Beach and New York.'

Palm Beach was the *total* community with polished chrome fire hydrants, pastel-shaded newspaper dispensers and manicured lawns. Palm Beach was insulated from the violence of West Palm Beach by a waterway. Palm Beach houses had the added protection of the latest surveillance equipment; they also had patrol dogs, electronic gates and sensors, video monitors, floodlights and perimeter fences with 'Armed Response' plaques. And they could always raise the drawbridges to try and stop criminals from reaching the mainland. There was talk of setting up video cameras on all roads leading out of Palm Beach, so that criminals could be identified and hunted down.

Mrs Lockham's dinner was held at one of Palm Beach County's one hundred golf clubs. We stood together and Mrs Lockham introduced each guest to me and simultaneously to each other, all the while maintaining a stream of polished small talk with the entourage of the moment. 'Hello Bill! How are you? You know the Ellsworths.' Mr Ellsworth had once gone game hunting in the Pamirs; the watchstrap to his Rolex was embossed with a miniature gold trophy of an ibex. Another guest had met Churchill. Membership of the club was based on your ability to pay the fees; to qualify your wealth had to be at least equivalent to the gross national product of Belize, your acreage equal to at least three county shires or your bloodstock of the most impeccable international pedigree.

I sat next to Francesca during dinner. It was fairly apparent that she had come under duress, a social obligation that couldn't be forfeited. She called the crowd the HB10s – Home or Horizontal By 10. The club's members had the ambition if not the energy to dance. Francesca saw the Palm Beach Waltz as the Dance of the Dinosaurs, 'slow, lead-footed and awkward'. Francesca didn't dance or play golf, but she enjoyed the occasional game of croquet especially when she could hit her opponents' ball east of Jesus.

It seemed a strange way to pass Martin Luther King Day, the third Monday in January 1989. When I returned to the hotel I switched on the television. One of the Spanish channels was playing a soap opera in Univision called *Vivir un Poco* (Live a Little); a cable channel offered a programme on the *History of Dieting* and on a local channel a Public Service announcement told us, 'Together we can make history.' The programmes were interrupted for a newsflash. Rioting had engulfed the black community of Overtown in Miami. Buildings had been set on fire, others were being looted and a huge pall of smoke lay over the suburb. The rioting had begun when a policeman fatally shot a black motor-

cyclist. The newsflash was followed by commercials offering sleek
sedans on unlimited credit, a Caribbean vacation and a skin
moisturizer. I returned to the *History of Dieting*: 'Check out
Cleopatra's features . . . Raquel Welch would never have survived
seven months in a cave . . .' Americans spend $5 billion a year on
dieting.

The riots brought home to me that I had been postponing my
work and a return to the places that had offered me the present
opportunities to travel in style and comfort. I longed to go back to
Afghanistan although I was apprehensive at the prospect of
returning to that war-torn country. I thought back to Herat where I
had lived with a mujahedeen 'Komiteh', a group of about twenty
men, during the summer of 1984. I had stayed there for fifteen days
and on ten of those days we came under repeated helicopter
gunship attack and MiG and Sukhoi jet fighter bombing raids. On
every single day during my stay in Herat we took casualties. Since
President Gorbachev's rise to Party Secretary there was a new
emphasis to Soviet foreign policy and, as part of the easing of
tensions with the West, the Russians were about to withdraw their
soldiers from Afghanistan. The Western media were predicting the
immediate fall of the Kabul government. Kabul was surrounded on
all sides by the mujahedeen who had battled with the Soviet forces.
In what was being seen as a potentially explosive situation Western
governments had taken the decision to evacuate their diplomats
and close their embassies in Kabul.

In February 1989 food and fuel in Kabul were in short supply for
the city was surrounded on all sides. The suffering of the capital's
residents was growing daily. I wanted to return to Afghanistan not
with the mujahedeen but with the Afghan government. Would
they know I had travelled with the mujahedeen? Would they give
me a visa? I was certain about one thing. One way or another, I was
determined to reach Kabul.

It wasn't easy to leave the comfort of luxury hotels and expense
accounts; it was a seductive way of life. But I left the United States in
the knowledge that I had passed the audition. The third largest
corporation in the United States had hired me for eight shows with
a line-up of stars that included Olympic athletics gold medallists
Florence Griffith Joyner and Jackie Joyner-Kersee, former US

ambassador to the United Nations Jeane Kirkpatrick, Daryl Hall and John Oates, and the singer and actress Dolly Parton.

It seemed both only yesterday and a million years ago that I had faced my first newspaper interview at a New York Mets baseball game. After the game I took the English reporter to an Irish bar where a nun sang 'Danny Boy'. It was 2 A.M. when we left; he offered to give me a ride home in his taxi. I took the subway. As he stepped into the taxi he asked me if I was attracted to danger. I wasn't sure. Does Dolly Parton sleep on her back?

The answers to both questions might become clearer in the months ahead.

5

FLIGHT 702 TO KABUL

Be a second Marco Polo, fly Ariana
Afghan Airlines.

Ariana publicity

February 1989

I first tried calling the Ministry of Foreign Affairs in Kabul on 12 January. I dialled the AT & T operator who in turn connected me to the international operator.

'To telephone Kabul you need to go via the operators in Pittsburgh and Paris,' said the international operator. She connected me to Pittsburgh. 'This is operator 412. How can I help you?'

'I would like to call Kabul, Afghanistan, please.'

'There's an indefinite delay, the first available call will be on the 28th–'

'The 28th! That's two weeks away!' I protested.

'No, sir; the 28th of February – there's a six-week waiting list.'

I tried again on my return to London. I was connected to an international operator in Glasgow. The delay was forty-eight hours. She explained that Afghanistan had only three international telephone lines to the outside world, one each via Paris, Glasgow and Moscow. The old manual exchange in Scotland took it in turns to receive incoming and outgoing calls to and from Kabul. Long delays were inevitable; the operators in Glasgow were handling calls from Australia, Japan, Pakistan and all over Europe.

Two days later I was awoken at 5 A.M. 'This is the Glasgow operator. We're trying your call now.'

After numerous attempts to arouse the Kabul exchange on the manual land line, Kabul finally answered.

'Hello Kabul. This is Glasgow. We would like Kabul 22352.'

'Okay. Okay, Glasgow.'

I had hoped to speak to Mr Amani, head of the Afghan government press office, to secure a visa. Instead, the Kabul exchange had connected me to an Abdul Khalid, a merchant, somewhere in the Morgh Khana bazaar.

I tried to explain I was calling from London. I wanted the Ministry of Foreign Affairs.

'*London!* Abdul Khalid!' Abdul Khalid shouted excitedly and repeatedly in the only English he knew.

'Glasgow, they've connected me to a wrong number!'

'*London!* Abdul Khalid!'

'Kabul are *yew* there!' screamed the operator in a heavy accent.

'Hello! Kabul!'

'Yes, Glasgow.'

'You have given us a wrong number. We want Kabul 22352.'

'Glasgow, we want London 257 2441.'

'Kabul, you haven't connected us to our call. First we want Kabul 22352!'

'No, Glasgow, it's our turn.'

The operators argued. The Glasgow operator eventually gave up in exasperation. She would try again later.

I eventually got through to Mr Amani on the phone. He agreed to a visa. I went to collect it at the Afghan embassy in London. An Afghan student was acting as secretary to the Afghan *chargé d'affaires*. When I was shown into the *chargé*'s office, I was handed an application form in triplicate. As I filled out the questionnaire I was given a stern lecture on the glorious revolution that had precipitated Soviet military intervention. I looked up at the *chargé*. Behind him, fixed to the wall, was a promotional calendar from an air transport company that specialized in the transportation of the deceased. On dangerous assignments I become superstitious; I wondered whether it was a bad omen.

As I came to the end of the questionnaire, I hesitated to answer the last question – Had I visited Afghanistan before? And if so, how many times? I thought of leaving it blank, but felt it wise to fill something in. No, I answered. After all, I reasoned to myself – I had entered the country clandestinely with the mujahedeen and I had recently got a new passport so that the *chargé* would not see my safe-conduct pass from Ismail Khan, the guerrilla leader, in the old one. In this way there was no official record of my previous visit.

It did not come as a total surprise that there were no excursion fares, package deals or discounted tickets to Kabul. Only Aeroflot, Indian Airlines and Ariana Afghan Airlines flew there. However, in the previous month Indian Airlines had withdrawn its flights and Aeroflot had reduced theirs to a weekly service from Moscow. I decided to fly Ariana. But I did find a discounted ticket, from a bucket shop in Southall, West London. For £320 I bought a return ticket to Delhi with stops in Prague and Kabul. I would simply deplane in Kabul and hold onto the Kabul–Delhi portion of the ticket.

I arrived at Heathrow Airport half an hour before the 7 P.M. departure of the OK Czechoslovak Airlines flight to discover the plane had not yet left Prague. There were only a dozen passengers in all, mainly Sikhs but also a handful of budget backpackers to India dressed in loose clothes, jewellery tied to leather thongs and sandals. Most had bought their cheap tickets unaware that they would be landing at Kabul, an airport considered too dangerous by the pilots of desperately needed United Nations mercy flights because of the risk of mujahedeen missile attacks.

When we did eventually leave four hours late we were handed plastic cups and offered a choice of reconstituted powdered orange juice poured from a jug or Czechoslovak beer poured from large communal bottles. The in-flight meal was a choice of chicken or vegetarian. I tried the chicken; pummelled boiled potatoes squashed into one corner of the tin foil container, greasy chicken in the other. I asked if I could try the vegetarian instead. I could. They simply removed the chicken.

We arrived in Prague in the early hours of the morning and were scheduled to change planes immediately, but the pilot of the Ariana plane had decided he was too tired to fly back to Kabul. Some of the passengers became alarmed. They asked Prague's Ariana representative when we would be leaving for Delhi and Amritsar, and were told we would set off when the pilot had recuperated. In the meantime, Iva, at the airport transfer desk, had handed me a single voucher covering an overnight stay for twelve passengers not in the usual airport hotel in Prague, but in a boarding house some thirty miles away in Kladno. Kladno was very beautiful and romantic, we were told. There were no tourists – that was why Czechs went shopping in Kladno.

We arrived at 4 A.M. The boarding house was squeaky clean, the towels like sandpaper and the radio played a single channel which couldn't be switched off. I slept fitfully, hoping we would be able to spend the next day in Prague, and woke to find beautiful, romantic Kladno a sterile prefabricated appendage to a small town. The Ariana representative called on us in the morning to tell us the pilot would be ready to leave some time that evening. We should be at the airport no later than 7 P.M. 'The plane won't wait for you, but you will have plenty of time to wait for the plane.' I decided to hire a taxi for the day and visit Prague. I asked the man in charge of the boarding house if he could arrange for one. The taxi arrived within half an hour but the driver had misunderstood – he had expected to take me to the airport and not spend all day in Prague. He would have to go home first, change shirts and drink a cup of coffee. I was invited to go with him to his house.

We drove into the old part of Kladno. Here quiet, cobbled streets were in stark contrast to the dirty, industrial complex that surrounded the boarding house. Bohumir parked his Skoda in the street and opened the double doors to a covered driveway. It was filled with a curious assemblage of steel tubes, welding equipment and a large white disc. He explained gleefully he had once been a factory worker at the steel complex, but now that he had retired was building satellite dishes in his spare time. This was his tenth. He had sold eight of the others and had kept one for himself. He handed me a visiting card with his name and the information that he handled television repairs, video cassettes and satellite dishes. He sat me down in his large living room while he made some coffee. In one corner a rubber plant had grown into the shape of a question mark. On his return he scanned the forty-one channels he received through his satellite dish. There was *Dallas* in Flemish and ice hockey from Canada but, he told me, 'I don't watch *shit* TV. I watch MTV (Music Television),' which showed

videos of current and past rock music. We settled down to watch
Bob Marley and the Wailers.

I didn't wish to drag him away from the television, but I was keen
to see as much of Prague as possible. He donned a brown suede
waistcoat and cloth cap and we set out for Prague thirty miles away.
In the event we made cursory visits to the Castle, the town centre
and Wenceslas Square. Sadly, many of the baroque buildings were
badly in need of repair and their frescoes had all but faded away.
We spent most of the time eating and drinking in taverns and bars,
as pleasant a way as any to spend the day. Bohumir smoked and
wheezed a lot, no doubt the cause of his pacemaker. He boasted
about his German friends and Kopernik which I presumed to be the
town where they lived until he explained it was a satellite in a
stationary orbit three degrees west of Austria.

Remarkably, the Ariana flight left an hour after we had been
asked to check in at Prague airport. It was not announced at the
time of our departure, however, that we weren't going directly to
Kabul as scheduled but to Moscow. And from Moscow we were
going to Tashkent! This last stop was required because of the
shortage of fuel in Kabul.

The plane's rear cabin remained empty during the flight except
for boxes of supplies that had been taken on in Prague. Whilst
Ariana officials had refused to give a discounted rate for emergency
medical supplies from a British charity, we were now carrying
boxes of Budweiser. The few passengers that had set out from
London were joined by a group of youngsters from the Democratic
Youth Party of Afghanistan, Afghanistan's equivalent of the
Scouts, and by a group of Afghan students who had been studying
in Prague. The flight also provided me with my first glimpse of
Afghan women. In the two-and-a-half months I had spent with the
mujahedeen I had seen a woman only once. Here they were
smartly dressed in the airline's blue livery; they wore make-up and
had the dark features, jet-black hair and piercing eyes of many
Iranian women.

Although Ariana Afghan Airlines had once been partly owned
and run by Pan Am, the airline had dispensed with most of its
American equipment. Its DC 10 had been sold (after one engine had
been hit by an anti-aircraft missile), and instead they flew two

Soviet-made Tupolevs. I visited the cockpit and asked the American-trained pilot about the difference between flying a Tupolev and a Boeing. 'It's like driving a truck when you've been used to a sports car.' I looked at the primitive controls, gauges haphazardly screwed into a utilitarian galvanized dashboard, the enormous footpads and a clumsy flight control stick. (There appeared to be no oxygen masks, life jackets, emergency chutes or fire extinguishers.) I was surprised we were still in the air.

During the course of the war many Ariana crews had sought political asylum. The cockpit crew of flight 702 couldn't talk freely – KHAD (the Afghan secret service) had ears and eyes everywhere. However they did mention the poor pay and long hours. They earned a basic salary of $38.00 a month and often flew an average of twelve hours a day. I asked the crew where they would live if they were free to go anywhere in the world. 'America,' said one of the pilots. 'And your second choice?' I asked. 'There is no second choice.' The other member of the crew added, 'Everything in America is great: their planes, their houses, even their eggs are the best eggs in the world.'

We were into our second day of travel when daylight broke over Soviet Central Asia. I struck up a conversation with Robert Wilson, a thirty-one-year-old bricklayer from London's East End on his way to India. His face had remained a ghostly shade of pale peach for the duration of the flight. I remembered seeing Robert anxiously clutching a bottle of Scotch as we left Heathrow and had wondered whether it was intended to steady his nerves. 'There isn't enough Scotch on board for that,' said Robert regretfully. In fact there wasn't any alcohol on board except for the boxes of Budweiser at the back of the plane. And we had lost most of the Coca-Cola when the metal refreshment trolley had collapsed under its weight and showered the cabin and passengers with the opened bottles' sweet stickiness.

'Will you be going home on the same flight?' I asked.

'Unfortunately yes. If I had enough money I'd be going home by boat.'

I sat next to Zivi, a student from Bristol. She had seen the advertisement for cheap flights to Delhi in *Exchange and Mart*. She had paid for the tickets by postal order, but when the tickets failed to arrive by return post had become alarmed. She called the travel agency: 'They promised me they had sent the tickets. I asked them how could they be so sure that they had been sent. They were sure – I was the only person who was booked on Ariana.'

Had she taken any precautions? 'Yes, travel insurance that covers delay, sickness, lost baggage and hijacking.' She was anxious. 'I've already suffered the delay; I'll probably be sick; in all likelihood I'll have my bags stolen; but hopefully I won't be hijacked!'

I returned to the cockpit as we approached northern Afghanistan at 31,000 feet. The great Amu Darya river marked the border between the Soviet Union and Afghanistan. Two weeks before, it was across this river that the last Soviet troops had left Afghanistan. The pilot was soon pointing out landmarks below us; to our right was the city of Mazar-i-Sharif controlled by the government, to our left the town of Tashgourgan controlled by the mujahedeen. There were towns that straddled the Salang highway – a fine pencil line twisting its way across the sides of mountains and along valley floors. It was Kabul's lifeline and umbilical cord to the Soviet Union. In some places one side of the road was controlled by the mujahedeen and the other by the government. In the interior, the provincial capital of Bamiyan was contested by seven rival mujahedeen groups.

There were no other clues to the cruel war below. The dramatic scenery of isolated peaks and deep valleys hid the brutality the way a Walkman blocks out the noise of traffic. Within half an hour of the Amu Darya we were above Kabul. I was asked to return to my seat for the precipitous landing.

From 31,000 feet the plane began a tight corkscrew descent over the capital to avoid the mujahedeen's heat-seeking missiles on the normal approach. We banked sharply and spiralled downwards as if spinning on a coin to stay as far away as possible from their bases in the mountains that surrounded us on all sides. We flew through a sky filled with the white trails of smoke from missile-deflecting magnesium flares fired from massive Soviet Ilyushin transporter jets that were jockeying for the restricted airspace above and below us. I discovered we didn't have any flares – the pilots hoped the mujahedeen wouldn't fire on a civilian plane. I tried to reassure myself and then thought of the DC-10 that had been hit on this descent. I looked at the stewardesses; their faces were lined with anxiety.

On our final approach we came in low over the city. Hardened mud-brick dwellings with courtyards flashed past beneath us as in a movie on fast forward. Rural compounds clung to the city, where only one humble skyscraper broke the horizon. In seconds we were over tarmac. Helicopters buzzed either side of our aircraft as we touched down. The airport was a hive of activity. MiG jet fighters screamed into the air. Venomous-looking helicopter gunships bristling with weaponry swept across the runway only feet above the ground. As we taxied to the terminal we could see bomber aircraft and helicopters nestling behind mud embankments. Outside the terminal soldiers in full battledress were lining up to board Antonov transport planes.

We walked out of the plane into bright daylight; it was bitterly cold. We had arrived in Kabul over a day late and most of the passengers still hadn't reached their destination. They were escorted to a bare airport lounge which would, in the coming weeks and months, serve as a pitifully exposed shelter against incoming rockets as the mujahedeen tried to sever the city's last link with the outside world. I headed for the arrivals hall where I was greeted by a bored immigration officer. He was dressed as a soldier in a military tunic and broad peaked cap. He spoke some English.

He turned the pages of my passport until he reached the Afghan visa.

'What's the purpose of your visit?'

'I'm here to take pictures for a German magazine.'

'Your visit is very timely. Business will be good – there are many rocket attacks.'

6

KABUL

I grew up in an era marked by tragedy, cruelty and terror. Many elements interacted to produce an extraordinary atmosphere: the persisting revolutionary élan; hope for the future; fanaticism; all-pervasive propaganda; enormous social and psychological changes; a mass exodus of people from the countryside; and, of course, the hunger, malice, envy, fear, ignorance and demoralization brought about by the seemingly endless war, the brutality, murder and violence.

Andrei Sakharov, *Memoirs*

March 1989

Imagine you are surrounded on all sides by the mujahedeen. They are closing in on you. Supplies of food and fuel are so short that the suffering of the city's residents grows daily. There is little chance of escape unless you are wealthy or have secret links with the resistance. They are invisible, but they are out there: in the mountains, in the valleys, on the plains beyond the city and as fifth columnists in cells within the city. Their stated goal: nothing less than total victory and death to all who served the government.

The picture was the same in all the Afghan government's shrinking and increasingly isolated enclaves; the pressure was mounting daily. Two provincial capitals had already fallen and others were expected to fall soon. With the Soviets gone Kabul itself was expected to succumb within weeks if not days. When I had

travelled with the mujahedeen they were the underdogs with the
odds stacked against them, given little chance of lasting out against
the Red Army. Now the tables had turned. The Soviets had been
forced to leave the theatre of war, the mujahedeen held all the
cards; they controlled the countryside, held the moral high ground
and had a tide of victories behind them as one government outpost
after another collapsed into their hands. Some, however, had no
mercy for either conscripts or government officers who had held
out or who had surrendered – they were immediately executed
once captured.

If the government had weakened on the original goals of the
revolution, to impose a Communist social order, it at least
remained steadfast in its bid not to relinquish all the reins of power
into the hands of the mujahedeen. I was intrigued to see and know
how 'the other half lived' – city dwellers not yet under mujahedeen
control. During the course of the war it had been rare to hear about
conditions amongst the Afghan resistance fighting against Soviet
occupation; now it was rarer still to hear of the conditions in
government-held towns under siege by the resistance fighters who
had so bravely fought the Soviet Red Army.

Two weeks prior to my arrival in Kabul, it had been a different
story. The Soviet army had withdrawn from Afghanistan under the
glare of the world's media. Troops and cameras had left hand in
hand, and now media attention was elsewhere, Afghanistan was
no longer in fashion. Only a handful of expatriate United Nations
officials and International Red Cross personnel remained in the
capital. Before the Soviet withdrawal was completed all Western
diplomats had fled the country; they had closed down their
missions and evacuated embassy staffs believing that without the
help of the Soviets the Afghan government could no longer
guarantee their security. They feared a bloodbath – a wave of
lawlessness and pogroms by the mujahedeen against those who
remained in Kabul. The British Foreign Office had warned me in
the strongest terms not to travel to Afghanistan. I was under no
illusions about the dangers I might face if the mujahedeen pushed
their way into town; there would probably be a lot of street fighting
and I could only hope in the event of a mujahedeen victory that

questions would be asked of those who survived the onslaught. As a precaution, I had hidden amongst my camera equipment letters from several mujahedeen guerrilla leaders confirming that I was known to them and that I should be given assistance should the need arise.

The government had declared a state of emergency, suspending constitutional rights, and a dusk-to-dawn curfew had been imposed. Transport was costly and scarce, but I found a shared taxi to take me from the airport to the Kabul Hotel. The streets were eerily quiet; we passed the Microrayan district of austere prefabricated concrete tenements built by the Soviets to house their advisers, but now occupied by government party members and cadres. We also passed the abandoned and padlocked United States embassy in the Karte Wali district which was still guarded by a group of Afghan soldiers. Major crossroads and some government ministries were protected by tanks, armoured personnel carriers and barricades of sandbags. Soldiers manned roadblocks with heavy machine-guns and rocket-propelled grenades.

On that first day I argued about the taxi fare, which seemed outrageously expensive, but I subsequently discovered that there was a severe shortage of fuel. Power cuts were frequent and electricity was only available on alternate nights with no power during the day. On the unofficial market a gallon of scarce petrol cost almost one month's salary.

The hotel was guarded by a soldier who lounged in a chair, his machine-gun on his lap and a cup of tea in his hand. The lobby was shrouded in semi-darkness. I had considered staying at the Intercontinental but the receptionist at the Kabul told me that I would be safer here: 'The hotel was built by the Germans in the twenties and its thick walls are good protection against incoming mujahedeen rocket fire,' he said unconvincingly. I looked around the lobby. It seemed little had changed since pre-revolutionary days. Layers of dust, faded tourist posters boasting dramatic mountain settings and badly worn Afghan carpets marked the passage of time. I signed the hotel ledger next to a 1970s BOAC timetable holder that now held news bulletins from the Soviet press agency Novosti.

The receptionist called for the hotel bellboy to show me to my room. He warned me to keep my windows open in case a bomb blast should spread shards of glass across my room. 'But doesn't it get very cold at night?' I asked. 'It gets very cold, minus 20 degrees sometimes.' It was a choice between frostbite or lacerations.

I stayed in room 116, apparently next to the room where on 14 February 1979 the kidnapped American ambassador Adolphe Dubs had been shot dead by Afghan police when, on the advice of the Russians, they stormed the hotel room where he was held hostage. I recalled the alarm a friend of mine had felt some months before Ambassador Dubs was gunned to death. He had been staying in a similar room at the Kabul Hotel on the eve of the Saur (April) Revolution of 1978 that had brought the Afghan communists to power. When he was woken up in the middle of the night by a soldier pointing a gun at his nose he drowsily asked the soldier what was going on. 'What time is it?' he asked. 'Revolution time,' the soldier answered.

I was about to go to the press office of the Ministry of Foreign Affairs to present my credentials as a *bona fide* photographer for *Tempo*, a German magazine, when a large blast rocked the hotel and rattled the windows. It was the first of several mujahedeen-fired rockets to land on the city that day. Two more followed in quick succession. I rushed down the stairs and into the street. Some distance away a huge pall of thick black smoke rose into the clear blue sky.

I was new to the city and didn't yet know the name of the neighbourhood in which the rockets had struck. When I eventually found a taxi I asked the driver to take me to the scene of the explosion. My few words of Dari, an Afghan language akin to Persian, were already coming back to me. I could remember the words for missile, mortar fire and which way to run from an enemy attack, but I had never learnt the words for building materials, restaurants or cutlery.

We drove right up to the fire engines that were dousing the flames. I got out of the taxi to see one of three bodies charred beyond recognition being removed on a charpoy, a wood-framed bed strung with rope. I felt sick and found it profoundly disturbing to photograph this aftermath. Three rockets had landed on a vegetable market; the wooden stalls and packing boxes had ignited like tinder. Those closest to the explosion had been burnt to death, those farther away had been cut down by wooden splinters that had torn through them at the speed of a bullet. I walked across the ground in ankle-deep mud into the billowing smoke. I coughed from the acrid fumes and tears ran from my eyes. The firemen were ill equipped with old secondhand Scottish-made fire engines. One fireman's only protection from falling debris was a Second World War German helmet painted red. Just visible through the smoke was a young man standing on top of an intact stall doing his best to help. He repeatedly poured water from a green plastic pitcher used for performing ablutions before prayers. No one could say exactly how many people had been injured; one fireman had counted five, but others had already been taken to nearby hospitals.

Kabul, the quiet overgrown residential town with a population of 800,000 before the war, had over the last two weeks turned into a charnel house. For the past decade, as the war had escalated and the fighting and bombings spread across the country, refugees had fled the surrounding areas and much of the countryside and had poured into neighbouring Pakistan and Iran and into the capital itself to seek sanctuary from the fighting. Today almost half the population were either dead or abroad. From the pre-war population of 15 million, over 5 million – one third – had fled the country. Two million had become internal refugees seeking shelter in the government-held provincial capitals, and well over a million are thought to have died in the conflict. Afghanistan's once predominantly rural population was now concentrated in the cities. By the time of the Soviet withdrawal, Kabul was overburdened and ragged with an estimated population of two million, although no one really knew.

I called on Mr Amani. The government press office of which he was the chief was housed in a colonial building built by the British. I entered his office under a dark painting – a present from a visiting foreign statesman – of an erupting volcano. It seemed appropriate. Mr Amani was tall, slim and dressed in a suit. The Afghan government had granted me a visa because I had organized an international conference on Afghanistan at London University's School of Oriental and African Studies in December 1988, so they were somewhat confused that I should be here working as a

Refugees East and West

Wishing upon a star – homeless in Hollywood; wild in Washington DC – a guitar in search of an identity; Kurdish refugee in Turkey

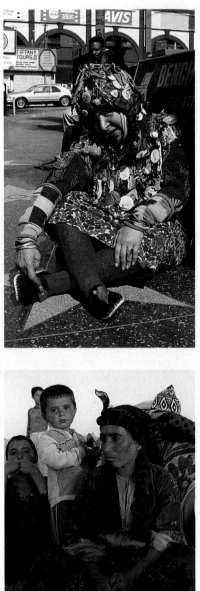

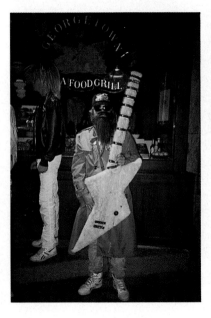

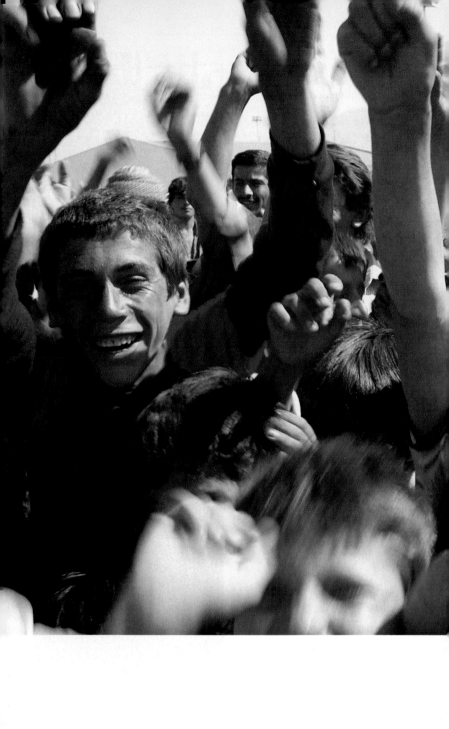

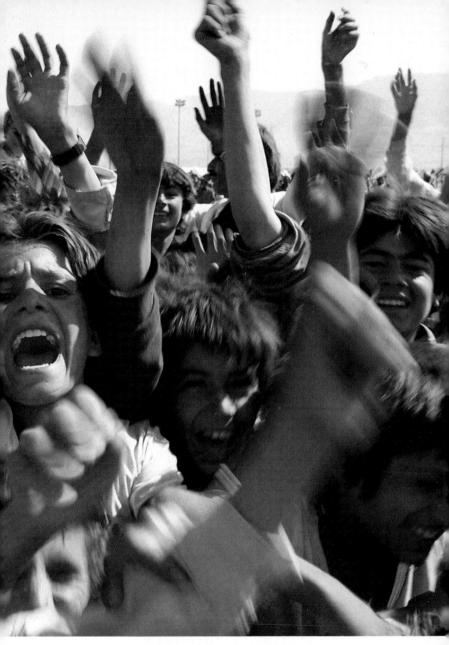

Kurdish refugees seek safety in a
Turkish camp after fleeing Saddam
Hussein's chemical weapons attacks
soon after the Iran–Iraq war ended

Right:
Faizullah, the 12-year-old puncture
man in Kabul

Below:
Young Afghan boy speaking during
International Women's Day, Kabul

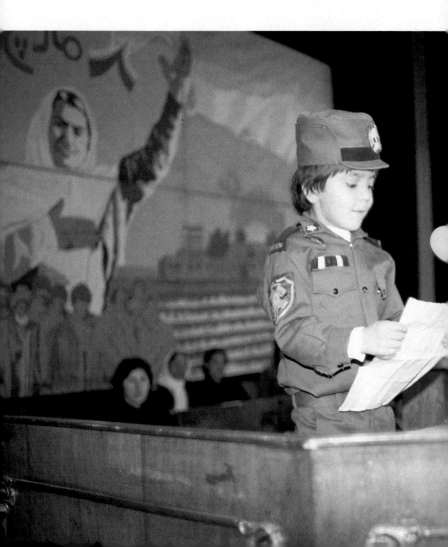

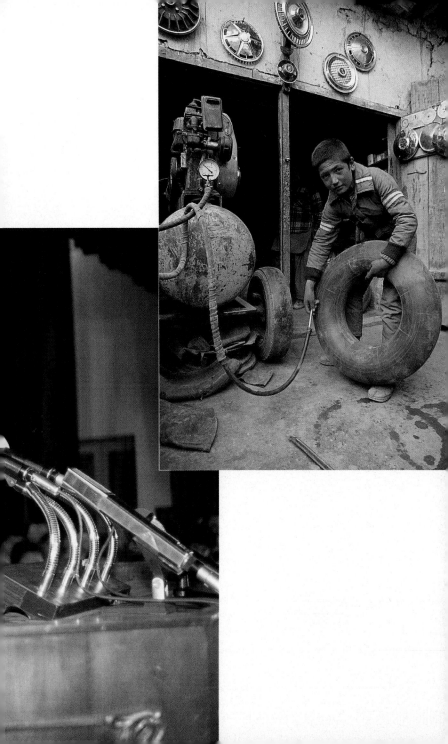

In Kabul the children's entrepreneurial flair is astounding. Mahrouf is a 14-year-old welder whose assistants are even younger than he is. He makes wheelbarrows, cots and doors out of dismembered goods containers

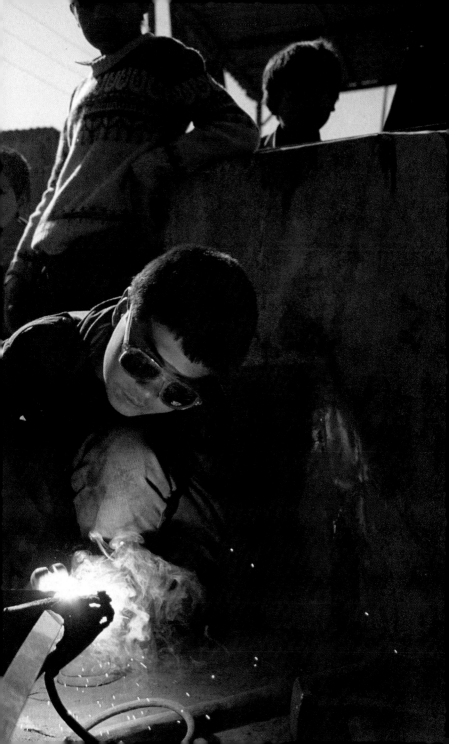

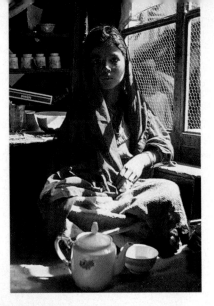

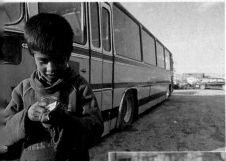

With so few Afghan men available, the children effectively run the economy

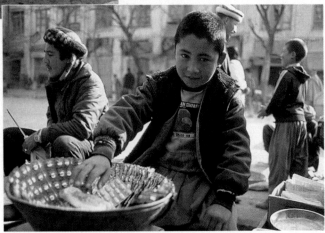

photographer for a German magazine. To begin with they insisted
on calling me 'professor' and wanted to show me the archives and
the National Museum. I was happy to go along with this, but I was
in Kabul on an assignment to produce a photographic essay. I was
advised that every day at five o'clock there was a government
briefing on the latest military and political developments. It was
like being back at school. You took pen and paper or a tape recorder
to the briefings in order to take notes. Afterwards you could ask
questions. If you played truant, one of the government press
officers would reprimand you and in the case of repeated
absenteeism they became suspicious. And if you didn't play by the
rules you were unlikely to get interviews with government officials
or permission to visit 'off limits' locations. In theory, all such
requests had to be channelled through the press office. At worst
they could expel you.

The press officers were in charge of 'facilitating' foreign correspondents' visits; they helped with translations and acted as
guides and interpreters. They were a mixed bunch. Depending on
nationality Mr Amani tried to pair the couples as he considered
most appropriate. If you were from France there was an elderly
Afghan gentleman who had been a professor at the Sorbonne in
Paris. He had returned from France on a sabbatical one week before
the revolution. Caught off-guard by events, he had become a
prisoner of circumstances. If you were Spanish you might be
escorted by Roshan, the dour and overweight figure of President
Najibullah's brother. He had spent six years studying in Havana
and spoke Spanish with a Cuban accent. There were others who
had received nicknames appropriate to their stock-in-trade
phrases, such as Mr No Problem who for a fee could fix it and
whose wealth was rumoured to be equivalent to Adnan
Kashoggi's. Mr Amani's assistant, Mr Unfortunately, had studied
how to handle the press in the Soviet Union and was a master at
excuses: 'Unfortunately, due to circumstances beyond my
control . . .' My escort, Dr Sadiqi, had spent more time in the West
than all but the Sorbonne professor. Sadiqi was a family man like
the rest of the escorts, but he was also fond of whisky, women and
Latoya Jackson. He had studied in the midwest of the United
States before the revolution and had retained fond memories of the

country and its people, but not of its paternalistic attitude or its money-equals-success formula. The highlight of his American sojourn and crowning memory was his date with Miss Ball State University 1969. All the press officers had one thing in common: a deep hatred and fear of the mujahedeen, and some were equally profane about the government. Some of them were party members; some quite possibly members of KHAD, the much feared and loathed Afghan secret service; all would have the hardest time convincing the mujahedeen they were good Muslims.

Many people I talked to spoke with equal vehemence of their hatred for both the government and the mujahedeen. They were tired of the war and frightened for their lives. An atmosphere of communal paranoia had built up. Everyone was frightened to talk openly. Depending on which rumour you listened to, Kabul taxi drivers were either all mujahedeen sympathizers or all working for the secret service. The more time I spent in Afghanistan the more I realized the two were not mutually exclusive; many Afghans who had survived the war thus far had a foot in each camp.

Because of the difficulty of finding transport it was suggested that I rent a car. This could only be done through Afghan Tour. Their office was in the Shar-i Now district of town and the staff lounged in chairs inside the dilapidated building and outside in the street. The president of Afghan Tour (a bloated bureaucracy meant that many government employees could call themselves president) was out to lunch so the vice-president suggested that in the meantime I should take a look at the official Afghan tourist brochure.

The brochure had been printed in 1977 and the country's turbulent recent history was reflected in its pages. On the first page, 'Democratic' had been penned in above 'The Republic of Afghanistan' only to have been recently crossed out. On page 3, under 'History of Afghanistan', I found several layers of stickers had been fixed across the typeset history after the last visible entry: '1929–1933 King Nadir Shah rescues the country from anarchy.' The first sticker read: '1979 . . . under the leadership of Hafizullah Amin.' I peeled it back and found another sticker that read: '1978 . . . under the leadership of Mr Noor Mohammed Taraki.' Both stickers were glued to the printed page, which read: '1973 . . .

under the leadership of Mohammed Daoud,' who had come to power that year by deposing none other than his cousin, King Zahir Shah. In recent years the country had had more bloody *putsches* and leaders than Leeds United had had managers.

For 2,500 years, since the time of Alexander the Great, foreign invaders had tried to conquer Afghanistan. The country had witnessed the passage of Genghis Khan, Tamerlane and the British. All failed to make a lasting impression. The current troubles that brought the Marxists to power grew out of a frustrated desire for social progress in a country with one of the world's lowest living standards and with strict social mores enforced by the mullahs who had wide secular influence and superpower politics. After the coup of 1973 which brought Mohammed Daoud to power with the help of Afghan Communists, Daoud remained committed to pursuing the country's traditional policy of non-alignment – ready to light his American cigarettes with Russian matches, as he was fond of saying. Five years later, in 1978, Daoud's decision to crack down on the local Communist Party, the PDPA (People's Democratic Party of Afghanistan), and the reported dismissals of Soviet-trained army officers resulted in the Saur revolution. The following year, in 1979, the first leader of the Saur revolution, Noor Mohammed Taraki, was killed in a factional dispute by his blood-crazed right-hand man Hafizullah Amin. An ultra-leftist and hardliner, Amin imposed on an unwilling populace literacy campaigns, redistribution of land and mixed schooling. Thousands of political prisoners were arrested and killed and a counter-insurgency campaign under the leadership of the clergy, landowners and disaffected army officers began. The resistance grew quickly and were known as mujahedeen or holy warriors. The Soviets were worried about the impact of the Iranian revolution, concerned over the possible spread of Islamic fundamentalism in its own Central Asian republics and nervous about the close ties of General Zia ul-Haq, Pakistan's military leader, with Saudi Arabia. The Soviets hoped to restore stability to their neighbour by installing their own man, Barbrak Karmal, as President of Afghanistan and brought 120,000 troops into the country to reimpose order. The United States and its allies immediately poured hundreds of millions of dollars into backing the mujahedeen through Pakistan's Interservices Intelligence Agency, the ISI, who had and continue to have their own agenda for the war and have often run the guerrilla war directly. The United States saw the conflict as an opportunity for revenge for Vietnam, the Chinese to stop Soviet expansionism and hegemony in the area, and the religious governments of Iran, Pakistan, Saudi Arabia and the Gulf States to further their influence. In 1986 Karmal was replaced by thirty-nine-year-old Dr Mohammed Najibullah, then head of the KHAD secret police. Najibullah has since denied that he or his associates are, or ever were, Marxists. He has referred to the 'numerous mistakes, and even big ones' that were made before he took power. But still Najibullah and the PDPA remain in power and are heavily backed by Soviet economic and military aid, and still the mujahedeen are financed and supported by the United States, Britain, China, Saudi Arabia, Iran, the Gulf States and western Europe.

I rented a bread delivery truck. There hadn't been a choice. Afghan Tour's Russian-built Volga's steering was shot, their Land-Rovers mothballed. I would also have to choose a driver and find petrol before I could get the vehicle on the road. But first I needed to change some more money. I chose not to return to Bank Melli where I had spent nearly an hour waiting to be handed enough Afghan currency to fill a suitcase – nearly 3,000 banknotes for one hundred dollars. Instead I went to Kabul's unofficial money market where dollars were exchanged openly on the black market and where the government was often forced to borrow.

I walked the short distance to Kabul's bustling open-air bazaar by the river where many of the city's two million residents buy their fruit and vegetables. To move amongst the crowds was to be on the threshold of Central Asia's crossroads – a bewildering mosaic of peoples, the descendants of countless civilizations whose fortunes had followed the crosscurrents of Central Asian conquests. They had come to trade and exchange news and gossip. There were the tall, Semitic-featured Tajiks with their aquiline noses and deep eyes. There were the jet-black hirsute Pushtuns or Pathans, the Ghilzais, the Durrani, the Mohammedzais and the Barakzais – different clans whose common link was a mutual distrust of one another. There were the Hazara from central Afghanistan, shorter powerful men

with narrow eyes and high cheekbones reputed to be the descendants of the armies of Genghis Khan. There were others: the
weather-tanned Baluch from the southwest; Turcomens and
Uzbeks of Turco-Mongol descent from the north; the Aimaq and
Firouzkohi from northwest and central Afghanistan. And there
were the 'Kutchis': campers or nomads drawn from different clans.
Styles of dress were varied and often revealed further clues to
cultural, tribal and social identity. The Panjshiris and Nuristanis
wore flat woollen caps with a rolled brim made from camel, goat or
sheep hair. The Badakhshanis donned long turbans wound around
a bright *colar* or hat. Civil servants and government officials wore
Western suits and ties in public. The poorest of the city's residents,
most merchants and men from the countryside wore traditional
dress: a long shirt to below the knees and baggy trousers.
Sometimes the traditional shalwar camise was worn in combination
with a Western-style sports jacket bought from one of the city's
many secondhand clothes markets instead of a *patou* or sheet
draped over the shoulder. Government officials and party members sported neatly trimmed moustaches, despising the long
flowing beards that were the mark of a peasant, *reesh safed* or village
elder representing the old feudal order. Later during my stay I was
gently reprimanded by several of the press officers for not shaving,
which was considered unkempt and backward. When they half-
joked that my growing six o'clock shadow was 'mujahedeen', it
was said with a suspicion that my unshaven appearance might
indeed have some sinister purpose.

The money market was a hive of activity. Money traders and
lenders gave the forecourt inside the open-air mall the frenetic buzz
of an anxious stock exchange. Traders shouted rates and wads of
notes were flourished in the air. For a small commission on the
transaction agents would seek out and take clients to a kiosk where
one could sit down to discuss business over a cup of tea. Many of
the traders were from Kabul's Sikh and Hindu communities. I was
taken to Jalil, a thin intense fourteen-year-old Hindu money-
changer on the market's first floor. His pockets were stuffed full
with wads of Afghanis. Jalil traded in dollars, pounds, francs,
Deutschmarks, roubles, rupees, Iranian rials and Abu Dhabi
dhirams. He knew all the international exchange rates and some of

the cross rates. I exchanged my dollars for Afghanis. I asked him about the Soviet departure from Afghanistan. 'Before the Russians left profits were much higher,' he told me. 'Now there are no foreigners. War is good for business,' he added. – 'Maybe peace is better.' – 'I don't know about that,' he said. 'I've never lived in times of peace. Listen, I can do you a good deal on Swiss francs and British pounds for dollars.' I bought the pounds at a 10 per cent discount, more to see Jalil at work than because I needed them. I noticed he also had French francs. We traded these as well. He deftly tapped out the international exchange rates on a pocket calculator; he'd do well on the Manhattan commodity markets. He could also arrange cash for cheques drawn on my Royal Bank of Scotland account – for a small commission.

In the bazaar children sometimes called me 'Tavarish', Russian for comrade. It felt like an invitation to be stabbed in the back and I was quick to point out that I was English. I wasn't alone in wanting to distance myself from the Russians; the vast majority of Afghans even on the government side held an ill-concealed hatred for Russians and anything that smacked of their influence. One young Soviet-trained teacher complained to me that he had to teach Russian at school. He trembled at the thought as if he had been given a dose of cyanide to swallow. As a foreigner I was often approached by Afghans in the street either out of curiosity – they thought I must be mad to choose to go to Kabul – or because they were eager to talk about their predicament. In the same way that they believed in Westerners' medicine to cure all ills, they set great store by the foreigners' ability to put an end to the war – many, for example, believed the United Nations was a country and couldn't understand why they weren't doing more for Afghanistan. I bumped into a soldier on the Pul-i-Khishti bridge. He was young, unshaven, carried a Kalashnikov and smoked a cigarette. He spoke some English and told me he had spent two years of a three-year sentence in jail (one with an Italian journalist who had been captured with the mujahedeen) for carrying a Jamiat-i-Islami mujahedeen party card. He had been paroled a year early but bound over in the army for three years. I asked him what he was going to do at the end of his military service. 'My brother's a mujahedeen commander in the Panjshir, I will go and join him.' He asked me if I wanted some 'dope', and I wondered whether he was for real. Most of the conscripts I met were politically apathetic and just wanted to survive. However, some young men had undoubtedly been influenced by the Communist regime if not the Soviets, like the adolescent who approached me in the street and repeated parrot fashion the Marxist maxim: 'We are building a nation free from exploitation, man by man!'

Remarkably, even though tens of thousands of Soviets had been in Kabul for over a decade, visible evidence of their presence had been all but erased from the city. The populace's real tastes could be seen on walls and kiosks hung with picture postcards of Indian film stars and posters of a steroid muscle-flexing Bruce Lee and a pouting Samantha Fox. A photographic shop offering hand-coloured portraits displayed examples of its traditional portraits with a 1970s poster of a porcupine-hairstyled Rod Stewart. Hoardings that once had murals emblazoned with bold socialist designs promoting Afghan–Soviet solidarity had disappeared as had the Soviet red stars above their former military and hospital compounds. Only in the Microrayan district could one find Cyrillic signs outside shops. Most of the city's signs were in either Dari or Pashtu although some English signs had remained from bygone days as in the shop advertising ACID DEALS – for car batteries.

One of the most dramatic and visible examples of the divisions that existed within Afghan society was the sight of Afghan women wearing make-up and dressed in blue jeans or skirts beside other women covered from head to toe in the all-encompassing veil called the burqa. I watched them passing in front of a poster of the pop star Madonna.

The issue of a woman's place in society went to the very heart of the Afghan civil war. One of the main reasons for the outbreak of fighting in 1978 was the Taraki and Amin government's insistence on forced literacy and mixed education for women. When I had travelled with the mujahedeen in the Afghan countryside women had been hidden from view and remained isolated in their houses. In the refugee camps in Pakistan Afghan women fared even worse; they were denied basic human rights and remained heavily secluded and dominated by the mullahs. It had been impossible for

me to see, let alone talk to, Afghan women in the countryside or in
the refugee camps.

Kabul's educated and working women were scared of losing
their new-found freedoms in the event of a mujahedeen victory.
On 8 March, International Women's Day, hundreds of women
packed the auditorium of the Zainab cinema in a rally of solidarity.
Many were enlisting in the militia and regular army units. A recent
volunteer, Hawa, was presented with an award by a deputy
commander of the women's 33rd regiment whose *nom de guerre*,
Razminda, meant 'Struggle'. Hawa climbed the steps to the
theatre's stage. The backdrop was a gigantic portrait of a scarfed,
matriarchal woman whose arm was held out in a gesture the
significance of which I didn't grasp. Hawa was dressed in
camouflage military fatigues and was visibly nervous despite her
partisan and captive audience, but she spoke forcibly of the
women's role in defence of the 'Watan', translated for me on
different occasions as Homeland or Fatherland and, in deference to
present company, as Motherland. Speaker after speaker spoke
against the reactionary and backward forces amongst the fundamentalist mujahedeen groups. The women went into rapt delight
when a tiny boy, dressed immaculately in a replica military tunic
pinned with medal portraits of Lenin, stood on a chair behind the
lectern to read from his prepared text. He basked in the women's
approval and received a standing ovation as he left the stage.
Unfortunately all too often hatred and prejudice are instilled from
an early age.

After the meeting I talked to several women who had been in the
audience. They spoke of their fear of the mujahedeen and related
the story of how before the war one of the fundamentalist leaders,
now in Pakistan, had allegedly sprayed acid in women's faces at
Kabul University because they were not veiled. Only last week,
they said, a woman had driven a minibus to one of Kabul's outlying
villages and had been dragged from the vehicle and knifed to death
by men who found her breaking of traditional mores unacceptable.

Several days after the meeting at the Zainab cinema I bumped
into Hawa in the street. She was no longer dressed in military
fatigues but in a long skirt and bright mauve woolly jumper with a
brooch. Her neat black hair curled around her shoulders, and she

smiled coyly when I spoke to her. She had only just joined the militia. No, she wasn't a Communist or a party member although she had benefited from the modernism promulgated by them. She admired the mujahedeen for the resistance they had shown the Soviets. I hesitated to ask her about her marital status; she had a boyfriend, but she was angry with him – he had fled the country and was now living in Australia. 'He should return home,' she said. They corresponded regularly.

'What sort of music do you like?' I asked.

'Afghan music and Madonna, Michael Jackson, Pet Shop Boys, Modern Talking.'

'Do you like dancing?'

'Yes.'

We talked about different styles of dress. She told me, 'The way I dress doesn't affect my ideology.' She considered herself a good Muslim.

I watched the women's 33rd regiment go through their training paces. They took up various combat positions with a Kalashnikov, practised loading and reloading ammunition clips and paraded around a courtyard. They wore loose-fitting green military tunics, soft kepis and high-heeled shoes.

Everyone had something to fear. Some mujahedeen groups had run riot pillaging and looting the towns they had captured; women were raped, the civilian population massacred, and machinery, including power plants which could have been turned to their own use, destroyed. The PDPA government had reigned by terror; torture had been commonplace; tens of thousands of people had gone missing; they had committed untold atrocities; families had been imprisoned; hundreds of villages had been razed to the ground and prisoners executed and buried in communal pits. And yet on my travels with the mujahedeen and now in Kabul the people displayed a resilience, a patience and good humour that seemed strangely unaffected and little diminished after a decade of war.

As a result of the massive influx of refugees into the city, thousands of people had colonized hillsides within the town where they had built houses of dry stone and mud-dried bricks. There was no sanitation or running water. Other refugee families had occupied the houses of Afghans who had fled the country. In the old part of town conditions amongst the dilapidated two- and three-storey hardened clay dwellings were as they had always been. Raw sewage poured from a channel in the buildings' external walls into the narrow maze of lanes below. Young boys and men who had lost limbs to anti-personnel mines hobbled on crutches through the thick glutinous mud begging for donations. I met a ten-year-old who had a prosthesis, but Ahmed didn't wear it because he was more successful without it when asking the bakers for bread.

It was a desperate existence for most of Kabul's residents. Most desperate of all was the plight of the women and children, malnourished and living in constant fear, each day a fight for survival. Young children and mothers risked arrest for breaking the dusk-to-dawn curfew in order to be in line for pitiful rations of bread. They trudged through the mud and across frozen pools of slush for eight pancake-size pieces of *nan* per family. They waited patiently in long queues in the freezing cold for hours until the bakeries opened. As the mujahedeen tightened the noose around the city food became increasingly scarce. Two dozen eggs cost the equivalent of an average week's salary. I remember seeing a crowd massed around a small bakery in the Old Town. The bakery wasn't yet open but children had climbed onto its roof. The crowd began to push forward, they swarmed around the hut pressing against its sides. Some youths had forced a side door open, grabbed loaves of bread, struggled free of the men inside and then pushed their way back through the scrum clutching their stolen loaves like American footballs. The men inside the bakery struggled to keep the angry chaotic mob from storming the flimsy hut. Gunfire broke out as plain-clothes militiamen fired into the air to restore order. Scenes such as this were commonplace and were repeated right across the city.

Nobody knows exactly how many Afghans have died as a result of the war. The figures generally quoted were between 1.2 and 1.5 million dead, approximately one in ten of the pre-war population. Comparable figures for Britain would be 6 million dead, for the United States 22 million. Several hundred thousand Afghans had been maimed and orphaned, tens of thousands of children left as breadwinners for their families. Children had become carpenters, mechanics, pharmacists and labourers. Many were successful entrepreneurs; others were apprentices working for slave wages.

Salam was eight years old; he had an untreated sore on his forehead; he wore torn overalls and his face was obscured by grease and metallic dust from the Volkswagen Beetle he was sanding down. His father had died in the war and he now worked as a trainee panel beater and paint sprayer for his uncle. He worked six days a week for fifty Afghanis (equivalent to two pieces of *nan*). Others had been more 'fortunate'; twelve-year-old Faizullah's father had been conscripted into the army. Faizullah had taken over the running of the family car tyre repair shop. I often went to see Faizullah and when I subsequently returned to Kabul was able to give him a picture of himself at work. Six days of the week he bicycled to work at dawn and returned home just in time for the curfew. He paid for his family's rent, food and clothes. When I first visited Faizullah he was struggling to make ends meet; initially his father's customers hadn't trusted him to do a competent job. Subsequently business had picked up; even the army began to patronize him for pit-stop repairs to punctured tyres and he occasionally employed a ten-year-old when he became too busy to clear the backlog of orders. He had little time for relaxation or games, though he enjoyed playing football, flying kites or watching the dog fights on the Sabbath. He had never seen television and had only been to the cinema once in his life. It was an Indian movie that had left a lasting impression on him. I thought he would be concerned about his father's safety, but he told me he didn't think much harm would come to his father. He explained, 'He's with Sayed Jaffar in Baghlan Province. There's not much fighting there.' How's that, I asked, curious. 'We're Ismailis, we've made peace with the government and we don't fight the mujahedeen.' Independent agreements were being worked out between regional resistance commanders and bribes were being offered to keep open the Salang Highway, Kabul's umbilical cord to the Soviet Union.

I was to hear a lot more about Sayed Jaffar, local warlord and self-proclaimed King of Afghanistan. He has been described as one of Britain's 'more dangerous old boys'. He was sent to school in Birmingham where he was a pupil at the Blue Coat prep school until he left for the United States where he attended the Hiram W. Dodd Elementary School and South Mountain Junior High in Pennsylvania. He was expelled from Junior Mountain High sixteen times for being a wild and crazy teenager (once for punching a teacher). He joined a motorcycle gang and worked in the local McDonald's in Allentown, Pennsylvania, and now rode trail bikes across his territory. He was a fan of Heavy Metal music and rock-and-roll, his favourite song 'Highway to Hell'. The government had made him governor of Baghlan Province north of Kabul and bestowed on him the title of general.

It was to the children I turned when I wanted to buy scarce petrol. They ran the black market in petrol, kerosene and diesel fuel from the Khair Khana district or 'Container City', as the area was appropriately nicknamed after the profusion of containers which had been recycled into everything from shops to garages and dismantled to provide doors, walls and building blocks. Many of the children were from the Panjshir, a valley to the north of Kabul, and were secret admirers of the Tajik guerrilla commander Ahmed Shah Massoud. I was taken to Abdul Latif, a young boy not much higher than my waist with a cocky smile and grubby appearance. His office was in the carcass of an abandoned bus in a wrecker's yard. We exchanged polite formal greetings and began to chat. He had recently arrived from a mujahedeen-controlled village. I listened in awe as he recounted with obvious relish his adventures crossing unhindered between warring factions and past Kabul's three security belts under the noses of government checkpoints. Fascinated, I wondered whether he was one of the children who carried messages between the city's fifth columnists and the mujahedeen. But he was running out of patience with my tiresome questioning. He had business to attend to: 'Do you want to buy petrol or not? I haven't got all day to stand around talking to you.' He counted my wads of notes with great dexterity and slipped them under his Princeton sweatshirt.

Children not only risked death and mutilation through the vagaries of war, but for a few pennies they risked life and limb out of economic necessity. Fuel was so scarce that children took to stripping the city's trees of their bark. Once stripped, the trees were felled. When there were no more left, they strayed beyond the city's limits into unmarked minefields in search of firewood.

Nowhere were the horrors of war more evident than in the city's primitive hospital wards. Statistics revealed only part of the story. Prior to the war Afghanistan had one of the lowest life expectancy rates in the world. Since the revolution life expectancy had been further reduced to about thirty to thirty-five years. To find a similar level in Europe one has to go back to the beginning of the seventeenth century.

Before the Soviet departure there had been some 200 doctors in Kabul. Fearing a mujahedeen victory, abysmal living conditions and the prospect of starvation, doctors, nurses, teachers, civil servants and university professors fled the country, swelling the ranks of professional Afghans who had already taken the same action to escape government persecution. One woman told me how she would arrive at work to find that colleagues had secretly slipped out of Kabul on the Sabbath or the previous night or that the luckier ones had flown to New Delhi. Now only sixty doctors remained, many medicines were unobtainable and those that were had to be bought in the bazaar. In the countryside an almost total lack of medical aid considerably reduced the injured's chances of survival.

The government's air force bombed mujahedeen-held villages. Within hours the casualties were brought into the government surgeries. Coated in grime and infested by cockroaches, the Kabul hospital wards and corridors were overflowing; wounded children often shared a bed. To me it was like a scene from Dante's inferno: Amputees, Neurological and Spinal Cord Injuries, Burns . . .

Outside the Wazir Akhbar Khan Hospital a row of stretchers caked in layers of blood were lined up to dry in the sun. The injured were brought in from the countryside with untreated festering wounds, carried by friends or relatives like broken toys. They had gangrene and deep bedsores. Many had gaping wounds and raw stumps where limbs had been blown off. Their stumps were wrapped in filthy flyspecked and bloodstained bandages. The families who had staggered into the hospitals with their injured had nowhere to stay and camped wherever they could, often next to their relatives in the wards. Every day the casualty list grew: six, eight, a dozen people killed and more injured by rocket attacks on Kabul. In the city of Jalalabad, where a major battle was being fought, the casualties ran into the hundreds and there were no official figures from the countryside where farms and paths were littered with mines and where thousands of refugees continued to flee the country to Pakistan and Iran or moved into the capital to escape. The government's continued bombing and shelling of the countryside hadn't abated since the Soviet withdrawal and in some areas had increased.

The government had run out of prostheses. They had a waiting list of over 4,000. In the recently built International Red Cross rehabilitation centre they could prepare a maximum of thirty-six prostheses a month; thousands more were needed. There was a shortage of wheelchairs. I witnessed young legless children being carried about in ordinary chairs. Along one wall of the centre, a forest of crutches waited for those who had graduated from the physiotherapists' exercises. The Red Cross's prostheses were fitted with modern trainers; they stood in rows on top of workbenches waiting to be filed, shaved and fitted to sit snugly on a stump. Several of the trainers boasted designer labels such as 'Maradona'. The Argentinian footballer's talent was matched in every way by the stoicism, strength and good humour of the disabled, even amongst children who had been cut down before their lives had begun.

The people's suffering made the government's past dogma all the more unpalatable. Each day the sky was filled with cascading flares and resounded to the drone of giant Soviet Ilyushins. It was a reminder that the government wasn't going to give up without a fight and that the Soviet airlift, which continued into 1991, resupplying ammunition and new arms, was going to ensure that, whatever the outcome, it would be a bloody one.

Some of the flares didn't burn properly on their descent and the hospital wards were full of casualties with appalling burns caused by magnesium flares that, instead of burning up in the air, destroyed men, women and children on the ground. I visited two small children in the Indira Gandhi Hospital. It seemed that only their eyes had not been exposed to the burning magnesium. They lay on beds unable to move, screaming with agony from skin that had been torched to a cinder. One of the children had a talisman tied to a thin rope around his ankle. That too had been charred. One mother and her husband and two of her three children had been horribly disfigured when a flare had landed in their garden.

Each day the government's tenuous hold over several provincial capitals became yet more uncertain. Apart from the government's northern enclave around the city of Mazar-i-Sharif, most roads were in mujahedeen hands. Even if they weren't, the risk of military convoys being ambushed was great. Resupply to the government's enclaves was by aircraft, but as they came under increasing mujahedeen ground fire and missiles they had to be abandoned. The government never admitted to losing military outposts. At the daily briefings Mr Amani read from prepared notes, Dr Sadiqi translated. Mr Amani was a master at camou-flaging emotions in the best diplomatic tradition and he had the politician's ability to invent, change the subject and give answers to questions that had not been asked. In answer to questions about the fall of the government outpost of Samarkhel near Jalalabad, the press office repeatedly denied that Samarkhel had fallen to the mujahedeen. After repeating the denials for days, the press office calmly announced that Samarkhel had been retaken by government forces. Several prisoners were brought before press conferences, their confessions no doubt either the result of fear or coercion. They included a number of Pakistanis, an Egyptian, a Sudanese and an Arab Wahhabi. Occasionally the government produced mujahedeen 'defectors' who spoke with little conviction and looked as if they had come straight from central casting.

Hardly a day went by when rockets didn't land on Kabul. According to the government they always struck soft targets, killing innocent women and children; they never hit military targets – or the government never told us about those. Detective-fashion I double-checked the number of explosions with ear-witnesses if not eye-witnesses. Since journalists were unable to move beyond Kabul and there were few independent sources it was easy for the government to stage-manage its propaganda. Facetiously I parodied one of their briefings in my notebook: 'Today twelve people were injured by extremists, of those thirty-six were women and children.' Later in the year when I returned to Kabul for a news service and as a radio correspondent, reporting became increasingly difficult. One day I stumbled across a battery of missiles being fired repeatedly at a distant mountain range. The soldiers manning the battery told me it was part of an offensive against a village some twenty-five miles away. It had been in progress for several days but the press office denied all knowledge and it went unreported in the local press. On another occasion a plane was blown up on the airport runway by a mujahedeen-fired mortar. I asked the press office for confirmation; they told me the billowing smoke was from an oil drum that had caught fire!

The government-controlled English-language *Kabul Times* was probably one of the world's few newspapers not the subject of a takeover bid by media moghuls Rupert Murdoch or Robert Maxwell, but the *Kabul Times* didn't have much to learn from the *Sun* or the *Daily Mirror* when it came to sensational articles. Under headlines such as CONFESSIONS OF AN ARRESTED EXTREMIST, PAKISTANI MILITARY AGGRESSION AGAINST AFGHANISTAN UNVEILED PART VII and EXTREMISTS ENJOY KILLING . . . the mujahedeen were variously described as 'cut-throat criminal groups' and 'sold-out warmongering extremists' who had, in language unconsciously borrowed from Dr Who's Daleks, been 'suppressed', 'exterminated' or 'eliminated' by the government's 'security organs', in 'tooth-shattering' and 'jaw-breaking blows'. And a commentary reflecting centuries of blood-feuds warned, 'The day will arrive soon and the people will take revenge of the blood of their sons upon them.' Killing was so commonplace that the newspaper could write in an article under the headline 'NORMAL LIFE REPORTED COUNTRY-WIDE' that 140 warmongers had been killed in action, 115 surface-to-surface extremist shells fired on the city of Gardez and tons of enemy ammunition annihilated. Simultaneously 472 patriotic youths had voluntarily joined the army (a government euphemism for press-ganged). This was a day when 'The military situation throughout the country has been reported as very normal in the last twenty-four hours,' and 'no incident has been observed'. The *Kabul Times* had not mentioned the final day of the Soviet withdrawal on 15 February.

* * *

As I returned to the Kabul Hotel along the city's empty streets before curfew, a momentary lull in activity took place before haunting sounds filled the night like the continuous buzz that fills the jungle. I often lay awake on my bed listening to the ravenous bark of scavenging dogs roaming in packs and the distant crack of automatic gunfire. I felt a thousand hearts were momentarily stilled when the rumble of rocket fire could be heard right across the city, but it was impossible to tell whether it was an incoming mujahedeen attack or an outgoing rocket fired by soldiers of the government. Tanks and armoured personnel carriers thundered along the tarmac beneath my window overlooking one of Kabul's main thoroughfares; great columns of armour crossed the city under cover of darkness to shore up the city's defences. And like clockwork, the drone from a low-flying spotter plane circled overhead. There was never a quiet moment. The city was far from asleep. In darkness families gathered in silence to rendezvous with a contact who for a fee would escort them out of the city and hand them over to a guide who would lead them along the treacherous path to exile. Mujahedeen sympathizers delivered *shabnama*, or night letters, to many parts of the city. They informed Kabul's residents of the latest mujahedeen victories and directed their supporters in actions against the government. Streets and neigh-bourhoods were cordoned off by the security forces and houses were systematically searched for members of the resistance, subversive literature, weapons, young conscripts and draft dodgers. Families too poor to pay bribes for their sons to be escorted to Pakistan or to receive a soft posting away from the trenches hid them in an attempt to prevent their being press-ganged into the army. I met one such family whose son had been caught and immediately drafted.

For the four weeks I stayed at the Kabul, the hotel was host and home to a bewildering variety of people. At night the waiters, cleaners and guests would crowd around the communal television set to watch the local news before switching to a Russian channel broadcast from Soviet Central Asia which played Siberian Westerns. If an electricity cut interrupted the programmes for more than a few minutes the recumbent audience wondered whether the city's power plant at Sorabei had been captured by the mujahedeen.

Among the hotel guests were several Iranian refugees including a family of five who had fled to war-torn Afghanistan to escape the ayatollahs' Iran. Everyone's plight was relative. The depths of despair had no limits. Whilst Afghans fled to Iran, Iranians were using the same route in reverse to seek temporary asylum in Afghanistan. The Iranian refugees dreamed of going to the United States, Britain and West Germany, but only Portugal and Finland had considered their requests for asylum. Several of the hotel's residents were mujahedeen defectors. One said he had been a bodyguard to the fundamentalist mujahedeen leader Gulbuddin Hekmatyar. He told me he had been shot seven times by the government whilst fighting for the mujahedeen and five times by the mujahedeen whilst fighting for the government. He had several bullet wounds to prove his point. However he said he was going into early retirement and was headed north to Mazar-i-Sharif.

Kabul had become official residence to several important exiles and defectors including two Baluch leaders from Pakistan and the most notorious of all defectors and one-time officer in the Afghan army, the renegade ex-mujahedeen commander and now self-appointed Field-Marshal of Afghanistan, Esmatullah Muslim Achakzai. He had been one of the mujahedeen's most resourceful and effective commanders based in the Kandahar area with his own group, the Fedayin-Islam, but had become disenchanted by the corruption surrounding the supply of weapons from Pakistan and the desire of Pakistan to consolidate the authority of the seven main mujahedeen parties. For a hefty bribe Esmat Muslim had defected with most of his men to the regime who confirmed him in control of his area when his men joined Soviet troops in 1985. He was now almost as useful to the government as he had previously been to the mujahedeen, controlling the supply routes between the city of Kandahar and the border with Pakistan. The previous year he had, however, received dozens of shrapnel wounds in a shoot-out with the Afghan security forces of which he was then a member.

Esmatullah was a wild character and a law unto himself. He drove around Kabul in his personal Mercedes protected by dozens of his machine-gun-wielding followers in a fleet of expensive jeeps. He owned several grandiose houses in the city and kept a harem of concubines. The field-marshal boasted he had ten wives all under the age of twenty-two. He had once said that it was lucky that his main personal bodyguard was an illiterate deaf mute, 'Otherwise he would have had to be shot because he knows too much.'

Each time I bumped into him in the street his glazed eyes were hidden behind a pair of dark glasses; he packed a magnum in his anorak pocket, was either stoned or drunk and was always with a different sulking but stunning Afghan bimbo. He could be as magnanimous in his generosity as he was ruthless in his dealings with anyone who displeased him. (He had reportedly been expelled from military school in the Soviet Union for stealing drugs.) Like other commanders who defected between warring protagonists at the flip of a coin, or at least the price of a Krugerrand, Esmatullah, who claims in his time to have worked for both the KGB and the CIA, was rumoured to be once again considering defection – back to the mujahedeen.

Another larger-than-life figure was the gregarious mayor of Kabul, General Hakim. I met him in his office and over cups of tea and a tray of assorted nuts we discussed the chronic shortages of everything from housing to sanitation and food, the new refugees who were arriving in their hundreds every week and his ambitions for the city. 'My ambition is to twin Kabul with New York or Washington DC, London, Tokyo and Rome,' he told me grandiloquently. As for the chronic shortages: 'I've witnessed the homeless and destitute in Atlanta, Georgia, and no one in Kabul has died of hypothermia,' he said. A voracious reader, the mayor was studying *The 2nd Long Term Plan for the Tokyo Metropolis* in the hope of turning Kabul into a modern city. It has often been said that the Soviet Union and the United States were fighting a war by proxy across a poor, small, defenceless country, but in General Hakim there was a cool, calculating man who made the Soviet Union and the United States look like Afghan pawns. Sent by King Zahir Shah on a US scholarship to train with the US Special Forces and the US Army's highly trained Ranger Force at various centres including the Kennedy Center at Fort Bragg, where he studied tactics for use against terrorists and in urban and guerrilla warfare, he returned to Afghanistan to use his US training with Soviet military aid to banish the monarchy and American influence in favour of a Soviet-supported socialist government. Like many Afghans in government ranks he shared a common background with the mujahedeen. Not only had he studied at school under Sibghatullah Mojadedi, now one of the mujahedeen leaders in Pakistan, but Sibghatullah Mojadedi was a distant relative. I asked the general what he did in his spare time.

'When I've finished answering letters from Switzerland and China requesting Afghan stamps and banknotes, I settle down to read books by Chekhov, Gorki, Steinbeck and Jack London. I also watch movies on my VCR.'

'Such as?'

'Clint Eastwood and Charles Bronson, and I have all the Rambo movies.'

'What do you think of *Rambo IV* in Afghanistan?'

He used words to the effect that it was bullshit. Not only were Rambo movies making the rounds in Kabul, but bootlegged copies of 'Top of the Pops' were a favourite amongst the children of the well-to-do.

The strains that had pulled the nation apart were still present after a decade of war which had brought tragedy and grief to every Afghan family. Even a few stolen moments of revelry at the lavish wedding receptions held at the Kabul Hotel were cause for the fundamentalists to take exception. The bride, who was in full view of the guests, was made up to look like a garish porcelain figurine. The guests were dressed in fashions held over from the fifties, sixties and seventies. Women were draped in secondhand sequins, glitter gowns and voluminous taffeta dresses. Men wore Bulgarian and Romanian suits, tweed jackets and bell-bottoms. The band played deafening tunes that were a curious mixture of Hindi and Salsa music, the product of a synthesizer which produced syncopated Latin rhythms and a long-haired bongo player dressed in a tank-top T-shirt. The volume of music was so loud, the men dancing with such abandon, that it was impossible to hear the muezzins' call to prayers from loudspeakers atop the city's minarets. Nevertheless, a section of male guests would always rise from the reception at the prescribed time and move to the hotel lobby to unfurl prayer mats and prostrate themselves in the direction of Mecca.

A great source for the study of Afghan history was a small

bookshop which although not fully stocked could produce rare
secondhand titles at a few days' notice. Page 65 of *Among the Wild
Tribes of the Afghan Frontiers* by T. L. Pennell was franked with the
Kabul British Council Library stamp, which made me suspect that
these books had not been legitimately acquired. I took Pennell back
to the hotel and read his opening chapter, written in 1908: 'The East
is a country of contradictions, and the Afghan character is a strange
medley of contradictory qualities, in which courage blends with
stealth, the basest treachery with the most touching fidelity,
intense religious fanaticism with an avarice which will even induce
him to play false to his faith, and a lavish hospitality with an
irresistible propensity for thieving. The vendetta, or blood-feud,
has eaten into the very core of Afghan life, and the nation can never
become healthily progressive till public opinion of revenge alters.
At present some of the best and noblest families in Afghanistan are
on the verge of extermination through this wretched system. Even
the women are not exempt.' This Pushtun code of honour and
vengeance was further exacerbated by the continuing war.

One man to whom foreigners turned for impromptu history
lessons was the 'Italian Mullah' or 'Christian Mullah', as Kabul's
priest was known to the local bazaaris. For the last twenty-five
years Father Panigati had resided in Kabul under an agreement that
allowed the Vatican to post a priest to the capital although he was
forbidden by the accord to propagate his faith beyond the foreign
community. One of his favourite duties was tending the Christian
shrine where the remains of ten British soldiers killed in 1879
during the second British–Afghan War were buried along with a
group of young Westerners described by Father Panigati as
hippies. Like many thousands of foreigners these hippies had come
to Afghanistan in the sixties and seventies for its dramatic natural
setting and the easy availability of high-quality hashish.

Father Panigati dressed in cardigans, poloneck shirts and a linen
cap. The sixty-four-year-old priest's unhurried, good-humoured
manner reminded me of retired men on the village green as he
recalled his previous parish in Leicester in the British Midlands. His
order, the Regular Clerics of St Barnabas, was Milan-based and
known colloquially as the Barnabites. His only links with the

outside world were a telex machine and his short-wave radio, on which he followed the fortunes of his favourite English team, Leicester City Football Club. A keen fan, he also knew the latest results for the leading English, Italian and Scottish football divisions as well as those of Formula One motor racing. On Vatican orders he would not have his comments about the war recorded, but before I left the modest bungalow in the Italian embassy compound where he lived with his two dogs, he opened a drawer which contained fragments of spent metal cartridges from the heat-deflecting flares that continually fell on his garden. He offered me one as a souvenir of my stay. No one could fail to be affected by the continuing horrors of the war. I wondered when and where it would all end. I thought of an earlier reply the Father had given me on the Soviet withdrawal, the closest he came to a political comment. 'The Soviets will leave Afghanistan fifty days after the end of the world,' he had said.

At the end of March, one month after my arrival in Kabul, I packed my bag as the rockets continued to fall on the capital, sometimes over thirty a day. Kabul was still under siege, but the mujahedeen were no closer to victory. For the same reasons the Soviets had not defeated the mujahedeen, now the mujahedeen had failed to take a single major town. The Red Army had fought a hundred armies with no central command; the mujahedeen were still deeply divided, which made a coordinated attack on the cities impossible.

The war had now dragged on for longer than the First and Second World Wars combined but the mujahedeen continued to fragment. Arms and money had acted as detergent does to oil in water, breaking the mujahedeen up into even smaller groups. The divisions within the ruling government coalition still existed but for the time being they had been set aside. Its members had to stand together for any chance of survival – if they didn't they could expect no mercy at the hands of the mujahedeen.

The civilians, alienated and uprooted, were pulled in different directions. The government drove them into the cities; into refugee camps in Pakistan and Iran where they were bonded to the mujahedeen leaders in exile. In the Afghan countryside some mujahedeen commanders forced peasants to stay in their valleys, while others forced them to leave.

In a game of poker called 'positive symmetry' each superpower had the right to arm its respective proxy whenever the other did the same. The protagonists had been armed to batter each other in a war of mutual attrition, and the superpower war games still continued two years after the Soviet withdrawal with weapons of ever greater mass destruction; 120mm mortars became cluster bombs, cluster bombs became 1,700-pound ballistic warheads; killing was breeding killing in a race towards obliteration.

The country was torn apart by a war to which there seemed no possible end. I was also torn by my own personal dilemma, having witnessed the terror on both sides: perpetrators turned victims; victims turned perpetrators. There were moral questions I had failed to address, or had avoided addressing.

I felt I had betrayed the mujahedeen. I felt tainted by my presence on the government side; they could not be pardoned for the holocaust they had inflicted on the nation, for whilst their policies seemed admirable in intent, they had been imposed on an unwilling populace. The vast majority of the people still supported the mujahedeen, but the women outside the cities had never had a voice. I thought of the cartoonist who had drawn two pictures of the same mujahedeen with different captions. In the first, above the caption 'Before 15 February', they were labelled: 'heroic, valorous, brave freedom fighters' as they pointed their guns at an occupation force; in the second, after the Soviet withdrawal, the caption read: 'reactionary, backward, fundamentalist fanatics', their guns now pointed at each other. But not all the freedom fighters were corrupt mujahedeen, nor all the militia gun-running, heroin-pushing mercenaries. Anyway, who were we to judge them? We were the mercenaries. The West had armed and equipped many Afghans in our common battle to prevent Soviet hegemony. The Afghan mujahedeen had been the West's footmen, our soldiers in a war in which no Americans or British or Frenchmen had shed their blood.

I had returned to Afghanistan in the hope of getting back to Herat to see the guerrilla commander Ismail Khan. I wondered whether he would now consider me a traitor. Personal shame was compounded by journalistic opportunism. I had for some time had more faith in the government's ability to defend itself than the mujahedeen's ability to defeat the heavily dug-in, well-equipped Afghan army. To be totally honest, I felt myself a coward too for not returning to the mujahedeen. I remembered the living nightmare of daily bombardments in Herat; to survive each day felt like a miracle and I was terrified at the thought of returning clandestinely from either Pakistan or Iran.

I had not been able to renew my links with Ismail Khan. The last I had heard from him was in a letter I had received three months before arriving in Kabul. But Afghanistan is a small country, and in a shop in Kabul I bumped into one of Ismail Khan's teachers when he had been a student at a Kabul military academy. The recently retired military officer seemed in a world of his own, self-effacing before my prying questions. He told me he had taught Ismail Khan psychology, military strategy and mathematics. He didn't say it but he must have felt wretched for he had trained officers to the best of his knowledge in the art of warfare only to see his class divide along cultural, clan and political lines and use the skills he had imparted to kill off their classmates.

Two days before my departure from Kabul I was approached by a Soviet journalist, a KGB agent. His motive in coming to see me at my hotel quickly became apparent. As we drove across town in his car he wanted to know if I would negotiate on the Soviet Union's behalf with certain guerrilla commanders I had met on my previous journey. So far they had been steadfast in their refusal to deal with Moscow. It was the kind of role I had always seen myself in, but the political ramifications were beyond my comprehension. I couldn't possibly accept; anything that might have opened a dialogue and served the cause of peace would have been worthwhile, but I hoped to return to Afghanistan again and the risk of being compromised by such a mission was too great. As I stepped out of the car I was puzzled that the KGB man was driving a brand new Japanese model. I asked him about this. 'It's a security precaution. We've traded in our Russian cars for Japanese ones. The Afghans have placed too many car bombs under Russian cars.' I watched him as he drove away – either through a breach in security or contempt for Afghan intelligence, they hadn't changed the licence numbers – the car still carried Soviet military plates.

Before leaving I returned to one of the hospitals to visit a young boy who had had a leg blown off whilst on duty for a government self-defence force. He had lost his parents; his mother had recently died when a rocket exploded on his house, his father had died a year earlier fighting for the mujahedeen, his elder brother for the government. He was left alone in the world with his one-year-old baby brother who had miraculously escaped death when part of their house had collapsed from the direct hit which had killed their mother. I also went to the women's ward to see Fatimeh. She was about fifteen years old and had small green diamond-shaped tattoos on her forehead and cheeks. (Few children knew their exact age; some told me they were born in the summer or the winter and that their fathers had grey hair.) Fatimeh was a wisp of a girl who belonged to the militia and had been defending the airport in Khost when a heavy enemy bullet had pierced her lower back. By the time she had told me how many cousins, uncles, brothers and other family members had been killed I had counted twenty-two. She lay motionless on her bed except to pick at pieces of bread that had been dipped in a bowl of soup that rested between her head and shoulder. She had been fighting for the militia for the last two years and I asked her if she would return to fight. She didn't appear anxious to do so, but said it was her duty to protect her country and village and if the government asked her, she would return to the battlefield. I passed the doctor outside the ward and asked him when her condition would improve. He told me she was paralysed below the waist – they hadn't told her yet.

On the wide asphalt road to the airport the twentieth century met the medieval age. A tank had stopped in the road, it had run out of diesel. The soldiers had probably sold it on the black market. A shepherd passed by with his flock of sheep. I stopped at the village of Bibimaru. It was difficult to tell whether the tumbledown sand-coloured houses had grown organically out of the ground or were being reclaimed by it. I watched a long line of children as they queued with buckets, jerry cans and pots for water from a standpipe. Beyond them several cows were tethered to a post where a child sat polishing a shoe glued to a detached prosthesis. There was a cemetery marked by simple stones and the green and red flags of martyrdom – one of thousands around the country. Like Tibet, Afghanistan had been changed irreversibly by an invading neighbour, but to have seen what was before the war as a quaint, carefree existence was to ignore the fact that it was poor, brutal and, for the individual, short.

I arrived for my flight minutes after several rockets had struck the airport. There weren't enough ambulances to take the injured to hospital; they had already used up their monthly rations of petrol. I had seen everything reduced to nothing; the fight to survive, the brink of starvation; the fear, terror and bitterness; the blind brutality; the primitive wards with the smell of death; the agonized screams and the abandoned children. Countless lives were being sacrificed on the altars of personal vendettas, blood-feuds, regional conflicts, spheres of influence and superpowers.

7

THE MAGIC KINGDOM

If we can dream it, we can do it.

General Electric

Go kill 'em! Let them eat bullets. We do
so much for all these countries, they're
selling us all these drugs, it's time we do
something for ourselves.

A gas station attendant on
sending 2,000 US troops to
Panama. Florida, April 1989

Florida, April–May 1989

Three days later Caroline took me shopping. She sat in a chair in the
Men's Department. 'Oooh, my, that's just how I want you to look!'
she said as I turned around in front of her dressed in a chic $500
blazer. She spoke to the tailor and then turned to me, 'This one's
fine, for the five nights I need you.' The tailor looked at me
knowingly; it wasn't what he thought. 'Excuse me,' said Caroline to
the tailor. 'Could you find him two pairs of slacks to go with the
blazer?' I tried on the trousers, selected a couple of shirts, ties and a
pair of shoes. She paid for them by American Express.

I tumbled out of Barney's into the clear New York morning
clutching boxes, carrier bags and a suit bag. Caroline hailed a cab. I
felt like the man in a version of a Cole Porter song, 'I get stocks and
bonds from faded blondes . . . I'm one of those pets they forget but
tailors remember – Thank God I'm a gigolo.'

It had all begun six months before in October 1988 at New York's
Asia Society, where I had been invited to give a lecture. I needed to
be more than usually inspired; I knew that my lecture agent had

brought along talent scouts to show them her 'find', like a football player whose transfer was subject to a closely scrutinized performance. I passed the test and, after a subsequent audition to see if I could read naturally from a teleprompter, was signed up by one of the largest US corporations for their $5 million recognition meetings. The corporate 'shows' took place in Miami Beach and Palm Beach – the Monte Carlos of the United States.

Before flying to Miami, Caroline, a producer on the corporate show, took me shopping – jeans were out of the question and Paul Smith designer clothes were considered too fashion conscious; they were looking for something more conservative – not Savile Row, but smart. After lunch my agent briefed me about my forthcoming tour. 'I have fitted extra lectures in between the business conventions to keep you busy. You will be talking to women's groups, universities and museums. The women's groups flipped over you. They can't pay the same as colleges, but it will be very good for you to go to them. The woman in Cleveland, for instance, is a trustee of a *wonderful* group in Palm Beach, where they do have money.'

That evening I flew to Baltimore to give a lecture and take a class at the university, so I arrived in Miami somewhat exhausted. In four days since leaving Kabul I had flown through Tashkent, Moscow and Prague, stopped in London overnight, flown to New York, given a class and a lecture in Baltimore, and was now being whisked in a thirty-foot limousine to rehearsals in Miami Beach.

The sleek smoke-glassed stretch limousine was something else. It was air-conditioned, had thick pile carpets and inlaid wood panelling, a 'liquid refreshment centre' (with thermo-cooled wine rack included), cut-glass decanters and glasses of different shapes and sizes, two electrical sockets, two telephones, a safe, vanity mirror, television set and videocassette recorder. 'Where's the paper shredder?' I asked the chauffeur jokingly. 'That's extra, only fitted as standard in the "Trump Line" model.'

My escort quickly laid down the rules. 'When you are on stage we don't want any dirty jokes, no ethnic jokes and you must not slight the competition.' By way of example I was told how a famous entertainer was not asked back because at the end of his act he told the audience that at one point in his life he had felt 'lower than a turtle's titties'. And only last year a comedian was fired for repeating a story that had appeared in the newspapers on a new African cult, an updated version of shrunken heads – shrunken penises. I was under no illusions as to what the corporation's terms and conditions did and didn't permit. I had signed a six-page contract – you either toed the party line or you were out.

I was driven to the Fontainebleau Hotel (pronounced Fountain Blue) in Miami Beach. The room, as I had come to expect from the American leg of my book tour, had enough shampoos, soaps, body lotions and conditioners, combs and shoe polishes to furnish a guest bathroom for years to come. On the TV, Channel 10 ran a programme on the hotel's facilities; Channel 12 began with the message, 'Welcome Mr Danziger. Press 1 for accounts, press 2 for account review, press 3 for account review and check-out.' I had only just checked in.

My first rehearsal was an utter disaster; I could hardly stand up for tiredness let alone read naturally from a teleprompter. The first show was in two days' time, and the producers began to panic as they questioned my ability to deliver the commentary to accompany an eighteen-projector slide show of my work which had been commissioned as a visual backdrop. But it was nothing a good night's sleep couldn't remedy.

I went to bed with my script and concentrated on learning my lines. The next morning I breakfasted in my room and readied myself for the rehearsal with Caroline. I was surprised to find her putting some of the company's vice-presidents through their paces. She had been speech coaching them, she later explained to me. 'They don't use their bodies or voices well. They offer unemotional analysis usually in a deadly drone, and the points they are trying to put across can send their audiences to sleep.' So Caroline was coaching the executives to deliver balance sheets in a lively fashion, walk gracefully and not fidget or tap the lectern. Like lawyers, who now consult actors and drama coaches, the corporation executives were learning how to improve their performances before their own judges and juries. Speech writers laced their speeches with suitable quotations and appropriate puns.

Caroline was part of a much larger team of producers, directors and stage managers. Ten gigantic trucks had brought in $10 million of equipment; the rigging came from Chicago, the video equipment from Atlanta, state-of-the-art lasers from Boston and projection equipment from New York. The outdoor events commanded an additional seven trucks: three for the marquee from Memphis and four for the generators. There were stage sets, sound and audio-visual systems, laser displays and dozens of video monitors. There were over eighty crew from around the States and a further ninety hired locally. In addition to the producers and directors there were projectionists, videotape operators, audio and lighting engineers, electricians, carpenters, flymen and assistants for this annual extravaganza in recognition of the corporation's over-achievers who had exceeded their sales quotas.

To cope with the 1,200 sales managers who were being flown in from every corner of the States, the corporation had set up a network of rooms in the hotel with computers, printers, copiers and faxes. It had its own switchboard with twenty telephone lines manned by a staff of managers, secretaries and nurses under the auspices of the Manager of Event Program, the Director of Special Communications Programs and the Program Event Coordinator, who had a team to check quality, make sure quotas were met and supervise the guidelines.

The size of the show was both daunting and intimidating. By the time of the full dress rehearsal Caroline had coached and coaxed me into a performance. During rehearsals she had periodically interrupted my monologue. She made me repeat one of the serious passages over and over again until I got it right. 'You don't have to be solemn to be serious,' she told me. 'Now take it again from the top of the paragraph.' Use your body, she told me; that would be difficult sitting on a stool, but I could and I did. I also used emotional control and mental imagery to add poise, drama to heighten the tension during moments of great danger, and smiled charmingly when I introduced amusing anecdotes.

The day of my first show I answered the wake-up call on the telephone. The recorded message spoke to me: 'Walk along the beach and witness a spectacular sunrise. The time is 6:54. It is 74 degrees.'

The stage was set and I didn't want to disappoint. My original script had undergone several changes. It didn't suit the corporation's image that I had been threatened with imprisonment on my journey across Asia and had at times been held by the authorities, so these passages were deleted, and only after a long debate was travelling 'clandestinely' permitted. They also had a problem with my description of a Syrian nightclub with a 'scintillatingly provocative' belly dancer. One producer wanted the passage removed because it might be considered sexist. I could live with the censorship to date, but this was the limit. We reached a compromise: the item would be kept although 'scintillating' was dropped because it was too much of a tongue twister and 'provocative' was dropped because the corporation didn't provoke. We now had the Parental Guidance version of my travels.

The show ran along a military schedule. Everything was immaculately choreographed, nothing was left to chance and continuity writers made sure one item flowed neatly into the next. The doors to the theatre opened at 8:15; the show began at 8:30 with an all-black choir or 'choral' from a High School in Plantation singing 'America the Beautiful'. This was followed by a video with the Stars and Stripes superimposed as a backdrop to US Olympic heroes telling the salesmen what makes America Great. Jackie Joyner-Kersee, 'The Greatest Woman Athlete in the World', explained her ingredients for success, 'The three "Ds": Determination, Desire and Dedication'. After the video the show's host, one of the corporation's vice-presidents, introduced Florence Griffith Joyner, 'The Fastest Woman in the World', and the 1,200 sales managers went wild with excitement. Flo-Jo, the woman with the longest nails in the world, walked through the theatre to a standing ovation that lasted minutes. Flo-Jo answered questions on what made her the fastest woman in the world: 'You've got to stay focused – when I go for the line, I want to be the first, the best,' and how she kept her fingernails in shape (they were painted with tropical scenes with palm trees, beaches and sunsets). She then proceeded to hand out the corporation's Presidential Awards – medals to the Sales Managers of the Year. Before she presented the awards Flo-Jo told the audience, 'I see a lot of champions out there just like the Olympics.'

'And now,' said our host, 'for this year's Rookie Sales Manager of the Year. From Cincinnati, Ohio. Joe Belushi.' (Wild applause.)

Joe bounced onto the podium and punched the air with his fist to shouts of 'Right on Joe!' 'Go Joe! Go!' Flo-Jo stepped forward, draped a medal over his head and shook his hand.

The host then said, 'Anyone else from Ohio here?'

'Yeah.'

'Yo, aw-right!'

It would be more than a slight exaggeration to say that Flo-Jo was my warm-up act, but I followed her on the stage. I waited nervously in the wings as the lights dimmed and the packed theatre faded from view. A two-minute multi-screen slide show introduced my story. 'The earliest stories devised by man are stories of a quest. A hero undertakes a journey . . . like Jason's voyage in search of the Golden Fleece. He undergoes many trials . . . Men have travelled all over the world and even into space . . . seeking supplies, trade, conquest, colonization . . . and something more.' As the preamble to my talk finished, I was introduced, 'Photographer, journalist, writer, artist and Fellow of the Royal Geographical Society . . . please welcome . . . Nick Danziger.' It was the cue for me to enter stage right, the spotlight following me across to the podium, from where I gave my talk aided by a teleprompter and a microphone. For those at the back of the theatre who couldn't see me clearly, two huge screens on either side of the stage projected magnified images of me dressed in the clothes the corporation had bought me for the occasion. I felt like Dean Martin!

I concluded the talk by focusing on our common humanity, 'not to judge but to try and understand others' way of life . . . to realize that the differences between us are what makes life exciting and constantly fascinating.' I left the stage to generous applause but no standing ovation. Backstage a corporate vice-president congratulated me. He agreed about the differences between us. 'But here at our corporation,' he told me, 'we are looking for people with the same chromosomes.' I looked around me. The sales managers all wore white shirts, dark blazers or suits, black shoes and blue ties – a red tie was a fashion risk that might result in unemployment. Success on the corporate ladder was based on your ability to sacrifice your individual personality in order to be consumed by the institutional identity.

After a coffee break there were other speakers. Former US Ambassador to the UN, the Hon. Jeane Kirkpatrick, was now on

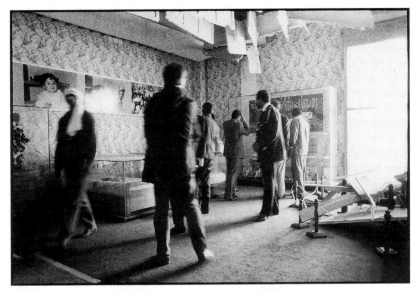

Colonel Qadhafi's house has been turned
into a museum in commemoration of the
US bombing raid. A photograph on the
wall portrays the little girl who was killed
in the attack – purported to be Qadhafi's
adopted daughter

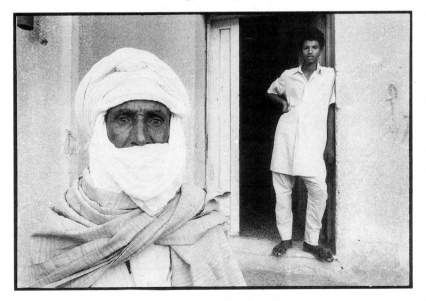

My search for the nomadic Tuareg ended in
a government-subsidized housing estate

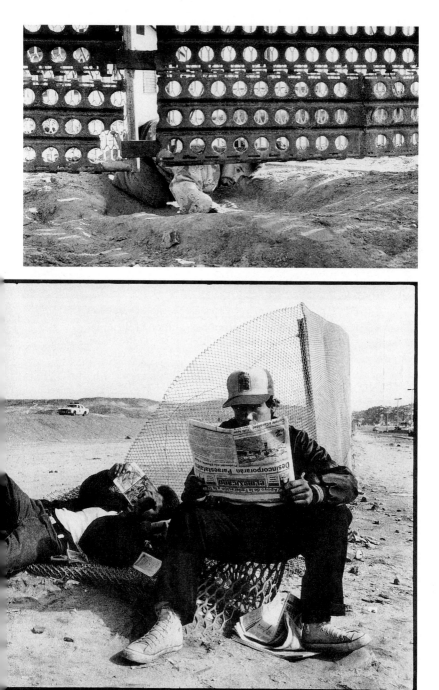

The US–Mexican border: every day thousands of would-be immigrants make a bid for theAmerican Dreamland. At the same time Americans freely enter Tijuana to escape restrictions enforced north of the border

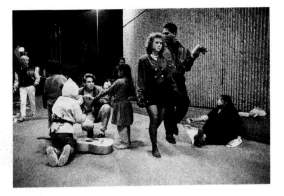

Left:
First World meets Third World as American youngsters pass local beggars on their way into the US immigration hall

Right:
A man tries to burrow his way out of Mexico into the United States

Right:
Between worlds: two young men sit on the fence that separates the United States from Mexico. A US Border Patrol car in the background is not much of a deterrent in stopping the tide of would-be immigrants

Below:
One of the thousands of people apprehended by the US Border Patrol. Like others who are caught, this young man will try and try again…until he succeeds in evading the Border Patrol

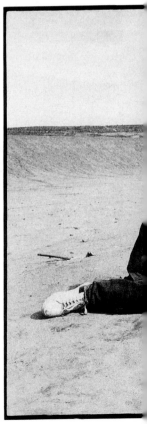

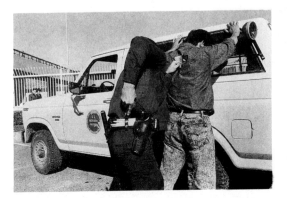

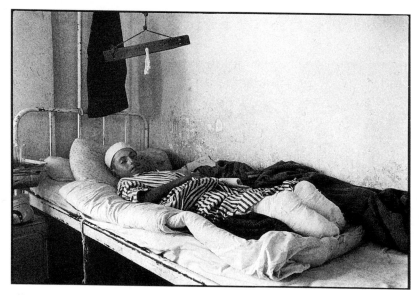

Millions of mines litter the
countryside

There is a massive waiting list for
artificial limbs

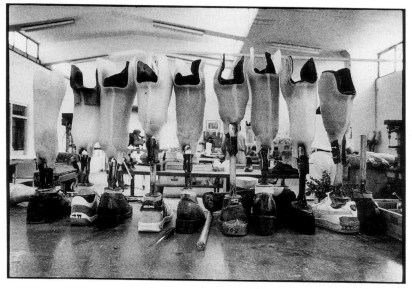

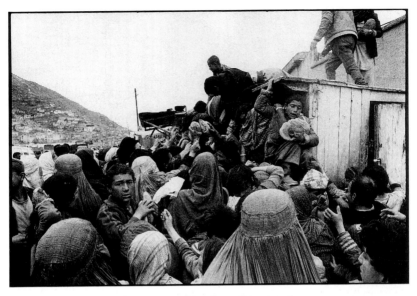

Shortages of food result in riots for
bread in Kabul

The war destroyed family support
systems, and Marastoon – a mental
asylum – is in reality a human
warehouse

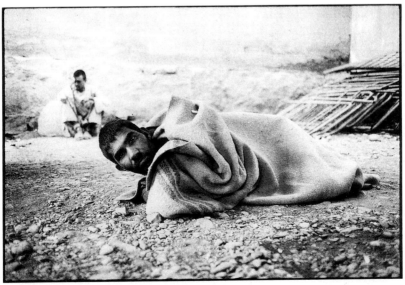

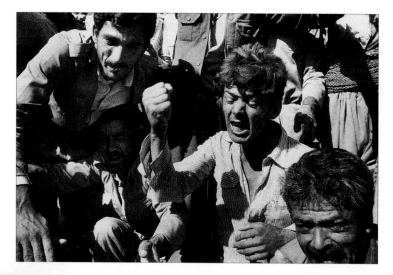

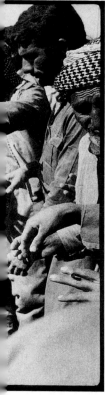

Above:
Rage and bitterness on the faces of unarmed refugees who fled from Saddam Hussein's chemical weapons attacks to the 'sanctuary' of a Turkish camp, where they were subsequently fired on by Turkish soldiers

Left:
One of the wounded refugees is dragged to a clearing

Below:
The picture that proved too graphic for the newspapers

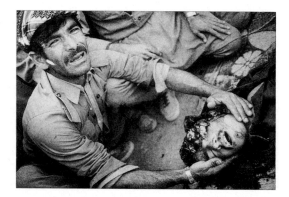

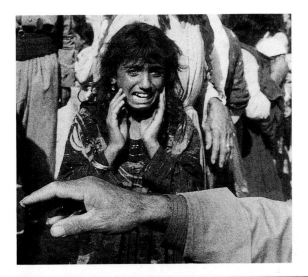

Pictures from the roll of film smuggled out of a Kurdish refugee camp in Turkey

A young girl witnesses the murder of a relative by Turkish soldiers

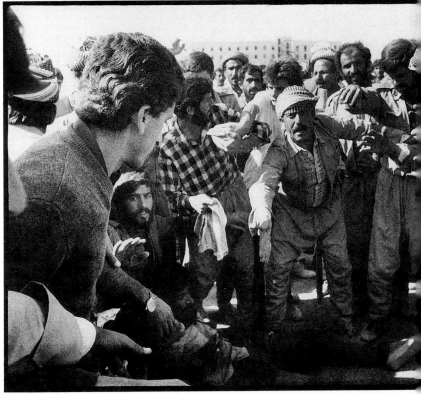

The desperate landscape of our inner-cities

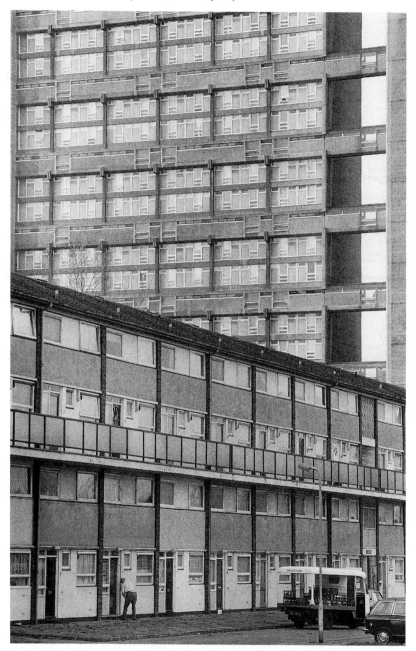

A council estate in the East End of
London, near where I lived

the Board of Directors of the American Foundation for Resistance International, an organization dedicated to the preservation of democracy, liberty and the rebirth of freedom of peoples under totalitarian rule. Her fiery talk could have been titled, 'Communism in crisis from Beijing to Belgrade'. She called Fidel Castro 'a bearded refugee from Berkeley who wears fatigues and a silly hat'. On elections in the USSR, she said, 'They were not elections by our standards, not even by South American standards, but were thrilling by Soviet standards. There's an attitude that all of us in this room understand, the whole's greater than the sum of its parts . . . partnership is the winning combination . . . stars and stripes. Communism has failed to produce the goods.' She quoted Mark Twain on Richard Wagner, 'That music is better than it sounds.'

The corporation was battling to remain near the top of the US Forbes 500 where it had stood for years. It was listed as one of the largest in the United States, employed over 388,000 people and with sales over $59 billion (net profits of $5.5 billion), its turnover was probably greater than the total GNP of Mozambique, Bhutan and Paraguay. Markets were now more valuable than territory, information more powerful than armies. The battlefield was the marketplace and the ethic was get it done, whatever the cost. This year's corporate motto was, 'Just say yes', the 'Can-Do' attitude was in. 'The corporation should be market-driven; you answer to the customer. Be both veterinarian and taxidermist,' the vice-presidents counselled the sales managers. 'Either way the customer gets his dog back.'

During the intermission I spoke to some of the executives; one had attended a business course at Columbia University called 'The Art of War'. Their conversation was littered with phrases such as 'bury the competition', 'select weapons', 'choose tactics', 'cut them off at the knees' or 'we've got them by the balls'. One of the invited speakers, a bestselling author on marketing strategies, gave a talk on 'How to disarm your opponent before going in for the kill'. The message was drilled into the sales force. Guest speaker Arthur Mitchell's moving personal story and that of his Harlem Dance Theatre confirmed the message: 'I want to convince every kid you can do it: you are the greatest. Even stars need a team,' said Mitchell, in a pointed reminder that we all owe our success to others.

Durwood Fincher, an Oliver Hardy-like character, added a comic touch to the proceedings. Durwood, an entrepreneur, was in his own right the inventor of Toe Floss, like dental floss, only for toes. It had brought financial security to Durwood's life. He gave me a dispenser of his successful remedy for prompt, temporary relief of foot in mouth. I read the instructions to the world's only 'footifrice', which had been developed 'after years of intensive research', and had been approved 'by at least one podiatrist'. Durwood claimed that studies had shown toe floss to be an effective mildew and dry-rot preventative, when used in a conscientiously applied pro-gramme of daily foot hygiene.

'I'm looking for a pharmaceutical meeting selling masochisprin. It doesn't help take away the pain, it helps you enjoy it,' said the comedian.

'Do you suffer from schizophrenia?'

'Yes and no.'

'Paranoia?'

'Why do you ask?'

'Do you wonder what styrofoam comes wrapped in?'

In the afternoons the conventioneers could go sailing, on organized shopping trips or play golf. Alternatively, you could relax by the pool or walk to the beach. Although most of the attendees loved to go out in the sun, the beach was empty because they worried about skin cancer. Many were on diets so they stayed away from the long buffet tables stacked with succulent meats, fresh fish and exotic fruits. There was enough to feed an Afghan village for a week. No, let me rephrase that – there were enough leftovers to feed an Afghan village for a week. They exercised relentlessly but lived in fear of heart diseases. Few walked, bicycled or took the stairs. But they did go to the gym. The hotel health club had stair-climbing machines, stationary bicycles and treadmills. The guests worked out in front of walls of mirrors, and computerized screens let the body toners know how many 'flights' of stairs they had climbed, the 'distance' they had bicycled and at what 'speed' they had walked. 'Do you know that men who climb more than five flights of stairs a day have 25% fewer heart attacks than those who stick to elevators and escalators?' said the sales manager from Detroit. He held a magazine called *Longevity*: 'A Practical Guide to the Art and Science of Staying Young', with articles on 'Aging after 30: How to Prevent 50% of it' and 'Rejuvenation Drugs, Do the Europeans Know Something We Don't? Maybe'. Visits to the gym were augmented by a cabinet full of assorted vitamins and mineral supplements that were sure to turn your urine green.

The shows were repeated every three days as each new group of sales managers or retailers arrived. Each time Flo-Jo answered the same questions: 'What makes you the fastest woman in the world?' – 'You have to train your body and mind. Believing and succeeding is the key. Hard-headedness to work more, do more.' – 'And how do you look after your fingernails?' Occasionally the dress rehearsals, which included the medal ceremony, were delayed or brought forward. And timings to the actual show were sometimes altered –'Nick, we're moving your introduction up two minutes, you'll take the stage at 9:33 instead of 9:31,' said Laurie, the stage manager, handing me a revised schedule. But in the first break between shows I was off to Orlando and Fort Lauderdale to speak to a women's group and at a museum. I was intrigued. I had recently read that Orlando vacuums its streets at night and disinfects its public telephones, and the airport has a moat with live alligators. A film producer from Los Angeles had described the city 'like a city on overload, or Dennis the Menace on acid'.

I was greeted at the airport by the committee for an Orlando young women's community club. The two hundred women who had gathered for the talk weren't exactly young, but they had joined a charity lunch in aid of the city's homeless young women. Standing in front of them, I wondered whether I was at a white supremacist meeting of the Anglo-Saxon daughters of the *Mayflower* or at a Spot the Wrinkle competition. The women of Orlando society were the low sodium, high soluble fibre, vitamin and mineral enhanced grandmothers of US television soap operas and commercial breaks. This was the American Dream – a stress-free life with all the time in the world to focus on body and mind.

In the afternoon I asked to visit Disney World, which is one of the world's most visited shrines, only surpassed by Kyoto, Mecca and the Vatican. There wasn't much time, but I had got used to cursory visits of the 'If it's Tuesday it must be Belgium' kind. The theme park gleamed with cleanliness and good order. Legions of men in Beau Geste outfits spent all day sweeping and scraping up Coke cans, ice-cream and popcorn cartons and gobs of bubble gum. They were graduates of Disney University with degrees in cleanliness, godliness and profitability. I was fascinated by World Showcase, designed to show the glorious aspects of eleven great nations. 'Even the people are authentically indicative of the countries they represent,' ran Disney's advertisement. I sat in a German Biergarten and listened to a live Oompah band: 'Hi! I'm Annette from Baden-Baden,' said the pretty, blonde Fraülein dressed in Lederhosen who served beer brewed in 'strict accordance with the German Reinheitsgebot purity law of 1516'. Ten minutes later I was beneath a replica Eiffel Tower and beyond that in an English street that boasted eight different architectural styles. Imagine Edwardian, Victorian, Georgian and a handful of other styles all straddling the same street. You could also sup on British fare, stroll along cobblestone lanes, visit a miniature Hampton Court maze and drink pints of warm ale from the Rose and Crown. I watched a belly dancer in a Moroccan souk. I had seen parts of Europe, North Africa and Asia without the dirt, graffiti, foreign languages, poor lighting and lack of sanitation, and where prices were in US or Disney dollars and not open to negotiation. I looked at my watch. It was four o'clock and time to catch the plane to Fort Lauderdale. My hostess drove me to the airport along a six-lane highway. She told me that a regional planning group said the highway would need 22 lanes by the year 2000. In the distance we could see Orlando; it wasn't a pretty sight. Mrs Hope, my hostess, caught me looking at the clutch of skyscrapers. 'We're proud of our skyline. It's not pretty, but it's *new*.'

At Fort Lauderdale I had an anguished wait for my escort at the airport. Someone from the museum was meant to collect me, but no one had showed up and I had neither a contact number nor the hotel reservation. I called the museum, it was closed. A recorded message gave details of the gallery's opening hours, the price of tickets and the exhibitions on display. Desperate for human contact, I tried another number. A computer-generated voice invited me to leave a message at the sound of the tone; it was like the Twilight Zone. When I had completed my message the computer voice directed me to: 'Press 1 to review your message; press 2 to alter your message; press 3 if your message is completed; if you wish to talk to a human press 0' – I had already tried that.

I had given up and was about to go in search of a local hotel when I overheard an argument outside the terminal. A tall young blonde woman was pleading with a policeman, 'I have no money, I can't park the car. I'm late and I should be meeting a man from Orlando. Well, he's not exactly from Orlando, he's from England.' I stepped forward and introduced myself.

'Hi! I'm Misty, I'm sorry I'm late but I forgot my money and couldn't park the car.'

'I could have paid.'

'You've got some money?' She sounded surprised. 'I'm afraid you'll have to sit in the back of the car or climb through the front window – a car smashed into the front door and it won't open – it wasn't my fault.' I climbed in.

Misty was from Sunrise, Florida. She had cascading blonde locks and wore mirror sunglasses with starbursts in the shape of hearts etched onto them. Every time I spoke I could see myself clearly framed in her shades.

On the ride into town she explained that two weeks ago she had been stopped by the cops for a speeding offence, and she had been late arriving at the airport because she came straight from traffic school where she was attending eight hours' driving instruction in lieu of prosecution. 'It's not bad, you learn some pretty interesting things at driving school,' she said between bites of her snack, combing her hair in the rearview mirror and switching radio stations all at the same time.

'Once I get a certificate that I have passed driving school, I deliver it to the court – you don't have to stand in line for that. At my last court appearance for speeding the judge asked us questions; the first one to answer each one correctly got $5 or $10 deducted from their fine.' It sounded like a television game show.

It was difficult to believe the United States was going bankrupt. Fort Lauderdale's inland waterways were sprinkled with $50,000 and $100,000 pleasure boats. The local ads in the paper had columns for cigarettes, not the variety that were smoked but thirty-six-foot power boats. If you wanted to protect your property, in the classifieds under 'firearms' you could find firearm classes, or under 'guns and ammunition' there were clearance sales and Uzis, and according to the sales pitch from the ad placed by Guntown, if you bought any selected firearm you got a .25-calibre automatic pistol free.

This part of Florida was a scrupulously adult place where cash customers were treated with grave suspicion. Pensioners inhabited ocean-view condominiums with eighteen-and-over tenant policies enforced by condo commandos, the local neighbourhood committee – Florida's answer to Revolutionary Guards. It would be nearly a decade before Misty could enter the local country clubs without showing identity papers, which were required from anyone under thirty. Anyone over thirty was haunted by the local paper's advertisements for secondhand wheelchairs and hospital beds, or they considered treatment at the Dry Mouth Center of Aventura, or the Body Contour Institute where for $4,000 you could have a blepharoplasty. On Sunday, its health and fitness pages warned readers of the dangers of caffeine, on Monday, the associated maladies of computeritis. On Wednesday it became illegal to release ten or more balloons out of doors.

The fashion for adding the French article 'le' as a prefix to all merchandise to make it more attractive: le car, le baron and even le bus, had been superseded by a thirst to consume anything Russian. Russian plays were being staged, exchange programmes between colleges inaugurated and cultural tours of the Soviet Union organized. Misty had signed up for a tour called 'Journey of the Czars' but she vouched that if the Russian guides forced her to visit Lenin's mausoleum, 'I'll close my eyes and turn my head when I pass his tomb.'

The following day I had time to take a stroll along Las Olas Boulevard and browse in the shops. The only noise along the quiet street was the whir from the cars' air-conditioners when they stopped at traffic lights. I entered a gallery which offered bullet-ridden, knife-slashed plates by the artist Voulkos. According to the gallery owner, the series of plates was 'a masterful collection'. He told me that Voulkos had once said of his work that it was 'the result of bad toilet training'. 'How did he get into art?' I asked. He quoted Voulkos again: 'I heard artists didn't have to get up in the morning.'

Every other shop was a beauty salon; like Lilli's of Copenhagen, formerly Stefano's, with toning and body wraps and guaranteed inch loss, and a hair and nail salon called Curl Up and Dye which seemed inappropriate given the median age of the community's residents. Most of the street's shops offered beautification of the self. Sue Gordon bridal salon suggested, 'If your mother doesn't cry when you try on your wedding gown . . . Don't buy.' Next to the Art Ministry of the First Presbyterian Church, I entered a shop called Pyramid Treasures. Here the obsession with physical fitness went hand in hand with metaphysical health. I was looking for a book called *The Power of Nothingness* by Alexandra David-Neel. A man was standing in front of the sales counter talking to a synchro-energized saleswoman. She told the man, 'There is no beginning, no middle, no ending; there is only now. What is is. That's always been the way with me.' He told her he was looking for a present for his wife. 'We fell in love a month ago and we decided to get focused and begin new cycles of life together. I'm into higher conscious-ness.'

The shop had a bewildering array of gifts with explanatory labels: a shelf with rows of candles held orange candles for courage, mind building, and help in legal problems; brown, aids finance and attracts wealth and success; green, attracts money and promotes healing; bi-color, to balance extremes and bring two people together; and tri-color, to accomplish personal desires. There were shelves of different medicinal drops for loss of memory, guilt, inadequacy and failure; displays of oils to keep away your enemies and racks of 'Energy T-shirts' with unique 'channelled' colour designs and patterns to enhance your own energies. A video, *A Course of Miracles*, had been made by the Foundation of Inner Peace, and *Weight Loss* by Potential Unlimited was described as 'a subliminal persuasion video'. I found the bookshelves and searched for *The Power of Nothingness* without luck. However there were books on discovering your past lives, books on rebirthing and astral projection for journeys to infinity, and a self-help book called *Creating Money*. The shop also offered ESP cruises on a yacht called *Anticipation*. 'You can bring your own psychic or meet one,' said the saleswoman who saw me reading the ad. I felt embarrassed, as though I had been caught reading pornography. If you didn't want to buy anything for yourself you could give a 'Past Life Regression Gift Certificate', billed as 'the perfectly unique and marvelous holiday gift for yourself or a friend'. A man was trying to sell a turquoise stone from Jupiter. 'This stone has a lot of vibes,' he said to the saleswoman, who bought it to put alongside her collection of gems and crystals that offered to balance the emotions, ease anxiety and end mental inadequacy.

As I left the shop the saleswoman handed me a present. It looked like an ordinary credit card but she told me it was nature's charge card. 'This one,' she explained, 'emits a protective energy field and is a powerful tool for self-transformation.'

I had wanted to get Misty a thank-you present from the Pyramid shop but I couldn't think of anything appropriate. Misty was a Christian Scientist. Christian Scientists don't seek medical aid, instead they hold that faith is as powerful as medicine and that God's will is as well served by the former as the latter. I remembered visiting their Mother Church in Boston which was nearly as big as St Peter's, where in a crypt computerized tablets answered questions on the faith. I asked Misty for the answers to two of the tablets' forty questions, 'Do you just pretend evil is unreal? What do you do about broken bones?'

She gave me the answers and then asked me, 'Do you ever feel it's you alone against the world?'

'Sorry?'

'Are you searching for health, companionship, guidance?'

Misty wanted me to attend one of their lectures. She told me that Christian Scientists throughout the world had been following Jesus' example. 'You too can find out how to solve your problems through God.'

'I've got to get back to Miami,' I apologized.

'It's free.'

'Free?'

'The lecture.' Misty showed me a booklet with the locations of Christian Scientist churches. It looked like a car rental directory.

My limousine driver had come to take me back to Miami. As we entered North Miami Beach, I saw an illuminated neon sign on top of a tall condominium, it read MARC POLO – I couldn't see the 'o' in Marco; presumably it hadn't lit up. I pointed this out to the driver, who chuckled. 'We're more informal here in the States.' We drove up the ramp to the Fontainebleau and parked behind a black Mercedes 300SEL with the licence number HORNY.

From the air Miami had looked like a gigantic microchip. Wide boulevards and highways crisscrossed the city bisecting neighbourhoods and linking freeways. On the ground you could drive through an eclectic mosaic of architectural styles in the same way you could switch radio channels from doo-wop to Heavy Metal. Spanish colonial homes gave way to pastel-coloured Art Deco buildings, sputnik-like motels and stucco and plastic rococo mansions with pink parking lines. On the surface this was a fantasy land from the comic strip 'The Jetsons'.

The people who inhabited this tropical land were as diverse as its architecture. Tanned, muscle-rippling youngsters in neon lime and fluorescent orange beachwear passed serried ranks of deckchairs containing retired Jews from Queens and Chicago who could boast they were older than the thirties-style buildings which were now their retirement homes. And everywhere were the immigrants or exiles from Central and South America and the Caribbean who had fled from repressive regimes or economic deprivation. Many had arrived illegally on makeshift boats, risking exposure and shark-infested waters. Others, like Clark, one of the hotel's car jockeys from Nicaragua, whose father had named his five sons and daughters after famous North American movie stars (the others were Errol, Ronald, Bette and Grace), had arrived illegally by paying smugglers to help him cross the US–Mexican border. Over half of Miami was Hispanic and nearly half the Spanish-speaking population were from Cuba, but this was no melting pot. The Hispanic population move in a different world from the Anglo-Saxon one, and both moved in a different world from that of African Americans.

One evening I received a phone call at the hotel. 'Hi! I'm Ana Maria, a friend of Daisy's. She told me you were in town and I wondered if you'd like to come to dinner?' Daisy was a friend of mine from Geneva and Ani was her sister-in-law. I gladly accepted the invitation.

Ani lived in a large house she had designed near Coconut Grove
and spoke with an exuberance and passion that was not American.
She was tall with unruly black hair, wore designer jeans, Charles
Jourdan shoes, a white silk shirt and dark glasses. She made it quite
clear that I had been invited as a family obligation to her sister-in-
law, but soon warmed to me. Most of her family had come to the
States from Havana when Ani was ten. 'In Cuba we had been
wealthy; but we left everything behind. My father worked as a
driver when we first arrived in Miami; my mother has only just
retired from the United States Naturalization and Immigration
Service.' For many years even though thousands of Spanish-
speaking immigrants were being processed through her office, she
was the only one who spoke Spanish. 'As you know, I'm now
married to Daisy's brother-in-law for the second time; he's a
banker. I'm what they call a CAP.'

'CAP?' I repeated, taken aback and slightly intimidated by her
openness.

'You know, like a JAP, a Jewish American Princess, only I'm a
Cuban American Princess. That's not to say there aren't Jewish
Cubans.'

'What are they called?'

'Jewbans,' she laughed.

We ate a delicious meal of *pollo asado*. I sat sandwiched between
two striking-looking Cuban women. There were no Americans but
German, Swiss and Argentinian boyfriends and husbands. A
Honduran woman babysat Ani's two children. She was the same
age as Ani, but the years of working first in Tegucigalpa (where six
of her eight children remained) and then as a maid without papers
in Miami had taken their toll; her wrinkled lines and weary look
made her seem old enough to be Ani's mother.

For many Latin Americans, Miami was Imperial Rome and a
Mecca for arms dealers, drug traffickers and business pirates
arranging deals that involved the sale of arms from China,
shipments from Colombia and transfers to and from Switzerland
through Panama and Liechtenstein. Even if not involved in illicit
activities, Cubans and Americans viewed one another with mutual
suspicion. Both felt they were being used and yet at the same time
believed they were using the other; contempt was high on the

agenda, the plundered and the plunderer appeared to be one and the same. But the Stars and Stripes culture, by far the most accessible the world has yet offered, left an indelible mark on all who arrived from foreign shores, be it clothes, music, cinema, female emancipation, freedom of speech or democracy. In an American-educated generation the seeds were sown even amongst those who lived within a culture that was other than North American.

After speaking to recently arrived Haitians, and having driven through blighted neighbourhoods, it was easy to see how resentments had built up over the last three decades. The economic stagnation of one community was seen as ineptitude by the others, and the influx of refugees had been blamed for either the loss of jobs or as a weakening of the country's heritage and a dilution of its bloodline. Racism and resentment were like a cancer under the surface of the city. In this respect it resembled so many others.

When the corporate shows ended in Miami, I rented a car and drove south to Key Largo and from there north to Palm Beach for the next series. The South Dixie Highway offered a hard-shoulder landscape of nude dancing shows, revivalist meetings, Baptist churches and Midas car tyre repair shops.

In Palm Beach it was the beginning of Suicide Prevention Week. I turned right just past the beware sign – golf carts crossing – to stay at the Breakers Hotel where $700-a-day suites were rented for a season and used for a couple of weekends. The hotel air-conditioning remained cold enough for the women to wear their furs and it was cheaper to fly to Orlando than order a steak in the grill.

The corporate show moved to the local Playhouse. The corporation was like a religion, not just a job but a way of life, an almighty power that governed your daily routine and your whole working life. The format of the show remained the same even if the characters had changed. The fastest woman in the world was replaced on stage by . . . 'Jackie Joyner-Kersee, the greatest woman athlete in the world'. (Applause and standing ovation.)

'Jackie, what makes you the greatest woman athlete in the world?'

'I am positive, I focus on myself and I get out there and do it. I work harder, strive for newer goals. I am a Christian. I talk to God a lot. I think, no, I *know* he helped a lot [applause]. I'm blessed to have been able to do both a team sport and an individual one.'

'Thank you, Jackie,' said the vice-president. 'No one can beat Jackie for determination! [Applause.] She reminds us of what we can do when we refuse to accept the limits people set on us.'

JJK came armed with her own newsletter and she gave me one backstage. According to the newsletter Jackie had recently made in-store appearances in St Louis and San Juan, Puerto Rico, for local 7-Up bottlers and had appeared at a fundraising dinner for the choreographer Katherine Dunham.

Evening entertainment at Palm Beach for the winning sales managers of the year had also changed. Kenny Loggins, who had replaced Hall and Oates, was himself now replaced. Court jesters fell from grace like Third World dictators toppled in bloodless coups and were sent packing with handsome paycheques. Hall and Oates had had their contract severed after two appearances, because their T-shirts and Oates's long hair with the 'windswept look' which required two wind machines didn't fit the corporation's image. Worse, the lyrics to their songs were counter-revolutionary; the corporate managers had been heard singing along to the chorus – 'No can do' – it was not a tune to inspire pride or self-confidence.

The managers and their spouses were treated to a foretaste of what was in store for their balmy Palm Beach evenings. After the show's intermission a polo pony was brought onto the stage of the Ponciana Playhouse. (The producers insisted the horse must rehearse before each show.) 'Tonight,' said the host, 'we will celebrate the game of kings and your high achievement in an exhibition game of polo.' A fleet of coaches and a police escort whisked two hundred couples to the Palm Beach Polo Club. After the exhibition game of four chukkas, the spectators entered a football-pitch-sized marquee fitted with plastic Georgian windows, air-conditioning and decorated with classic cars where they feasted and then danced the night away to the Platters, the Diamonds, the Coasters and Lesley Gore.

However, their biggest treat was yet to come. The star guest for the third and final night, the climax for this year's nine-to-five over-achievers, was the irrepressible Dolly Parton. Introduced as the Queen of East Tennessee, Dolly chose a different outfit for each of her appearances. They fitted so tight to her 40-inch bust, 20-inch waist and 36-inch hips they seemed painted on. Her tantalizing Southern drawl, stunning looks and country-and-western songs with their diet of broken hearts, booze and dead horses sent the audience's collective pulse rate soaring. Her hillbilly lifestyle at the family's shack in Locust Ridge with no running water or electricity, where she and her eleven brothers and sisters were raised (six had shared a bed) was far removed from her present circumstances, a $200-million empire that included a $75-million Dollywood theme park, 'I love Dolly' T-shirts, Dolly dolls, Dollywood watches and her White Limozeen.

Every day the hotel's guest activities broadsheet arrived under my door with the local newspaper. A pet macaw named Horace and her mate Decino had made front-page headlines and in another story a woman who had been mugged was quoted as saying, 'I knew the attackers didn't belong to Palm Beach.' In the paper's useful tips an advertisement ran under the headline HOW TO DRESS LIKE A MILLION ON SOMEBODY ELSE'S MILLION. 'In Palm Beach,' the article went on to say, 'if you're lucky you marry money . . .' In Palm Beach secondhand furs were referred to as 'gently worn', secondhand cars as 'pre-owned'. Limousines were to Palm Beach as yellow taxis are to Manhattan. I looked at the list of hotel activities. There was a croquet clinic, limousine tour of the beach, bodywork dance studio, an etiquette camp and golf clinic for children, or you could discover scuba diving off the hotel where a 1967 Rolls-Royce had been sunk in eighty-five feet of water to create an artificial reef.

It was ten o'clock on a lazy Sunday morning when I decided to go for a drive. I crossed from the Haves in Palm Beach to the Have-Nots in West Palm Beach. I drove down Flagler past the Unity Church of Practical Christianity where the congregation had gathered to listen to Lassie Rosencrans on 'Living your childhood'. Palm Beach County could boast seven pages of churches in the local Yellow Pages with something for everyone from the Finnish Pentecostal to African Methodist Episcopal Zion. 'For spiritual renewal Dial for

Christ,' read the graffiti with a telephone number on the wall of a transmission repair shop. (The Yellow Pages had several numbers listed under Dial-A-Prayer.) On US1 I passed a huge highway sign outside a Victory Baptist Church that read, KINDNESS IS LOVE IN ITS WORK CLOTHES and outside the Bethel Temple Assembly of God a sign informed me that a group called the Missionettes were playing. Churches were as numerous in Florida as pubs are in Britain. Having driven past several more, curiosity got the better of me and I dropped into not a church, but a gun shop next to the local McDonald's in Riviera Beach.

The Village Gun Shop sold handguns, shotguns and rifles; it also specialized in guns for ladies. I entered the shop as several Christian motorcyclists with leather jackets painted with the words 'Truckin' for Jesus' were leaving. Inside a woman with immaculately coiffed hair was examining a counter of pistols. They were laid out on felt mats behind a glass display case like jewellery.

The salesman offered her a wide variety of products including the new Ladysmith. He said it was 'a sleek pistol which comes in frosted blue or red with a matching case by Smith and Wesson.' I looked at the gun. It had the word Ladysmith delicately scripted along its side. He also showed her the Titan Tigress. 'It's a gold-plated gun with matching gold lamé case and faux ivory handle.' It was inscribed with a long-stemmed red rose. 'Or there's the Bonnie and Clyde, a his-and-hers set made by Charter Arms of Connecticut.'

Whilst the woman handled the latest in deadly fashion accessories, the salesman served a man who wanted a gun to fit an ankle holster. He then turned to me, 'How can I help you?'

I hesitated. 'I'm looking for a sub-machine-gun.'

'You name it, we've got it – if it's an Uzi, AK-47, AR-15 or Hoch and Kochler. I've got guns that can knock airplanes out of the sky.'

I asked him if there was one he recommended. 'It boils down to money. The Hoch and Kochler is the Rolls-Royce of semi-automatics. It will outlast you and me; you can hand it down to your kids.'

'And the Uzi?'

'It's accurate even when fired from the hip, after a hundred rounds you start to feel good, but the ammunition is expensive.'

There was a steady trickle of shoppers; two kids just out of school were looking for a pair of assault rifles. He let them hold the guns. 'That one you are holding is a version of the M-16 used in Vietnam.' I later learnt that after conversion by a skilled gunsmith it was capable of firing 900 rounds a minute. The kids left without purchasing. They said they already had Uzis but had wanted one retooled with an extra-long barrel for greater bullet velocity. The manager couldn't help them. As they left a man came into the shop with a harpoon gun that fired .22-calibre bullets. 'I need a new firing pin.' – 'It'll cost you; you'll have to kiss $50 goodbye.'

I asked the salesman if he was concerned about selling guns to kids. 'If they're over eighteen, it's okay by me. Sixty per cent of Palm Beach County own guns. I know boys who could hold off the whole police force.

'So what will it be?' he said.

'I'm looking for a good deal.'

'We've got a good buy on an AKM.'

'AKM?'

'Chinese version of an AK-47.' He pointed to a Kalashnikov lookalike. 'At $750 it's still a bargain.'

'$750!'

'Yeah, I know it's expensive, but it's still cheap compared to the others. A month ago I couldn't sell the AK at $350, but now that they're trying to ban assault rifles, I can't get enough, I've been selling over thirty a week.'

I was looking for a way out.

'How can I pay?'

'Cash, Mastercard, Visa.'

I tried a different tack.

'Do you need any ID?'

'A driving licence will do and the last one is yours.'

'Thanks, but I'm looking for the original version of an AK-47,' I apologized. 'I think I'll wait.'

'Seven fifty and I'll throw in an extra ammo clip,' he said hopefully.

It seemed incredible that I could buy a semi-automatic and a round of ammunition, walk out of the shop and, within the space of time it has taken you to read this sentence, shoot at least thirty people.

I entered another gunshop. Here, between racks of semi-automatics and rifles there was a poster with a gunsight pointed at Colonel Qadhafi's face. The words beneath his head read SHOOT THE MAD DOG! My accent immediately made the shop assistant and a prying customer suspicious. The customer was dressed in a T-shirt depicting a soldier with an assault rifle over the slogan WASTE THE RED BASTARDS. He had just lifted some books from a book bin and I looked at the titles as he placed them on the sales counter. *Get Even: The Complete Book of Dirty Tricks; Improved Explosives: How to Make Your Own* and *To Ride, Shoot Straight and Speak the Truth*. He stared at me menacingly; he guessed I was a journalist. 'University people are liberal assholes, liberal assholes are faggots,' he said and went on to tell me that politicians were faggots and 'lawyers who came bottom of their class'.

He based his philosophy on 'Might is Right'. Here the three 'Gs' had supplanted Flo-Jo's three 'Ds'. The shop assistant told me, 'The things America has got going for it are God, Guts and Get Up.'

Meekly, I asked about Vietnam.

'Tenacity counts for something,' said the man in the T-shirt, explaining the Viet Cong resistance.

'We did the wrong things for the right reasons,' the shop assistant said. 'America won our freedom through violence and firearms and that isn't going to change. There's a threat. We have the right to reply. The history of the world is one of being better armed.'

As I left the shop he repeated a National Rifle Association slogan I had heard before, 'Guns don't kill people, people kill people.' I wondered if the people who died each sixteen minutes in the United States from a gunshot wound would have agreed.

One of my last lectures took me to Cleveland, Ohio. I arrived at the local country club at 1:15 A.M. after a seven-hour journey and several long delays. A note on my pillow read, 'Welcome to the Country Club! We would like to acquaint you with some house traditions. Proper attire is required on the club premises. On the main floor of the Clubhouse, including the Dining and Cocktail Terraces, men and older boys must wear coats and ties, except for the South Porch where sports attire is permitted during the summer season . . .' I slept soundly in the knowledge that the corporation had let me keep their clothes.

The next morning my hostess drove me to her house in a leafy suburb. It could have been Epsom in Surrey only the mansions were much bigger. She asked the date of my birthday. 'Aries?' – 'No, Taurus.'

'There are a lot of Taureans in Cleveland,' she informed me.

When we reached her house, she asked me if I would like to go for a swim. 'The indoor pool or the outdoor pool?' she asked.

'Whichever is most convenient for you,' I said politely.

She showed me the outdoor pool and then took me to see the indoor pool. I didn't want to appear rude, but I couldn't see how it was possible to swim there; the pool was only about fifteen feet long.

'At the touch of a switch, you can swim against the current at speeds up to 4 mph. My father loves it.' But the guests were already arriving and I thought it ungentlemanly to leave the ladies to themselves.

The average age of these women was younger than in Florida. Over a buffet lunch I chatted to a group of charming wives about Marco Polo and the silk roads. An older woman interrupted our conversation. 'Did I hear you talking about Napoleon? Well, my great-great-grandfather was General Junot, Napoleon's best friend. We have a Napoleon society in Florida, but I can't stand the humidity in the summer.' The conversation eventually returned to China. One of the women said China was dirty, India wasn't too clean, but Kashmir was wonderful. 'I'd like to bring some of their girls over here.' Another woman, the wife of a corporate president, said she had been in Tiananmen Square twenty-five years ago. 'It isn't what it used to be,' she said regretfully, 'and communism isn't cracked up to what it's meant to be.' – 'What do you think of Red China?' she asked her friend. 'I think it goes well on a blue cloth.'

I had engagements in New York, Washington DC and Miami before returning to Kabul, and I stopped in Philadelphia *en route* to Washington to see a woman I had met at one of my lectures. She talked about Lord and Lady so-and-so, Philadelphia's cricket grounds, famous gardens, Mark Phillips, Prince Charles, Jackie O and fox hunting in Shropshire. 'I taught my daughters everything, fox hunting, sailing, skiing. They say I'm a vanishing species,' she said, more surprised than hurt. 'But then, I suppose it was easier when my parents brought me up; we had the little people, lots of servants: gardeners, cooks, cleaners and chauffeurs.'

For my last stop, in Miami, I stayed in a suite in the pink Key Biscayne Bay Hilton. It seemed incredible that in two days I would be back in Afghanistan, in the middle of the 'fighting season', as their summer was now called. For the last two months I had been living out a dream. I had been seduced by fair-skinned, soft women, a Puerto Rican woman with long jet-black hair that reached all the way down her back, and a friend of Ani's whose spiritual home was somewhere between Miami's Little Havana and the South Dixie Highway. It had been a hedonistic, carefree existence with no responsibilities other than the keys to a convertible rent-a-car. It was my last evening in Miami; tropical sunsets, beaches, palm fronds, and Eighth Street or *Calle Ocho* seemed worlds apart from the daily terror of rocket attacks and scorched earth policies. And yet Miami Beach was connected to Kabul by air routes just like those between London, Paris and Milan. In the physical sense the world has been reduced, brought closer together, and yet enormous gulfs separate us. The United States offered a surfeit of freedom and choice to those who could afford it.

Ani drove me to the airport. Mia, her daughter, had just had her seventh birthday. I thought of the children in Kabul, as I often did. Would they be on the same street corners plying their wares when I returned, or would their brief lives have been prematurely ended by rocket attack? I turned to Mia and asked her about her birthday presents, a drawing set, some books and a doll – small gifts, but beyond the reach of most Afghan children. But Mia sounded disappointed. She hadn't received what she really wanted. 'What was that?' I asked.

'An American Express card.'

8

GRENADE FISHING

If we didn't invent kites, we certainly
invented fighting with kites.

Afghan children

In practice missiles land more or less
randomly and one accordingly either
accepts them as a fact of life – like traffic
accidents and muggings elsewhere – or
becomes a nervous wreck.

United Nations official
on life in Kabul

Kabul, May 1989

The Ariana Afghan Airlines' descent over Kabul followed the
regular tight corkscrew pattern to avoid incoming missiles. The
snows had melted from the surrounding mountains. From the air,
the city which had been sodden with mud had taken on the colour
of English tea. The dry weather signalled the beginning of the
fighting season. The mountain passes were open and the supply
routes to the interior passable.

I had flown to the Afghan capital for three weeks before I had to
return to the United States for a corporate show. In the meantime, I
hoped to persuade the government to grant me permission to travel
to Herat. Although I had no assignment, I planned to continue to
photograph daily life. However, once again fortune seemed to
follow me on my travels, and on arrival in Kabul the departing New
Delhi bureau chief for Agence France-Presse asked me to file news
reports for them. Even though the expected seasonal fighting was
about to begin there were moments to savour. I arrived in the

capital as the government began its preparations to celebrate the 200th anniversary of the French Revolution.

The mood was surprisingly cheerful; the airport customs officer told me that there hadn't been any rocket attacks on the city for a few weeks. Outside the terminal a soldier with three pistols tucked into the front of his trousers waved me past the checkpoint. I headed for the Kabul Hotel and my old room 116.

Within hours of my arrival the calm that had recently descended on Kabul was shattered by renewed shelling. In the first twenty-four hours, eleven rockets landed on the city, killing at least four civilians and a soldier, with many more injured from shrapnel and falling debris. I filed my first report as a stringer for Agence France-Presse on the resumption of rocket attacks.

Although the government provided casualty figures, they could not always be relied upon. I double-checked the official figures with the hospitals. At one hospital a woman with a broken leg lay on a bed. In the initial panic, after an explosion had rocked her apartment, she had jumped from her second-floor balcony to rescue her child who had been playing outside the building. In a separate attack, a woman and child were killed walking to kindergarten. I interviewed a woman who had been in the apartment block next to where the explosion had taken place. She had once studied at Westminster College in London, and made a passionate denunciation of the superpowers, criticizing both the United States and the Soviet Union for supplying weapons to the protagonists. She raised her voice in anger. 'The Soviets have left, what is there to fight about?' A neighbour had joined her in the apartment; they sat cross-legged on the floor in traditional Afghan style in front of a wall-sized poster of a Caribbean beach. The friend added with great bitterness in her voice, 'The mujahedeen are our brothers; it is the West and Pakistan that are continuing to arm them.'

As I left the apartment I noticed a small crowd gaping at the devastation: a charred Volkswagen van and the pockmarked first and second floors of the apartment block. A soldier was extracting a mangled child's bicycle from the debris, and children who had clambered onto the splintered wood and broken glass offered me chunks of shrapnel.

Later in the day I telexed AFP in New Delhi to offer them a feature report on the 'Tour de Kaboul' bicycle rally, and the forthcoming Afghan first division soccer championship match between Hadayat and the army club (who had recently won the Afghan Cup Final 1–0). At first they were puzzled. 'Football and bicycle rally???' they asked in their telexed answer.

In spite of fears of mujahedeen guerrilla attacks and continuing rocketing of the capital, residents of the ever-expanding city gathered in the streets during a temporary lull in the fighting to cheer the hundred bicyclists taking part in the 'Tour de Kaboul'. The ten-kilometre race was not without incident. From the start at Darulaman Palace, some cyclists, many of whom wore jerseys emblazoned with the joint Soviet–Afghan cosmonaut space launch, crashed into each other, whilst others suffered punctures on the potholed roads. It was an uneven contest for those who rode old-fashioned Chinese and British shopping bicycles rather than the modern, lightweight racing bike. The eventual winner was twenty-year-old Kabul University student Mohammed Sarwar in a time of 14 minutes and 25 seconds. Mohammed, reflecting on his victory, declared he was so happy, 'I can't fit into my clothes', an Afghan expression meaning 'over the moon'.

When I tried telexing New Delhi with the feature on the race the message repeatedly became garbled. I telephoned the Kabul exchange to complain. Within minutes they sent a tall gentleman in an ill-fitting suit to fix the telex machine. When he had finished repairing the antiquated machine, he telexed his office with the international call sign to check that all the keys were functioning: 'the quick brown fox jumps over the lazy dog,. –1234567890().' Someone at Kabul's central exchange replied, 'Now is the time for all good men to come to the aid of the party.'

He gave me a wry smile. Like most Afghans, it was unlikely that the humble telex repairman was a Communist. If he had joined the party he had done so, like many others working in government ministries, to gain access to ration coupons and to remain employed. He confided to me that his son had escaped to Pakistan to avoid the draft. Could I help his son get to the West? he asked.

Whilst the war and the rocketing of the besieged cities continued, the bicycle race and the football match were just two events in a much larger series of races and contests to be held over fifteen days for eventual qualification to the 13th Annual Youth Festival to be held in Pyongyang in North Korea. They hoped to send two or three athletes. Two thousand athletes from government institutions, schools, sports clubs and the university and polytechnic were taking part in games of volleyball, football, basketball, table tennis, weightlifting, wrestling and handball. The eventual winners were to be awarded Russian radios, Hungarian sports shoes, Mongolian socks and cash. Smaller qualifying meetings for the finals to be held in the capital were taking place in the provincial capitals of Mazar-i-Sharif, Kunduz, Herat and Sheberghan. From Jalalabad, where there was still heavy fighting and intense shelling between government troops and the mujahedeen, the local sports committee sent a letter to Kabul. The message was translated for me: 'We regret that we will not be able to take part in the games as our sportsmen have not recently had the opportunity to train for their respective events.'

When I had finished telexing, I passed a group of armed militiamen sitting in the hotel lobby watching a Soviet Siberian Western on television. One of their trucks bristled with new weaponry, a gift from the government. It was parked in the hotel car park and guarded by a turbaned young militiaman with a Kalashnikov and a pair of Ferrari designer sunglasses. They asked me to join them for tea, but the concierge told me I had a phone call.

It was the former professor of the Sorbonne, inviting me to the inauguration of the Afghan Commission for the Celebration of the 200th Anniversary of the French Revolution. Twenty Afghans had been charged by President Najibullah to organize a fitting tribute to the revolution. All the members were Francophiles, most of them graduates from Kabul's former French lycée. Their debate could have been one that takes place daily at cafés on St Germain-des-Prés. At the head of the commission was Monsieur Habibi, head of the Afghan Senate.

The twenty members sat at two long tables in a building that housed the Afghan Journalists' Union. At each setting Chinese pencils printed with the slogans UNIVERSAL LOVE and FRIENDSHIP sat like cutlery above a notepad. M. Habibi opened the meeting with a keynote address: 'In the name of Allah, the most merciful and benevolent, I hereby inaugurate this commission with a statement from our esteemed president who has decreed to celebrate the 200th anniversary of the glorious victory of the French Revolution . . . *"Liberté, égalité, fraternité . . ."*. It is necessary for the Republic of Afghanistan which has observed these points to celebrate this great event.'

The president's sentiments were echoed by the committee members in a headstrong rush to praise the French Revolution. One member spoke of the stirring strains of the Marseillaise; another, the Declaration of the Rights of Man, the will of the people, and the epic struggle in which the archaic feudal order was overthrown by the masses. Although recent Afghan history resembled Europe's in 1789, the committee made only oblique references to Afghanistan and its own revolution. The terror that Robespierre represented wasn't mentioned, but the emergence of a nation state from the ashes of a monarchy was.

In many ways the Afghan Revolution had taken the same course as the French. Both had grown more and more radical as their leaders justified the terror by 'circumstances' – the dangers posed by the counter-revolutionaries. Presidents Taraki and Hafizullah Amin shared Robespierre's half-crazed self-righteousness. *'Des erreurs ont été commis,'* was how the committee described the excesses of the French Revolution in an oblique reference to their own past mistakes, as if you could de-Hitlerize Nazism by announcing that Belsen was a mistake. *'Napoléon avait supprimé des droits pour certains temps'*, was another way of explaining Dr Najibullah's State of Emergency. The triumph of the French Revolution, of good over evil, was being used as an apology for the tyrannical rule of past Marxist Afghan governments, as well as the continuing belief that the suppression of individual rights, like the tyranny of citizens, had been justified for an ideological goal that was for the country's collective good.

After the polemics, they turned their attention to more practical matters, organizing the celebrations. Someone suggested that the ordinary man in the street didn't much care about the French Revolution. Dr Farouk, academician, addressed the problem: 'The [Afghan] man in the street doesn't know about French history, but he must be enlightened; it is our duty to organize a commission to educate him.' There was general agreement. They suggested a television and poster campaign. Another member of the commission added, 'We must also teach the ordinary man in the street the history and revolutions of Latin America if we want to study a great blow against feudalism . . . against imposed taxes . . . and the egalitarian demands. The inefficiencies and privileges of the ruling classes as seen from a remarkable stage in the development and emergence of an urban proletariat . . . the financial and industrial bourgeoisie . . .' The man sitting next to me whispered in my ear, 'Il y a toujours un emmerdeur qui adore parler. [There's always a bore who loves talking.]'

'The financial problems that led France to a revolution and its social evolution are separate topics that must be addressed at a later date,' said the committee's vice-president, who saw only one cloud on the horizon. 'Unfortunately, the 14th of July coincides with the third day of Id-e-Qorban' (the Muslim celebrations of Abraham's willingness to sacrifice his son Isaac). But the main points of the campaign were agreed: 'We must build a constituency – a party of patriots. The French Revolution is a model revolution which has inspired all other revolutions. A commission should be elected to study this in detail.'

'I thought this was the committee?' I said to Dr Masim.

'Ah, mais oui, mais il faut construire un comité commun.'

Early one morning, when I had finished filing, I left the hotel in search of a cab. The first to stop was a clapped-out Opel. I quickly made friends with Mohammed Nur, who had been leasing the same taxi for years. He was a giant, and looked like a buccaneer with unkempt black hair and beard. Mohammed lived alone because he couldn't afford the dowry that would have been needed for marriage. He was permanently stoned and his shalwar camise was stained with drops of oily hashish; he told me the best dope came from Imam Sahib near Kunduz. He drove his cab like a ship weaving between slow-moving vehicles. When we were stopped by a traffic policeman for driving in and out of a column of tanks like a dodgem, he handed the policeman a piece of hashish. I pretended that nothing was happening, the policeman slipped the dope into his breast pocket and sent us on our way with nothing more than a mild reproach for not showing more respect to a military convoy. When we stopped at checkpoints and waited in line to be searched, Mohammed often fell asleep at the wheel. How we avoided a major accident or arrest was Allah's private mystery.

Mohammed had the remarkable ability to communicate in English with the two words he had picked up from foreigners in the seventies – 'fuck' and 'hashish'. The army, the Communists, the government were 'fuck'; everything else was hashish. Later in the week he took me to see a friend of his who spoke English and who had once worked as a driver for Afghan Tour. His friend seemed pleased to have a foreign guest in his house, although he was apprehensive that someone might have seen a foreigner enter his home; but Mohammed knew the risks that an Afghan ran for being in the company of a foreigner, and he had taken the precaution of driving his taxi down the narrow lane right up to his friend's front door. Over lunch his friend showed me an album of faded photographs. 'This is me with Susan from Albuquerque,' he said, pointing to a picture of himself with an arm around a young blonde American woman in Bamiyan north-west of Kabul with an enormous statue of Buddha in the background. He turned the page. 'This is me with Jane.' Jane had long brown hair and was smiling naturally; they were standing in front of the Band-i-Amir lakes a little farther to the west. There was also Anna from Oregon, Laura from Phoenix and Chris from Missouri; each stood in front of a different backdrop making the album something of a lovers' guide book to Afghanistan. After lunch Mohammed and his friend unfurled prayer mats and prayed in the direction of Mecca.

In the afternoon I went to visit Giorgio and Maurizio, two Italian journalists who were staying at the Kabul Intercontinental. Although no longer part of the international hotel chain, the hotel still liked to call itself the Intercontinental, until the end of the summer when they were pressured into changing the name. This they accomplished by dropping the 'Inter', so that in one simple stroke the Kabul Intercontinental became the Kabul Continental. Not more than a handful of the hotel's two hundred rooms were ever occupied at the same time, and as a precaution against incoming rocket fire from the mujahedeen-controlled Paghman hills to the north, the management only rented rooms on the lower

floors facing south. Later in the summer the penthouse 'presidential' suite received a direct hit. Like the Kabul Hotel, the Kabul
Continental existed in a time warp; there were brochures for the
London Portman Intercontinental, advertising single rooms for
£9.00 and doubles for £13.00, timetables for Green Line tours to
Windsor Castle, Hampton Court and Chessington Zoo, and a
pamphlet on Westminster Abbey with a 25% discount on all brass
rubbings on production of a Super Tour ticket. You could no longer
dine in the hotel's Pamir Supper Club or the Nuristan lounge and
bar, but food including golden pancakes was still served in the
Bamiyan Brasserie. The bill came franked with a stamp that hadn't
changed for twelve years; it read 'PAID JULY 1977'. Although the
hotel still advertised a tennis coach and a photographer for special
occasions, neither of these services was available, and the empty
hotel pool was now home for a goat which was tethered to its steps.

One morning Mohammed Nur suggested Giorgio, Maurizio and I
go and eat at his local kebab house. First we went shopping for
Maurizio's wife. We found a shop selling burqas – the traditional
all-masking Afghan veil with only a small mesh window to see
through. Until we approached, the tailor had been sitting like a
cross-legged deity in his small shop. He stood to attention, bowed
slightly and uttered polite greetings with his hand on his heart.
Outside two young men were dyeing the veils a glorious shade of
mauve in two enormous vats, stirring the dye with sticks. When
they hung the veils to dry on long clotheslines in the sun, they
fanned out like curtains.

At first I had thought the cut of the tarpaulin or tent was one of
strict uniformity; if there was variety it was in the description:
completely faceless, totally anonymous or entirely masking; but the
tailor explained the veils came in a variety of cloths and styles. The
cheapest were made of Russian cloth, the most expensive of
Japanese; the smartest veils were tightly pleated. As I had already
discovered in the streets of Kabul and at several shrines where
women visited weekly, I could tell something about an Afghan
woman, her class and a clue to her age from the colour and type of
veil she wore, the cut and the cloth of the trousers visible below its
hem and the style of shoe; and equally, the smarter the veil the

more pronounced were her posture and gait and the more decipherable her figure. Maurizio and Giorgio chose emerald-coloured burqas for their companions back home, as attire for a fancy dress party.

As we drove through the streets of Kabul, Giorgio imagined himself still in Saigon or the Via Veneto in Rome; he marvelled at the beauty of some Afghan women. Even though Kabul girls liked to listen to Michael Jackson and George Michael, I never considered that they might be interested in Western men. Giorgio, however, actively entertained the possibility. When he thought he saw an Afghan woman wave at us as we passed her in the street, Giorgio asked Mohammed to swing the taxi around and double back towards her. Maurizio tried to reason with his hot-blooded Roman companion.

'What technique are you gonna use to pick up the girl?'

'I winking,' replied Giorgio confidently.

'Maybe you make mistake?'

'Never.'

'No?'

'Is international technique.'

By the time we had caught up with her it was too late to try Giorgio's sure-fire international technique; the lady in question had boarded a military bus. Not that this deterred Giorgio, who had us follow the bus until it got away.

After our little charade I suggested we go to Qarga lake, on one side of which the battered remains of the Kabul Golf and Country Club stood on the edge of government-controlled terrain. From the other side of the lake as far as one could see to the Paghman hills, the ground was controlled by the mujahedeen. There was a regular exchange of fire between the government- and mujahedeen-controlled sides: on the one hand they were being martyred by the 'criminal, puppet regime', on the other they were being martyred by the 'criminal, cut-throat warmongers'. It wasn't always possible to reach the country club without being turned back by soldiers. Some taxi drivers refused to drive to Qarga, but Mohammed was game, even though it wasn't Friday, the Sabbath, when in theory there was some sort of understanding that the mornings should not be disturbed by the regular exchange of rocket fire. In practice each side cried foul and the duelling continued.

At the last checkpoint we found a soldier slumped in his chair in front of a kettle, his gun on the ground next to him and an ammunition pouch hooked over a nail above him. With a tug on a rope he was able to release the pole that blocked our way without having to get up from his seat. As the taxi climbed the hill to the lake, we looked down on the nine-hole golf course whose fairways were littered with discarded ammunition boxes, and putting greens or 'browns' now landing pads for helicopter gunships and resupply. Bunkers had become entrenchments for tanks and artillery pieces. We arrived unopposed at the Qarga Country Club. The complex was deserted; it had once been overrun by the mujahedeen before being reclaimed by government forces who now used it as an outpost guarding the approach to the capital. Its walls were peppered with bullet and shell fire; the restaurant sign had been severed from its fixing and hung limply from its last mount. We wandered over to the club's terrace overlooking the turquoise lake. The water looked inviting and I was drawn to the beach where I stripped off down to my boxer shorts.

The water was cool, and as I paddled about in the lake blissfully giving myself over to the pleasures of recreation, all thoughts of the war receded from my mind. However, I was rudely awoken from my daydreaming by a group of soldiers who had gathered on the terrace's parapet. I had swum into the middle of the lake and they were shouting at me to return to shore. As I swam towards the beach they continued to shout at me, 'Do you know where you are? Do you know who is over there?'

'Yes, the mujahedeen.'

'Get out of the water!' an officer ordered.

On the beach a soldier was standing at the water's edge. As I got out he ordered me to move behind him; the officer, other soldiers, Giorgio, Maurizio and Mohammed Nur were standing in a line on the parapet some way above us. I was annoyed that the soldiers had interrupted my pleasant swim and thought they were being excessively protective. Annoyance turned to alarm as the soldier in front of me pulled a grenade from his ammunition pouch, and then with his free hand pulled the detonating pin. I looked askance, the grenade was never going to reach the other side of the lake; puzzlement turned to fear; why the hell wasn't he throwing the grenade? The seconds ticked by. He arched his arm backwards and threw the grenade into the lake.

It hit the water like a stone and then a muffled bang erupted in a mushroom of water that broke the surface of the calm lake. I looked up at the officer, who smiled at me. I looked at the middle of the lake. Two dead fish had floated to the surface. I looked back at the officer. He wore a broad grin as he pointed to the fish. I got back in the water, swam to the middle of the lake, collected the fish and returned to shore with one in each hand. I made several journeys swimming out to the middle of the lake and back. Each time I reached the shore another group of dead fish had floated to the surface. On the third excursion, I took an empty tin to gather the remaining fish. When I brought them ashore they were cleaned and gutted by the soldiers and the two Romans.

We had a barbecue of freshly-caught fish on the terrace. I was too exhausted to eat; the exertion of swimming backwards and forwards and the extreme heat had taken their toll and so I rested on a bench whilst the others feasted. Mohammed sat on the back of another bench pointing to five soldiers sitting in front of him who were heartily tucking in. He was trying to tell me something. At first I couldn't read his lip movements and he mimed the same two words over and over again. By the time I understood what he was saying his English vocabulary had nearly doubled. 'Fuck Communists!' he repeated, pointing to the soldiers.

In the background the government and mujahedeen artillery continued to exchange fire. We could see huge plumes of smoke rising above the Pagmah hills along a canopy of trees and cultivated fields as shells exploded sending fountains of earth, trees and debris into the air before the distant rumble of the explosion reached us. There were days when the dust never settled. When the mujahedeen returned fire their target was the Qarga garrison and the capital itself. They scored a hole-in-one with a rocket on the seventh 'brown'. As Maurizio said over lunch, 'Not a bad shot from ten kilometres away.'

We returned to Kabul in the early afternoon. Near the Russian-built polytechnic, where in winter the children had been busy cutting trees for firewood, the children with no jobs were busy flying kites. Nothing was ever wasted: the children were carefully cutting disused plastic shopping bags into sails for the little bits of featherweight wood they had scrounged. Although it has been reported that kites with hand grenades attached to them had been used to bring down Soviet helicopters, I had never heard such a story during my travels in Afghanistan. However, here the children had turned their kites into fighting vehicles by attaching shards of glass to the kites' tails to bring down their rivals in a battle for supremacy of the skies. As a felled kite drifted down, a wild stampede ensued as the children scrambled to become the new owners of the captured prize.

As we drove into town, Mohammed lit a huge joint which he smoked like a pipe through an opening in his fist. His eyes began to water, and no sooner had he finished each enormous drag than he began to choke and wheeze with a vigour that was otherwise missing in his manner. Maurizio took a polite drag but preferred his strong-smelling Indonesian cigarettes. Before entering the Karte Parwan district of Kabul, we were stopped by a plain-clothes policeman with a semi-automatic. Mohammed whispered 'KHAD' (secret police). The policeman asked me for my papers. I asked him for his and he pushed the nozzle of his Kalashnikov under my chin and made a show of dropping the gun's safety catch. 'Your papers!' he shouted impatiently. Mohammed, Maurizio and Giorgio were already trying to calm the man, who spoke no English. We all pulled out our papers. Giorgio handed his over to the man, smiling. 'You belong to the biggest dickhead organization in the world,' he said politely. The policeman smiled back at him. It wasn't unusual to be stopped at checkpoints leading into the city. However, if the police or military saw foreigners in the car, they usually waved them on. Sometimes when taxi drivers carrying foreigners were stopped they interceded on the foreigners' behalf, reprimanding the soldiers for not respecting foreign guests, which seemed foolhardy but confirmed the Afghans' penchant for arguing given the slightest excuse and showed their contempt for authority even if at great risk to themselves.

Mohammed dropped us at 'Chicken Street' so the two Romans could continue their shopping spree. As soon as I entered this street, which had been a landmark on the hippie trail, I felt like an alien as dozens of Afghan shopkeepers emerged from their shops, each one trying to entice me in, each one experimenting with a string of languages one after the other. 'Good sir, please come . . . have some tea . . . wonderful carpets . . . no obligation, just look . . .' 'Monsieur . . .' 'Herr . . .' 'Señor . . .' It was difficult not to succumb to an Aladdin's cave, a treasure trove of shops with a vast array of intricately woven silk carpets and others with trinkets of silver that hadn't disappeared or been destroyed by the war but had been preserved in dust. It was just as hard not to succumb to their classic Eastern bazaar sales pitch: 'You are the first customer for four months, and the last ones didn't buy anything. Unless you buy something, kind sir, I will not be able to feed my children . . . Just choose one thing . . .' Prices were often halved and halved again with a desperate recklessness for a sale, which for me, the foreigner, added authenticity to their stories of hardship, but I couldn't buy the nation singlehanded.

The next day I took Maurizio and Giorgio shopping in the bazaar. You could find Cristal d'Arque glasses, spaghetti-making machines, Horse's Head Chinese toilet paper and, in tumbledown caravanserais – warehouses that had stood for centuries – boxes of seventy-two-piece china sets from Korea piled high to the eaves. We joined Mohammed for lunch at a crowded kebab house. A young boy cleaned the table of scraps of melon, grapes and pieces of bread by sweeping them onto the floor with his arm. He flicked a filthy rag at a cloud of flies that constantly hovered over the table. Then, seeing that we were foreigners, he gave us special treatment, placing a newspaper on the table for a cloth. The other patrons continued to spit bits of bone or gristle onto the floor. Maurizio lit a pungent Indonesian cigarette and began to fidget.

'What's the problem?' I asked.

'Is there an ashtray?'

We all fell about laughing.

Mohammed ordered the kebabs. When they arrived on skewers we found an unusual variety. In addition to the regular meat kebabs, there were liver and kidney kebabs and a fourth whiteish-coloured kebab which I hadn't previously eaten.

'What's this?' I asked.

Mohammed didn't answer, and for the first time since I had known him he looked rather embarrassed. I continued to press him for an answer. He looked down at his crotch and smiled – testicle kebabs – a popular Afghan dish. It was the first and last time I tried testicle shishkebab.

When it was time to pay for the meal I was surprised at the size of the bill. I protested gently. 'I only want to pay for the kebabs,' I jested in an oblique reference to past invaders who sought to conquer the whole country. However, the Afghans had always held most of the cards if not the balls.

The press office, which was part of the Ministry of Foreign Affairs, arranged for me to meet Abdul Wakil, the Foreign Minister, to discuss the possibility of my returning to Herat and being allowed to move from the government-controlled city to the mujahedeen-controlled countryside. Like all government officials, Abdul Wakil had tried to distance himself from previous Marxist Afghan governments, but in his case it would be difficult to deny past links. Rumour had it that he was on the first plane into Kabul after the Soviet invasion. Like all current ministers, he left me in no doubt that he remained confident that the government's position was growing stronger day by day. He dispensed with his English interpreter and showed a geniality and sense of humour which shouldn't have surprised me, considering all Afghans I have met shared this trait. Likewise his dogged look and quiet determination bespoke a ruthlessness that had been employed in defence of the revolution. When we broached the subject of my visit to Herat he seemed well prepared.

'You have visited my country before without permission or visas, I believe?'

I didn't answer.

'I also believe you have a habit of crossing borders in the same fashion,' he continued.

I nodded.

'Well, I want you to promise me that you will not enter Afghanistan again without a visa.'

To agree to this was to bar me from entering Afghanistan with the mujahedeen. 'I'm sorry, Minister, but I cannot do that. But supposing you were to give me permission to visit Herat and leave the confines of the city to visit Ismail Khan [the guerrilla commander] there would be no reason for me to enter your country without a visa.'

The Foreign Minister said he would consider the matter.

When I next met him later that summer I was still waiting for an answer. I pressed him for a decision. He gave it some thought and then told me, 'I want to meet him first.'

After my initial meeting with the Foreign Minister I remained hopeful that he would look favourably on my request. However, as I waited for his decision news reached Kabul of the Ayatollah Khomeini's death on 3 June 1989 and I cut short my visit to Afghanistan to fly to Tehran to attend the Imam's funeral.

THE AYATOLLAH'S
FUNERAL

A mass of upturned faces streaming
with the heat and all stricken and fur-
rowed with the cruel poverty and
hunger of such bitter lives – the tent, the
dust, the smell of the lamps and the
people! – the whole thing remained in
one's mind as a sort of nightmare chaos
which I should not like to see again.
And yet it was not even really pic-
turesque, it was too sordid and too
false . . .

Gertrude Bell writing in
Travels to Asia Minor and Persia (1911)
on the religious ceremonies
held in honour of Imams
Hassan and Hussein in 1892

The day I feel danger to the Islamic
Republic, I will cut everybody's hand
off.

Ayatollah Ruhollah Khomeini, May 1981

Tehran, June 1989

I first heard the news of Ayatollah Khomeini's death on the BBC
World Service. 'The lofty spirit of the leader of Muslims everywhere, His Excellency Imam Khomeini has gone to heaven,' was
how Ayatollah Khomeini's son announced the death of his father
the morning after he had died from five massive heart attacks and
severe cancer of the bowel. For years Western intelligence agencies

had declared that the Ayatollah was at death's door with cancer and kidney failure. For years rumours in Iran abounded that the Imam was dying, or indeed was already dead. One had it that he had died soon after the revolution in 1979 and had been impersonated by an actor ever since, and it was the actor who was now dying. What was certain was that the eighty-nine-year-old leader or his imper-sonator had died without fulfilling the 'great goal' of his revolution: 'the creation of a global Islamic government'.

I was desperate to return to Iran. For five years I had been applying for a visa to revisit a nation that had left a lasting impression on me. I had been enchanted by the magnificence of its mosques, its architecture and rich history, its fantastic desert expanses. But I was equally astonished by the fervour of its people, and bewildered by the size of the crowds of worshippers who were now guaranteed to turn out to pay homage to their leader who had put an end to 2,500 years of Persian monarchy, the legacy of Darius the Great and Xerxes, and replaced it with the first Islamic government since the reign of Ali, the fourth caliph, cousin of the Prophet Mohammed, thirteen centuries before.

I contacted my New York picture agency in the hope of securing a photographic assignment. They told me to head for Tehran as quickly as possible.

It wasn't an easy trip to Tehran from Kabul. I was set to join an Afghan presidential flight with a delegation of Afghan ministers, but the flight was cancelled at the last moment because the Iranian authorities refused landing permission. I was now in grave danger of missing the only flight out of Kabul for the next three days. The Afghan government, having been partly responsible for the hiccup in my travel plans, agreed to intercede on my behalf. They telephoned the Kabul airport control tower to stop the Ariana Afghan Airlines flight to Delhi from leaving. They gave me one hour to reach the airport. In that time I had also to find a new air route to Tehran and obtain a visa from the Iranian embassy.

The quickest and only route to get me to the Ayatollah's funeral on time was via Delhi, Dubai and Bandar Abbas on the south coast of Iran, opposite the Strait of Hormuz. At the Iranian embassy a group of Shiite Afghan mourners had gathered in the street to chant and wail in grief. A visa couldn't be issued in time, but the

Iranian *chargé d'affaires*, who was visibly shocked by his leader's death, agreed to give me an official letter of introduction for the authorities at Bandar Abbas airport. However, he was unable to find anyone to type the letter. Valuable minutes ticked by as he disappeared in search of a typist. With fifteen minutes to spare I received a letter typed in the Persian script and headed for the airport. The plane was still on the runway, but I didn't board for another 2½ hours as I argued over the correct ticketing. When I did eventually join the plane the passengers were covered in rivulets of sweat. I took my seat and waited for the engines to start.

As time passed with no sign that the plane was being readied for departure, the pilot informed us, 'I don't know what to do. I can't get the engines started.' But help was at hand. We were towed around the airport by a tractor to achieve a jump start.

On arrival in Delhi I was told that the flight to Dubai was full. This was also the case for the flight to Bandar Abbas. However, through a mixture of cajoling, pleading and a token of my gratitude, I was able to secure not only a seat to Dubai but an upgrade.

At Dubai I boarded the Iran Air airbus with some trepidation. On my only previous visit to post-revolutionary Iran I had spent a month and a half wandering around the country before crossing into Afghanistan with Iranian-based Afghan mujahedeen and all my subsequent attempts to obtain a visa had been refused. I might well be denied entry to Iran. Looking out of the plane down at the sparkling clear waters of the Gulf I remembered too that it was on the return flight, the Bandar Abbas–Dubai leg of the journey, that the USS *Vincennes* had blown an identical Iran Air airbus out of the sky by 'mistake'. The sailors had misread the data and passed the faulty information to the captain, Will Rogers III, who then ordered the launching of two missiles that destroyed the plane, killing all 290 aboard and adding another cause to Iran's continuing hostility to the West.

My fears of trouble with the authorities were confirmed on arrival at Bandar Abbas airport. Three other journalists and myself were not allowed to reboard the plane to Tehran. At immigration a surly young official quarantined us. In Khomeini's theocracy all differences and dissent were demonic; foreigners had corrupted the world with Judaeo-Christian values. We should have come stamped with an Iranian government health warning. The young bearded revolutionary treated us with great animosity, and I feared we were going to be sent back, but there were no longer any planes. We were detained for eight hours. When I raised objections at our treatment and protested that we had all the necessary documents, the official refused to listen to our explanations, but scowled at us and grew increasingly belligerent. I was caught taking a picture of a family in the arrivals hall and was forced to hand over my film. In an inhospitable airport surrounded by young Islamic Revolutionary Guards, prospects were not bright. Years of isolation had created a large degree of xenophobia. I thought of an Iranian delegate to the United Nations who said the Koran states that non-believers 'shall burn in the fire of Hell, a dismal resting place. There let them taste their drink: scalding water, festering blood and other putrid things . . .'

We watched several chartered planes ferrying mourners to Tehran. Over a hundred people had gathered in the departure hall. They sat in chairs and squatted on the ground to stare at a television screen with pictures of the Ayatollah's body lying in state inside a refrigerated glass box on top of a ship's container surrounded by a vast sea of black-shirted mourners. The Imam's body was wrapped in a white shroud and his black turban, denoting his family's descent from the Prophet Mohammed, was placed on his chest.

In the late afternoon, some twenty-four hours after I had left Kabul, a high-ranking city official came to the airport to apologize for the treatment we had received. 'Everything is all right. Your credentials have been established,' he said reassuringly. He offered to take us to a local hotel to freshen up, but our immediate concern was to reach Tehran in time for the funeral. The delay had caused us to miss the day's last scheduled flight to the Iranian capital. Once again he apologized; he would seek alternative travel arrangements. In the meantime he whisked us past the officials to the airport VIP lounge, a room with broken windows through which sand was encroaching. Tea and a selection of nuts were laid out in front of us. We were tired and frustrated – so near and yet so far.

The official returned with the encouraging news that he had arranged for a private jet to take us and one of the leading spiritual figures in India, Imam Bukhari, to Tehran. Imam Bukhari was an enormous elderly gentleman in a djellaba, a white dishdash and a vermilion skullcap. So great was his size, he had the utmost difficulty in moving; each turn or movement required the support of his walking stick, an enormous effort and the assistance of his two young manservants.

By the time we boarded the small jet, my bones ached from tiredness and I was asleep soon after we became airborne. I woke nearly two hours later to see the glittering lights of Tehran beneath us. In many ways the Iranian capital resembled Los Angeles for the heat, traffic and pollution as well as the size of the sprawling metropolis. Mehrabad Airport was a hive of activity. Half a dozen Iran Air 747s were parked on the airport belt. Inside the terminal hundreds of passengers filled every available space, their suitcases spread over a large area with each item, basic commodities such as decaffeinated coffee, cornflakes and deodorant – almost unobtainable locally – being scrutinized as if they might be dangerous contraband, which was of course what the authorities were looking for. Such was the confusion that we were able to march past the other arrivals towards the taxi rank.

The men were dressed in black shirts, the women in black chadors and black or navy ropoushes, a mackintosh-like overcoat worn with a scarf. We grabbed a taxi and drove out of the airport past portraits of Thatcher, Reagan and Saddam Hussein portrayed as child-murdering, bloodthirsty cannibals. The city's streets were empty; merchants had shuttered their shops and whole buildings were swathed in black banners. The unmistakable impression driving through the city was that a great tragedy had befallen the nation.

We headed for the former Intercontinental Hotel. Like the one in Kabul it too was under new post-revolutionary management. The Tehran Intercontinental, or rather the Laleh or Tulip Hotel, symbol of martyrdom, was now owned by the Ministry of the Oppressed.

The hotel was buzzing with activity. Over sixty foreign journalists had flown in from different parts of the world to cover the funeral. This was my first experience of the media circus which one journalist described as 'a Mongolian cluster fuck'. The correspondents renewed old acquaintances. Lee, a correspondent for

United Press International, shouted happily across the lobby, 'Dave! The last time I saw you was at the Istanbul synagogue massacre!' They embraced warmly. Two correspondents jested competitively, 'So I fucked you, I got to Hoxha's Albania before you did.' The Iranian guests and staff at the Laleh, normally patronized by Iranian clerics and foreigners with a suitably militant background, gaped in wonder at the dozens of journalists.

I found a room and then went to the coffee house to grab something to eat. I chose an Azadi salad, literally a freedom salad, described in the menu as 'a friendly mixture of apple, carrots, celery or lettuce'. The salt for the meal came from the Great Satan himself, packaged by the Embassy Lucky Boy Grocery Corporation of New York City and Washington DC. I overheard two cameramen discussing the day's events. 'It's a pity we didn't get there, they would have made great pictures – there was blood, groaning and people screaming.' – 'We chased an ambulance going like a bat out of hell, but we lost it.'

Back in the lobby television anchormen were fighting to obtain pictures. 'I don't care what it takes,' said an American correspondent waving a bundle of hundred-dollar notes at his Iranian interpreter and guide. 'I want the pictures!' His TV crew members shoved aside those of another network to get a better 'visual' of some mullahs entering the hotel. Others were concerned about meeting the deadlines for their prime-time newscasts, which reminded me of a media tale I had heard on my earlier travels. A television foreign correspondent covering a unit of government troops moving against a guerrilla post kept eyeing his watch and asking the commander when he would order the attack. The distracted commander said, 'Not yet, not yet.' The correspondent, losing patience, finally exploded, 'Goddammit, I've a bird, a satellite to feed to the network at six o'clock!' The commander, understanding perfectly, ordered his attack immediately. Nothing had changed.

I had arrived too late to take pictures of the funeral. I watched the scenes on television with some Iranian officials and some other journalists who had been shepherded away from the grave as hundreds of thousands of wailing, grief-stricken followers began to flagellate themselves, beating their chests and pounding their heads with their hands and fists in the wild abandon of a wave of intoxicating religious fervour. One journalist was still complaining to his escort from Ershad, the Ministry of Islamic Guidance, 'You don't allow non-Muslims! Shit! We allow you into the Vatican!'

Some journalists never left the hotel, opting for the security and comfort of their air-conditioned rooms, and filed their reports from the live Iranian television coverage. The scenes made for compelling viewing. The first attempt to take the Imam's body from where it lay in state to the burial ground south of the city was abandoned when the vehicle carrying it was stranded in downtown Tehran as a huge procession of mourners swarmed all over it. The corpse was then transferred to a helicopter to complete the journey to the cemetery at Behesht Zahra, where tens of thousands of the revolution's martyrs lay buried. A million mourners converged on the consecrated ground, many wailing and pounding their heads. They were packed so thick that people were crushed to death; the top of a double-decker bus collapsed under the weight of those fighting for a better view, injuring those inside. As the helicopter, described by the television commentator as the 'Chariot of Death', touched down, the frenzied crowd surged forward fighting to touch the body and snatch a piece of the burial shroud. Some managed to surge past the Revolutionary Guards. They clambered into the flimsy casket to plant kisses on the dead Imam; the corpse spilled to the ground; the Imam's feet and knees protruded from beneath the torn white shroud. The grave itself was occupied by mourners who refused to move and see their leader buried forever. The Guards, unable to control the crowd, fired shots into the air whilst others retrieved the body and shoved it and the broken casket into the helicopter. It lifted off with the coffin hanging precariously out of the door while several mourners tried to cling to the helicopter's skids.

Iranians watching the scenes on television broke down in tears, sobbing hysterically. They were inconsolable. The commentators heaped great eulogies on the Ayatollah, referring to him as the 'Saviour of Islam', 'Imam-e-azziz' or Imam, O dearest. Five hours later, as the Chariot of Death reappeared, the commentator wailed 'Hail Khomeini! You flew like a bird from your cage. We cried and shouted very much. We asked God not to let the bird go out of the cage, we need it. No one paid attention to our prayers. You were like Moses floating down the river [the television cut to a sea of flailing hands] . . . *Ya Khomeini! Ya Khomeini!* [Hail Khomeini!] *Allahu Akbar!* [God is Supreme!]' cried the overwrought Iranian television commentator.

This time the body had arrived encased in a metal coffin. As the helicopter once again touched down the crowd surged forward, arms flailing and chanting, '*Marg bar Amerika! Marg bar Amerika!* [Death to America!]' The Guards made a frantic rush for the grave. At the last instant the lid of the metal casket was removed, and the body rolled into the ground in keeping with Islamic tradition, which requires that the dead be interred in only a shroud. The grave was quickly covered with concrete slabs, and a large cargo container lifted on top to stop the delirious mourners from plundering the earth to exhume the corpse.

By the time the Ayatollah was buried at least eight people had been crushed to death, nearly five hundred had been hospitalized and 10,800 had been treated for injuries. In these moments few worshippers had taken into account the words laid down in the Imam's book, *The Practical Laws of Islam.* An abridged edition which I studied contained only a fraction of the 3,000 rulings, but included such matters as 'A Lost Item with no Owner', 'Mortgages', and 'Divorcing Women Who are Menstruating'. Under the heading 'Bathing the Corpse and Burial of the Corpse' they would have read that 'The shroud must not be usurped,' and 'A mourner must not injure himself in any way.' The sacred laws seemed far from the minds of those who were subsumed in a vortex of passion, and whose sole goal was to keep a piece of the Ayatollah's shroud or some earth from his grave, both of which were considered divinely blessed by a man some Iranians hailed as an Imam qualified to be the deputy for the Shiite Messiah.

For seven days afterwards hundreds of thousands of people continued to gather at the grave site, drawn relentlessly towards the body to pay their last respects. They came from all over Iran. Wailing men, women and children crowded to touch the makeshift shrine of cargo containers or to press their children, pieces of cloth, prayer beads or Korans against it in the quest for a divine blessing. For seven days the emergency services were overwhelmed by the hundreds of people suffering from injuries, heatstroke, exhaustion or heart attacks, and those who had fainted in the torrid heat and crush of bodies. For seven days the authorities did their best to provide hand-outs of bread, watermelon and refreshments, but like the masses that swelled around the shrine, the scene of each hand-out became another crush of screaming bodies and flailing hands under the sweltering heat. This place was called Behesht Zahra, the Gateway to Paradise.

Each day I travelled the twenty kilometres to Behesht Zahra, but I also found time to visit the Imam's former home in north Tehran, attend Friday Prayers at Tehran University and have dinner with Jalal Talabani, an Iraqi Kurdish resistance leader who had for years been used by the US State Department and the Iranians, under both the Shah and the Ayatollah, as a pawn in his fight against the Iraqi dictator Saddam Hussein. During dinner at his temporary home he espoused the merits of socialism and his thoughts on the small Soviet Kurdish population taking sides in the Armenian–Azerbaijani conflict in the Soviet Union, as if he didn't already have enough problems in trying to unite the disparate Kurdish resistance groups inside and outside Iraq. I also had time to speak with Iraqi Feili refugees (mainly Shiite Kurds) forcibly taken from their homes in the middle of the night and deported from Iraq, to go shopping in poor downtown Tehran where I was nearly beaten up by an anti-Western mob, and to accept several invitations to parties in uptown Tehran where stunning Iranian women removed their veils to reveal décolleté singlets. Here the wine and music flowed and the air was sweet with opium.

On my previous visit to Tehran I had visited the Shah's marbled palaces, which had been turned into a museum pointing up the contrasts between its blowzy wealth and the people's poverty. Now, not more than half a mile away in the district of Jamaran, I visited the Imam's house at the invitation of the Ministry of Islamic Guidance. I made my way there with Fred's Taxi Service. Albert, my Armenian driver, took me by way of the Ayatollah Sadr Highway and was forced to drop me at a roadblock manned by Revolutionary Guards on Hojatolislam Dr Bahonar Street. From the shahs' accession to the Peacock Throne to the present day, the cult of personality continued unbroken. Shah Reza Pahlavi's portrait had been replaced by the stern, taciturn face of the Ayatollah, icon and sword of the Iranian Revolution. As far as living memory could recall, the country had suffered an uninterrupted chain of corruption and dictatorship, torturers and executioners, with dissenting citizens who hadn't been summarily shot in exhaustive political purges forced into exile.

As I walked towards the Imam's house, a platoon of goose-stepping Revolutionary Guards, each with a picture of Khomeini pinned to his chest, marched past led by standard bearers carrying large floral-wreathed portraits of the Imam. Sorrowful youngsters and grey-bearded grandfathers followed. Many wore a red or black bandana inscribed with their willingness to continue Khomeini's revolution.

Around the complex of houses that surrounded the Imam's home, hundreds of grieving women had come to see where he used to breathe and to worship the ground on which he had stood. They waited in line weeping and praying. There were tears, screams and stunned silence as they waited their turn to enter the inner sanctum. In a side street women and children crouched by the Ayatollah's portrait; some kissed the image. One heartbroken woman clung to the hoarding, her hands abreast of the Imam's head. In floods of tears she wailed, 'I have been orphaned.'

Security in the covered street to the Imam's home was tight. Adjacent to his house was a mosque packed with distraught pilgrims trying to reach the temple's inner balcony to touch the armchair from which the Imam had once stared down at his followers. My guide ushered me past the gates to the house, a modest, rather shabby bungalow. I wasn't allowed inside but was permitted to walk along a raised gangway from where I could see into the living room. It was spartan, and the Imam's old man-servant, Haji Isa, stood forlornly inside its small confines which the Imam had rarely left since he had moved to Jamaran some seven years earlier. The Imam had stuck rigidly to his schedule, starting the day with prayers and half an hour of exercises. He occasionally received visitors but he kept one hour aside each morning and afternoon for his children and grandchildren. He watched television, read the newspapers and listened to the BBC World Service,

the Voice of America and Radio Israel. In the evening at precisely
nine twenty-seven he called his wife to serve him dinner. At ten
o'clock he would go to bed, sleep four hours, then get up to pray.
Each new day always began with gymnastics. The guide informed
me that the Imam led a simple life. He told me, 'He had no
furniture.' I pointed to two pieces of furniture. 'Those belong to the
Imam's wife,' said the guide. 'And the carpets?' I asked.

'They do not belong to the Imam,' he said. 'They must be given to
the needy *sadat* [descendants of the Prophet].'

'Did he leave any money?'

Again my guide quoted the Imam: 'There is a small amount of
cash in Tehran which has been donated as personal gifts.'

'What about the vast sums of religious alms and taxes paid by
people and kept at home or in banks in the Imam's name?'

'The Imam said they didn't belong to him and his inheritors had
no right to them.'

It was hard to overestimate the intensity of religious fervour, and
the theocracy tried to harness this devotion to the dictates of Islam
in all manner of ways. As the faithful flocked by the thousand to
Friday Prayers at Tehran University, a government ministry had at
some point organized their own Friends of the Earth campaign in
accordance with Islam. 'Allah commands the recycling of renew-
able resources' and 'Littering is a sin against Islam' read the slogans
on several posters above the crowds and on black banners that
lined both sides of the street.

Streets leading to the university were choked with worshippers;
traffic was at a standstill. Several thousand women in the head-to-
toe black chador were segregated from the men and entered
separate quarters to perform their devotions.

Outside Tehran University everyone was body-searched. Inside
was a vast ocean of worshippers. Several of the country's leading
ayatollahs and the speaker of the Majlis, the Iranian Parliament,
Hojatolislam Ali Akbar Hashemi Rafsanjani, were expected to
speak to the worshippers who sat facing Mecca in serried ranks. In
the meantime the audience listened to the warm-up act: several
mullahs who spoke from a dais flanked by portraits of living and
dead ayatollahs. Two security men stood on either side of the

speakers, each clutching the barrel of a Kalashnikov in his left hand like a walking stick.

The mullahs took it in turns to quote from Ayatollah Khomeini's thirty-page last will and testament. In it he raged against 'the atheist East' and 'infidel West'. At the top of the list was the greatest enemy of all, the United States in the guise of Satan, denounced as 'an inborn terrorist state which has set fire to the world from end to end with its ally, international Zionism'. Death was devoutly wished upon 'their affiliated agents, those notorious traitors the al Saud family [of Saudi Arabia] . . . May the curse of God and that of his angels and prophets be upon them all.' Jordan's King Hussein was branded a 'criminal tramp'. The President of Egypt and the King of Morocco were accused of 'treason'.

A tearful Iranian journalist who had been listening to the mullahs said, 'The Imam's will is indicative of his kindness.'

Each dignitary took it in turn to launch into an updated script that included the crimes of George Bush. Each rebuff was hailed by sections of the crowd who broke into a Simon Says chorus of *Allahu Akbar!* It reminded me of football fans cheering fouls, corner kicks and goals.

When the Imam's successors took to the podium they claimed fidelity to the 'Imam's line'. The Ayatollah's name was invoked to instil divine ordination, demonstrate allegiance and confer legitimacy on their policies. The kneeling congregation didn't know whether to applaud or pray.

The turbaned clerical revolutionaries left the university in their air-conditioned, smoke-glassed, bulletproof black Mercedes limousines flanked by posses of bodyguards on motorbikes. The lumpen masses spilled out into the streets to be bussed back home. When they saw the Western television cameras they began to chant 'Marg bar Amerika!' It spread like the plague through the crowd whose members began to shake their fists and beat their heads and chests. People fainted, roamed the streets distraught and confused. Four days after the Imam had been buried, I saw a devotee's head still caked in earth from the burial ground.

In north Tehran the mood was distinctly at odds with what I had witnessed so far. I had been invited to dinner by the cousin of a school friend I had bumped into a week before in Kabul. It was only the first in a series of remarkable coincidences, one later that evening and another two weeks afterwards, when I encountered the brother of the same school friend on the New York subway – I hadn't seen him for twelve years.

The other guests, like most residents of north Tehran, greeted the Ayatollah's death with relief. The mood was soporific, the climate cool, and the closest thing to religious fervour was the way in which people approached the smoking of opium. In the relative security of the spacious villa in a quiet tree-lined street beyond the tall unfinished luxury apartment blocks the women abandoned their black or navy ropoushes.

Everyone discussed the price of the US dollar. In a country so at odds with the United States, no currency was as closely linked to the dollar as the Iranian rial. The theocracy's every sentence was analysed for a hint at rapprochement or continuing isolation from the West, in turn reflected in the fluctuating exchange rate of a worthless currency. The men discussed the value of land, property development and the cost of bribing mullahs. One guest suggested to his friends that they invest in burial plots as a hedge against inflation, which was out of control. By way of example, another guest told me that the cost of living was so great that only if a government employee saved all his salary for fifty years would he be able to buy a plot of land to build a house. Another quoted a famous Iranian preacher as confirmation of the present hopelessness: 'If you give a penny to a mullah and you can't get it back from him, how can you expect to get the country back from him?'

The women also complained about prices – a week's salary for a hair perm. But some of these women were the wealthy Iranians with access to foreign travel. They wore the latest Paris fashions, and as the music and home-made wine began to flow their clothes revealed more curves than a scenic railway.

One well-preserved, sleekly attractive woman half-seriously, half-jokingly told me that for her the revolution meant that the latest in European *haute couture* took an extra week to reach Tehran. She complained that her six-and-a-half-year-old daughter nagged her to allow her to wear the veil like the grown-ups.

I struck up a conversation with Azadeh, a petite woman with chestnut hair who spoke English with little trace of an accent.

'Where did you learn your English?' I asked nervously, not finding a more original opening gambit.

'I went to school in England and I used to be married to an Englishman.' Younger than most of the partygoers, Azadeh was also more bashful, and unlike the rest of the guests she didn't drink either the home-made vodka or the wine.

'Where did you live in London?'

'Well, we didn't live in London when we were married, but Ronnie now lives in Brixton.'

I explained I also lived in Brixton. If that was a coincidence, imagine my surprise when it transpired her ex-husband and I lived in the same street. I asked her if she had considered moving abroad, maybe returning to England. 'I have no money. I work as a secretary and I am forced to live at home. Besides, it's impossible to get a visa, everyone wants to leave Iran and no one wants to grant visas to Iranians. When I was in the United States during the hostage crisis everyone thought Iranians were either terrorists, mad mullahs or religious fanatics. I don't think things have changed, there is still a great deal of suspicion.'

She spoke of the revolution as a stifling experience. Like other Iranians of about my age who weren't committed to the goals of the revolution, she complained that living in Iran was like 'being buried alive'. It was the same refrain I had heard across the world from educated young people who were hostage to the fortunes of their governments.

I wondered how one knew what was and was not permitted. Azadeh said they had a saying – 'If it doesn't make you tingle, it's okay.'

'There is nothing to do,' she explained. 'It's forbidden to listen to music, play cards, drink wine. Of course,' she said, looking around the room, 'all of this goes on behind closed doors.'

In one corner of the room our host had ceremoniously begun the preparations for smoking opium. He emptied a bag of charcoal into a *mangal*, an ornate brazier, which he stoked until it was hot enough to melt a small piece of opium on a pipe. He did this by drawing a piece of charcoal over the pipe, and holding it there with a pair of tweezer-like pliers, close enough to the opium to melt it, but not so close as to let it burn. When he drew on the opium through the pipe the charcoal glowed. The host's family and friends gathered around the *mangal* and the room slowly filled with the sweet smell of opium. When the melted opium covered the porcelain pipe's minute hole, a needle referred to as a *damad* (bridegroom) was pushed into the hole to clear the blocked opening.

The place settings, the stoking of the *mangal*, the carving up of the opium into *misqals*, a quarter of a *lul*, and the polite passing around of the pipe reminded me of family and friends sitting around a table for a traditional English Sunday roast. I pointed this out to Azadeh. 'You're right,' she said, 'only it takes place every day.'

I asked Azadeh what effect opium had on smokers. She said the only positive thing about it was it kept men from arguing with their wives.

'Aren't they worried about the local snoops, the Revolutionary Guards from the neighbourhood Komiteh?'

'No. Sometimes they come and join in.'

I thought this a little far-fetched until, several days later, when invited to another house in north Tehran, we were joined by the local Komiteh man. He was faultlessly polite and occasionally made a witty joke. He reminded me of the local bobby except he wore a suit and a collarless shirt and the revolutionaries' mandatory uniform – a two- or three-day designer stubble. He was in his late twenties with only a secondary education but his new ambition was to become a doctor. At first he declined a glass of wine, but subsequently took a few sips from a glass that had been placed in front of him. I felt the guests, who were all against the revolution, saw this as some sort of victory, that beneath the strident tones of the revolution life went on, albeit behind closed doors, in much the same way as it had under the Shah – everyone had a price.

I visited several of Tehran's large bazaars. At the Djomeh Bazaar collectors set up little stalls with their goods displayed on rugs. You could find all manner of things. Local stamps commemorating holy battles, hostage-taking and the blood of apostates as well as some of the 150,000 mullahs, ayatollahs, hojatolislams and elders. I found an out-of-date London *A–Z Streetfinder* and several books in

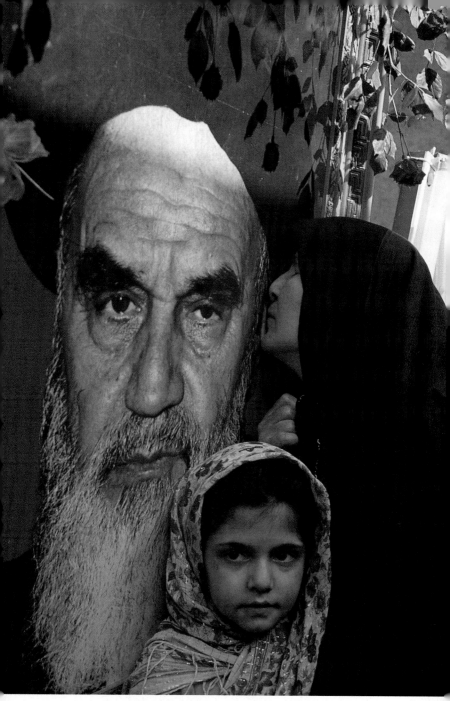

The Ayatollah's funeral. A Tehran side-street

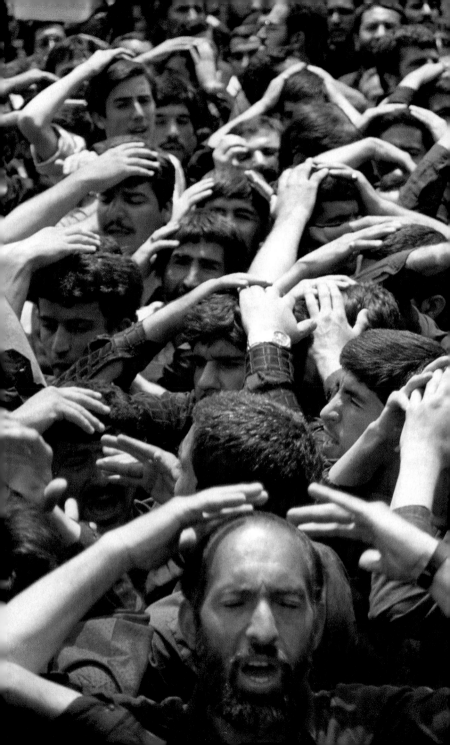

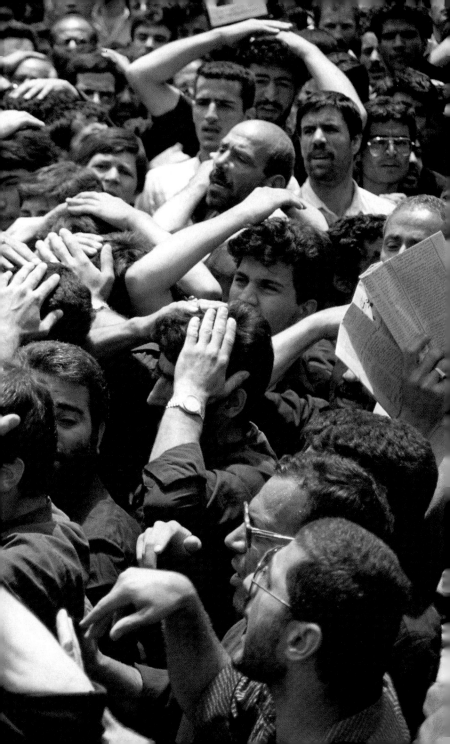

Overleaf:
Self-flagellation during
the first seven days
of official mourning after
the death of the
Ayatollah

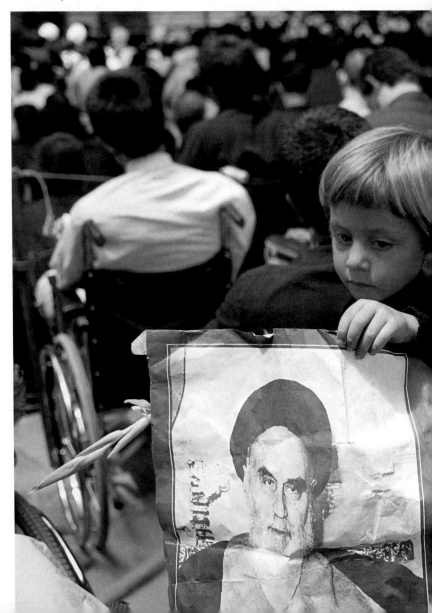

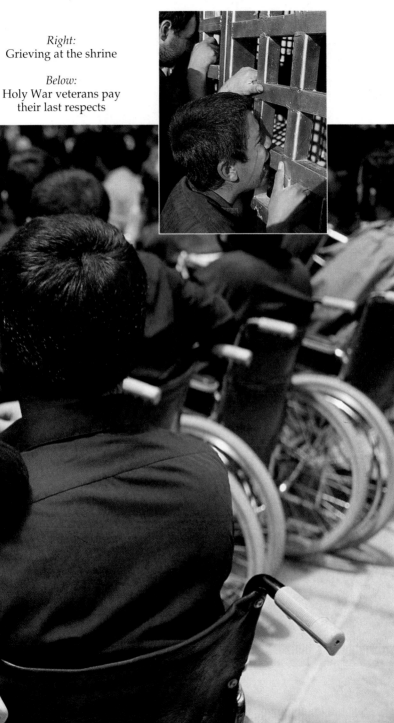

Right:
Grieving at the shrine

Below:
Holy War veterans pay
their last respects

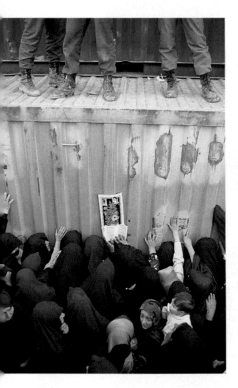

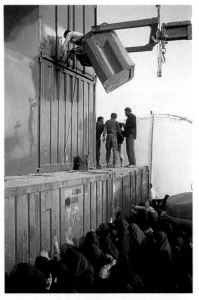

The Ayatollah's shrine being constructed out of goods containers. As usual, the women wait while the men watch

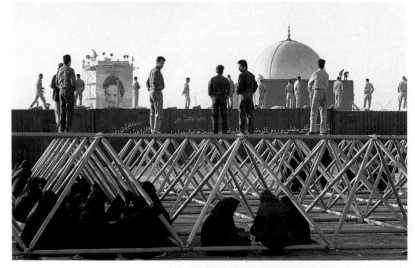

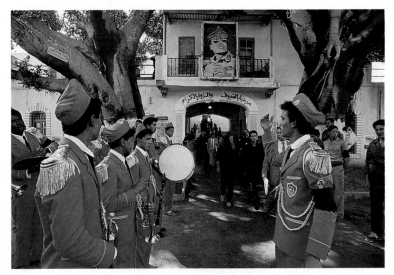

Libya

Above: 'Mourning Day' under the omnipresent
gaze of Colonel Qadhafi

Below: Sabrata, on the Mediterranean coast, one of
the many valuable archaeological sites in Libya

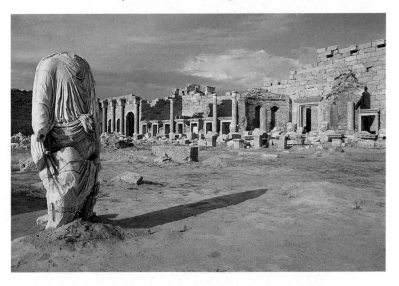

Young Afghan militiaman in Herat. Yesterday he fought alongside the mujahedeen, today he stands alongside the government

English, including *Zen and the Art of Motorcycle Maintenance*, a biography of Martin Luther King and a book entitled *Cuba: An American Tragedy*. There were also magic potions – mountain herbs to be infused in water to reclaim lost hair, old stethoscopes, carpet spot remover, a dismembered Barbie doll and a battered suitcase with a collection of medicines. However, the farther south you travelled from the centre of Tehran the higher the temperature rose in both climate and religious zeal.

Fate looked kindly on me the day I visited the semi-industrial sprawling bazaar of Saeed Ismail in the heart of downtown Tehran. Accompanied by a Turkish businessman, I travelled by taxi through the congested streets. The air became thicker and more polluted, and my eyes began to burn. Unlike north Tehran, here there were few parks and little shade from the unremitting heat. Here people lived crammed together in rundown houses in an urban nightmare of narrow alleyways. This deprivation was the fertile breeding ground of the desperation and fanaticism that continued to stoke the flames of the revolution. We had entered Khomeini-land where the poor had not benefited materially from the Imam's revolution but had gained spiritual salvation.

I went into part of the bazaar, a Shiite theme park where the Ayatollah's portrait loomed larger than anywhere else and hung alongside posters of living and dead divinities. In a small shop an elderly man was busy grinding and polishing recycled nuts and bolts into chains for self-flagellation; there were also masks, swords and helmets made from recycled materials. I asked the gentleman who his clients were. He told me he sold to theatres, those in mourning and the Pasdaran (the Islamic Revolutionary Guards). I picked up an ancient-looking helmet. 'To which dynasty does this belong?' I expected him to say the Achaemenid or Assyrian dynasty. 'Since the time of the Prophet,' he answered cryptically.

No day in the East is complete without several long breaks for cups of *chai*, and Bulent, the Turkish businessman with a homing instinct like a migrating bird's, found us a tea house just as we were about to wilt. It wasn't so much a tea house as a cupboard which three people could only enter at a push. Strictly speaking, the bazaaris ordered the tea from the tea house and it was delivered to their stalls. The owner had lived for thirty years in this little cubicle that was smaller than an average-sized bathroom, but he had made it his home with every available inch covered in picture postcards and magazine clippings. I scanned the walls. There were pictures of a Volkswagen Beetle production line, the city of Zagreb, Abraham sacrificing a lamb, cats, mosques, a picture from the early days of the Shah when Iranians wore Western clothes and hats (ties were now considered a symbol of Western decadence), and a drawing of the Prophet Mohammed. My attention was drawn to a pair of castanets pegged to the wall. 'I believe fishermen use these to attract the fish to their nets,' said the owner, his mind as imaginative as his cardamon tea was refreshing.

Along the bazaar's main avenue the smell of thick old grease hung in the air. Here the shops sold grandfather clocks, brass instruments – several tubas – broken-down Westinghouse refrigerators and weighing machines. As I raised my camera to take some pictures, I was set upon and nearly beaten up by an anti-Western mob. I was jostled by tough-looking men who cursed and shouted at me, 'You're not Iranian, you aren't allowed to take pictures!' Bulent, who had been inside a shop, rushed to my defence. He spoke fluent Farsi and explained we were Turkish. The men apologized, the Muslim brethren should be united, they said. 'Until America frees us from our yoke nothing will improve.' Unlike the north of the city, here the theocracy was not blamed for rising inflation, shortages and ration coupons.

It wasn't the first time I had been stopped for taking pictures. Apart from this incident and the one at Bandar Abbas, I had fought to save my camera from being smashed by one of the clerics' bodyguards after he saw me photographing a fleet of black Mercedes limousines hurtling away from Tehran University. I had also had problems at the burial ground, where I was stopped from taking pictures of the crush surrounding the free food distribution because, according to the Ministry of Islamic Guidance, photographs of the crowds fighting to get hold of the eggs, melon and bread might be misinterpreted in the West as riots by a populace on the brink of starvation. Luckily I had already taken the pictures. I was not so fortunate when I finally found the 3,000 mullahs who had left their seminaries in Qom to walk the eighty-five miles to Behesht Zahra. When I caught up with them at dawn on the final leg of their journey I was once again forbidden to photograph. This time I was not permitted to take what would have been a dramatic picture of thousands of mullahs asleep in the desert in ordered rows under blankets with their turbans placed neatly beside them, because the Revolutionary Guards said the West would see this picture and think thousands of mullahs had died. I was deeply disappointed, especially as I had left the hotel at two o'clock in the morning to catch them at sunrise against the vast expanse of open desert.

However, for seven days I travelled to the burial site to photograph the mournful procession of penitents who swirled around the improvised shrine of containers, drawn relentlessly towards the corpse. Each day thousands of wailing men circled the site lashing themselves with chains; each day sobbing and moaning women clung to the blistering hot containers; each day parents pressed screaming babies into the hands of Revolutionary Guards surrounding the shrine, pleading with them to rub the frightened infants into the dust of the wall to be eternally blessed. All the while the crowd chanted mournfully and continued to beat their heads and chests with their hands and fists.

Paint-sprayers, welders and masons worked day and night assisted by giant earthmovers and cranes to build the shrine. It was not unlike a scene out of the film *Mad Max II*: the noise of the construction machinery, the continuous wail of ambulance sirens ferrying the injured to hospital whilst helicopters and fire engines doused the crowd with rosewater and flowers.

I moved in to take pictures amongst the crush of sweating bodies in the blistering heat and choking dust. The distraught mourners stamped their feet, pumping their hands up and down against their chests and heads and crying 'Hussein! Hussein!' to recall the most tragic incident for the Shiites when the grandson of the Prophet was martyred in the battle of Kerbala over 1,300 years before. Everyone around me was excited, but it was an excitement that was supplanted by another emotion – ecstasy, rising to hysteria. There was an intense energy and I found it difficult not to be caught up in the intoxicating emotions. The hypnotic rhythm shook me to my bones and reverberated through me like an electrical charge. As I moved away from the dark power of mass hysteria I caught the dazed faces of the mourners transported by the opiate of religious grief.

I pushed forward searching for an open space to surface for some air. Several limp bodies that had fainted from the draining emotion, heat and exhaustion were passed over the sea of flailing hands. I was approached by a man who saw my cameras around my neck. 'Where are you from?' he shouted above the crowd. 'England.' A black-chadored woman moved between us. 'Where are you from?' she spat. Her face trembled with rage. 'Infidel!' she shouted in English. She cursed the imperialists, vehement with anger, and promised she would sacrifice her four sons to any future holy war as a gift to the Imam. The man who had first asked the question tried to calm her. 'He's only a photographer.' But the crowd had already launched into the refrain 'Death to America!' I was frightened, fearing the mob might set on me. In future I would say I was from Switzerland. The Turks were now out of favour, their Tehran embassy trashed and ransacked because the Turkish newspapers had published an article under the headline 'IN THE SHADOW OF MULLAH AFTER MULLAH' and had described the Imam's corpse in the fight to touch it as 'dragged like a dead dog'.

On the eve of the seventh day after the death of the Imam the site was cleared of worshippers. I arrived at dawn to find hundreds of people camped out in the dusty plain and on the motorway's central reservation near the shrine to ensure a good place when the ceremonies began. Already thousands of the faithful were streaming towards the grave, squashed into the backs of freight containers, packed into the beds of pickups; families of four and five arrived riding pillion on motorbikes. Others came by car – sometimes with women and children sitting huddled together in the boot – bus and taxi; some, like the 3,000 mullahs, came on foot. All but one other journalist were still asleep in their hotels, but I had spent a good part of each day capturing the faithful, and my persistence and badgering of the authorities had finally paid off. I was given admittance to the shrine to capture the final moments before the Imam's tomb was completed. I watched it being covered in slabs of marble. A young boy had broken through the security cordon. He clutched the tomb's protective gold-plated metal cage; tears were streaming down his cheeks. He kept screaming 'Agha!

Agha! [Sir!]' until exhausted. The shrine was swathed in green cloth and topped by a gold dome resembling the Al-Aqsa (Dome of the Rock) Mosque in Jerusalem. They called Khomeini's grave the Haram-e-Sharif after the tomb of the Prophet Mohammed. Nearby cranes and a tall scaffolding carried huge portraits of the dead Imam.

I returned to Tehran for breakfast. By the time the Ministry of Islamic Guidance bussed the journalists on the 'official' visit to the shrine traffic prevented us from getting anywhere near the tomb. People had simply left their cars parked where they had come to a standstill in the traffic jam. We began the long walk to the shrine. Half an hour after we had started our trek, a Chinook helicopter came to take us to the grounds. As it touched down in a field next to the motorway hundreds of Iranians had the idea of trying to hitch a lift and there was a mad, frantic scramble to reach the helicopter first. The crew of the Chinook fought to keep the ordinary citizens at bay whilst they hauled the journalists on board. Each scene grew more dramatic than the last. From the helicopter I had a bird's-eye view of the tens of thousands of mourners converging on the shrine.

We weren't the only ones to arrive by helicopter; leading mullahs were ferried partway in old American Huey helicopters and then whisked in limousines and jeeps through a concrete tunnel into the heart of the shrine. The mullahs talked about turning the shrine into a 'new Mecca' to be visited by millions of pilgrims from all over the world in gatherings as large as the annual *haj*. The future leader of Iran, Hojatolislam Rafsanjani, said that the centre of the shrine 'radiates heavenly light'.

I tried to reach the press stand, but the pull of the crowd was so strong that it was a struggle not to lose my footing. To fall would be to be dragged into the undercurrent of flailing feet as thousands of pilgrims pushed towards the shrine against the dead weight of the crowd. Security had once again broken down. Miraculously no one was trampled to death. When I reached the press stand it began to swing dangerously. The mourners chanted, 'We have lost our father,' and a group of Lebanese Hizbollahs whipping themselves with swords cried, 'Light of my eye, O Khomeini!' There were some signs in Armenian amongst the hundreds of hand-held portraits of the dead Ayatollah. One man carried a placard that promised: 'ALL

THE WORLD MUST BE SURE THAT WE WON'T DEVIATE FROM THE WAY OF
IMAM KHOMEINI.' Mullahs rallied the crowd to a fever pitch of
hatred of the West, and the clutch of cameras helped send the
mourners into their own refrain of 'Death to America! Death to
Israel! Death to England!' At the end of the seventh day the
authorities reported at least another two people dead. More than
10,000 had lost consciousness.

There wasn't a lot to do at night if you weren't into power mourning.
The television and radio played a steady diet of doleful music and
readings from the Koran. I watched a television show hosted by a
mullah called *Manners in the Family*, and a programme featuring
spine-chilling re-runs of blows against imperialism – the bombing
of the US embassy in Beirut with a reconstruction of the path the
'heroic' truck driver took in his vehicle packed with explosives. The
commentary described the events with a sense of practical purpose
which was frighteningly sober. Joining the bombing of the US
embassy in Beirut were the top ten imperialist acts against
humanity, among them the Israeli invasion of Lebanon, the US
invasion of Grenada, the US war in Vietnam and the British war in
the Falklands; each carried clips of injured American and British
soldiers.

I called Azadeh. She invited me to her house in north Tehran. To
have invited her to my hotel would have been as suicidal as
handing out copies of Salman Rushdie's novel *The Satanic Verses* in
downtown Tehran. She asked me not to come to the door in the taxi
in case the driver should report my visit to the Ministry of Islamic
Guidance. I was sure Fred's Taxi Service and my driver Albert could
be trusted, but nonetheless I asked Albert to drop me at Maidan
Mohseni, a fashionable square in north Tehran where well-to-do
Tehranis bought expensive jewellery, designer clothes and ice-
cream.

Azadeh's family lived in a comfortable house with precious
Persian carpets, Louis XV chairs, antique porcelain and crystal
vases. Her father had retired from the National Iranian Oil
Company, her brother as the only son had been exempted from
military service and had spent the last ten years in Los Angeles, the
last three studying medicine at UCLA. Azadeh's younger sister

was still at a local school; her parents had decided against sending her to school in England because they didn't want her to turn out like her sister. Instead part of her daily routine before beginning class was to stand on the American flag in her school playground and chant the mantra 'Death to America!'

Azadeh suggested we eat at a local restaurant.

'Aren't you afraid someone might see us?'

'It's a quiet neighbourhood; we would be unlucky if we were caught by the sisters.'

'The sisters?'

'The Khahar Zainab – I think it translates as the sisters of the Prophet – the female equivalent of the Revolutionary Guards who check on moral backsliding. They drive around arresting women for wearing lipstick, nail polish, colourful clothing, thin stockings; they even smell for telltale signs of perfume. A friend of my sister's was reprimanded for plucking her eyebrows.'

'What about hair protruding from headscarves?'

'You can be arrested for allowing locks of hair to curl out from under your scarf – that's a manifestation of corruption! Do you know one ayatollah said, "A woman's hair sends out special rays that arouse men." Actually, things are a bit more relaxed at the moment. Although the sisters still drive around in their Hillmans followed by the well-armed Pasdaran, the Islamic Revolutionary Guards, in Nissan patrol jeeps, you can find many women with their scarves pulled slightly back, it's a sign of defiance.'

In fact the scarf was a barometer for the revolution. In downtown Tehran women were strictly covered, whereas the further uptown you went the more the scarf was pulled back, but equally the government's level of toleration depended on how many curls, how much ankle or calf began to show.

Over lunch Azadeh told me she wanted to go to Europe or India, not to settle but to get away from the stifling dictates of the revolution. I asked her what she did in her spare time. 'I watch videos. We get the latest movies smuggled in from the States even before they have opened in London. Sometimes I watch *Ushin* – a popular Japanese soap opera.' She missed the little luxuries of life. 'I can't afford a brand name [imported] toothpaste – it would cost me a day's salary.' Her headscarf kept slipping off her head.

'Imagine what it's like wearing a school uniform for the rest of your life!' she said, referring to her navy ropoush and her headscarf which she kept pulling back in place. The movement came automatically to her, like a nervous tic.

My visit was coming to an end. All the journalists who had flown in to cover the interment after the lying-in-state had left, forced to go by the Ministry of Islamic Guidance. As soon as they had departed the Laleh Hotel was colonized by wounded Lebanese Amal militia who had been flown to Tehran for treatment. Even though I had formalized my stay with a visa, I had to leave for my corporate show in southern California. There were no hard feelings between me and the Ministry of Islamic Guidance. Before leaving they gave me a present: three volumes of *Documents from the US Espionage Den*, part of a sixty-volume set of classified CIA and US State Department documents which had been shredded, captured in the takeover of the US embassy in Tehran, and painstakingly reassembled.

I called my parents to let them know my whereabouts. I hadn't spoken to them for a month. My stepfather answered the phone: 'We thought you would be in China covering the events in Tiananmen Square.' He made Tehran sound like a holiday on the Costa Brava, which, if you lived in downtown Tehran, I suppose it was during the seven days of official mourning – not much to do other than pray, attend rallies, grieve and join the free bus excursions to Behesht Zahra, refreshments included.

For weeks afterwards I thought about the extraordinary scenes surrounding the Ayatollah's burial, the emotion of it all. In many ways the Ayatollah's own words on his revolution are a fitting description of the events surrounding his death: 'Its evaluation is beyond the capabilities of the tongue and pen.' But in the legions of his followers, mainly the disenfranchised, I could not help making the parallel with followers of many organized groups around the world: people who were searching for love, a sense of belonging, belief in a faith, a means of salvation.

I had spent two weeks in Tehran. It seemed a lifetime since I had left Kabul, and now I was departing for Los Angeles. I looked at the airline schedules. At Tehran's international airport a dour official at passport control examined my passport and checked his files. I began to worry that if they had a file on me it would show I had never officially left Iran in 1984. Instead I had crossed illegally into Afghanistan with the Afghan resistance. The official continued to study my passport closely. Anxiety was welling up inside me. He rechecked the index cards in his filing cabinet. For a third time he asked me to repeat my name. Twenty minutes later and in danger of missing my flight I was on the precipice of panic when the official handed me my passport. I would not feel safe until I was on the plane and airborne. As the Turkish Airlines airbus left the ground I breathed a deep sigh of relief. I felt as if I had emerged from a nightmare.

I stopped in Istanbul for breakfast. On the way into the city my taxi driver asked me where I had come from.

'Tehran.'

'You went for the Ayatollah's funeral?'

'Yes.'

'The Ayatollah was a great man,' sighed the driver.

When I reached America I sent Azadeh a tube of Colgate toothpaste. Seven months later she made it to France; the British wouldn't give her a visa. Her brother still lives in Los Angeles; he hasn't seen his family for ten years. The shrine at Behesht Zahra continues to be visited but within a year it was shut for urgent repairs to prevent its golden dome collapsing.

Now, instead of forecasting the Ayatollah's death, the world seeks to predict the country's political future between Islamic orthodoxy and pragmatism, moderates and radicals, continuing isolation or rapprochement with the world community, light and dark, like the ancient Persian religion Zoroastrianism with its dualistic nature. Most Tehranis I met were more worried about inflation and the cost of food than the Imam's line, in direct opposition to the Ayatollah, who once said the revolution was about Islam, not the price of melons.

10

THE SUMMER
FIGHTING SEASON:
DESCENT INTO CHAOS
AND MADNESS

We do not believe it is either appropriate or possible for the United Nations to try to force a settlement in Afghanistan at this time.

Testimony of US Ambassador Tomsen
to the mujahedeen before the House
of Representatives Select Committee
on Hunger, 27 July 1989

I against my brother; I and my brother against our cousin; I, my brother and our cousin against our neighbour; all of us against the foreigner.

Afghan proverb

Nations have no permanent allies or enemies, only permanent interests.

Lord Palmerston

Afghanistan, July–September 1989

'It's the only place in the world where we are killing Russians,' explained a Texan Democrat and a member of the House Permanent Select Committee. The Big Red One, as the Soviet invasion of Afghanistan was called by some American politicians, was over, but the Afghan war was still in full swing. Unable to secure a photographic assignment I had arrived in Washington DC in search of a job that would take me back to Afghanistan for the coming months. I found two. I would be working for both United Press International and the Voice of America radio service as a stringer. Being in Washington also gave me the opportunity to meet US policy planners, military and Afghan experts in think-tanks, journalists, State Department officials and groups that made a profession out of lobbying for disparate causes, and to hear their views on the continuing war and US policy towards Afghanistan.

Entering the corridors of power was like moving into the set for the sixties television series *Get Smart*. At the State Department I was handed a locator map and a light-sensitive identification badge. Once I left the building and my pass was exposed to sunlight all the security details would vanish within seconds and stop me from re-entering. The locator map was necessary to find my way around the spotless corridors. Each door was as anonymous as the previous one. Behind them, when the politicians and bureaucrats weren't sending war-o-grams to their foreign adversaries, they were fighting wars around the globe and working out dollar-per-kill ratios in the margins of agency memos.

My appointment with officials on the Afghan desk was on the same floor as the Arms Control and Disarmament Agency. I heard a lot about politics, strategic interests, alliances. There were statements and schemes that would have befitted a bad B-movie, like the proposal to offer every Afghan government party member a visa to the United States; I was told they would all take up the offer and one morning President Najibullah of Afghanistan would wake up as the last party member in the country, with a pistol at his head. Far-fetched as the scheme sounded it had already paid some dividends. The President's brother had defected and in return for a denunciation of his brother, whom he called a homosexual and child molester, he had received his visa and now lives in San Francisco. But it seemed that the US policy on Afghanistan – when there was a policy, because I was told by one State Department official, 'We have a policy vacuum' – ran headlong into contradiction with itself. Whilst elsewhere in the world the US was doing everything in its power to stem the tide of Islamic fundamentalism, it had supported the Afghan mujahedeen for the greater strategic interests of stemming the tide of Communism and reaping revenge

for Vietnam. Also, by encouraging the mujahedeen against the
Soviets, they hoped to gain a toehold of influence over events in the
Muslim Soviet Central Asian Republics.

Earlier I had visited the Congressional Research Library where I
saw impressive computer flowcharts on casualties and arms
movements. There were reams of statistics to fit half-baked
theories, but the harsh realities, the pain, the death and mutilation,
were abstract numbers. It did not come as a surprise to me when on
a flight from Tehran to the States I read a secret report issued by the
US embassy in Kabul dated August 1979 in Volume 30 of *Documents
from the US Espionage Den*. It concluded: 'The United States' larger
interests . . . would be served by the demise of the Taraki–Amin
regime, despite whatever setbacks this might mean for future social
and economic reforms in Afghanistan,' which pointed to United
States funding of the Afghan resistance even before the Soviets had
invaded. The Afghan resistance, the mujahedeen, became the
United States' friend by becoming the enemy of 'our' enemy, the
Soviets.

Since the Soviets had left Afghanistan the United States' political
and military aims in Afghanistan were no longer as clear as they
had once been. There were inter-agency disputes over policy,
intelligence failures, errors of judgement and flights of wishful
thinking. Everyone had expected the Afghan government to
collapse in a matter of days after the Soviet withdrawal; then the
consensus was modified to a few weeks, then months. It was now
coming up to six months after the Soviet withdrawal. The
mujahedeen had not taken a single provincial centre since 15
February 1989 when the last Soviet troops crossed the Oxus into
Soviet Uzbekistan. The unofficial, official position in Washington
was that the mujahedeen would, if necessary, be given another
fighting 'season' to defeat the Kabul government. In Washington-
speak this was called 'a chance to exert military ascendancy' or 'to
give more time for the Kabul regime to start unravelling'. What was
clear to me was that, no matter what the cost in Afghan lives, the
White House was bent on backing the mujahedeen until they
achieved outright victory. The CIA were taking over more direct
management of military strategy and United States supplies and
weapons to the mujahedeen now included cluster shells that

spread exploding bomblets over a wide area and runway cratering mortars to knock out airfields. At the same time the Soviets seemed prepared to double their military aid to the Afghan government, providing hundreds of Scud missiles, new tanks and armoured personnel carriers. The coming months promised to be bloody as I flew back to Kabul.

It was with some fear and trepidation that I returned, for the summer fighting season was in full swing. The sound of exploding shells punctuated the day, buildings shook and windows rattled as plumes of smoke continually rose above the city. The wail of ambulances ferrying the dead and injured was all too frequent. Up to a quarter of Kabul's residents had fled to Pakistan and the north of the country. Each day the incoming rockets killed and wounded dozens of those too poor to pay the bus fare and exorbitant 'guide' fees charged by smugglers. My arrival in the capital was delayed by a day because Kabul's airport had been temporarily closed due to fierce rocketing.

Rumours of an impending *coup d'état* by the Defence Minister Shahnawaz Tanai and army officers were rife. The army, like Afghanistan's ruling People's Democratic Party and the mujahedeen, was riddled with political differences, personal feuds and Byzantine intrigue.

I checked in to my dark and dingy room at the Kabul Hotel, which had recently been hit by a stray mujahedeen rocket, but my stay at the hotel was brief. Soon after my arrival I contacted the old school friend whom I had bumped into on my previous visit to Kabul. Masti was working as a programme officer for the United Nations and she suggested I move in to her rented house in the fashionable Shar-i Now district. It would make a pleasant change from the Kabul Hotel.

She told me the enormous house had stood empty for some years. This no doubt had something to do with the fact that it was behind the Ministry of the Interior and the KHAD secret service headquarters and was therefore a prime target for rocket attacks. The Ministry of Foreign Affairs was somewhat concerned that I wouldn't be in one of the hotels in which correspondents were expected to stay and cited security reasons for this arrangement.

But if they had visited Masti's house they would have noticed that I was afforded the best protection in town with several armed guards outside the house and two armoured personnel carriers and a tank to defend the ministry in case of attack. Masti had taken her own precautions, affixing United Nations regulation plastic film to the house's windows to stop shards of glass from a bomb blast flying through the air.

To the small international community from the United Nations and the International Red Cross she was known as Mastaneh. I called her Masti, and the Afghans called her affectionately *Bibi* – duchess. Masti was originally from Iran. She walked as if she didn't have a care in the world, but I knew she cared passionately, to the point of personally supervising the distribution of international humanitarian assistance to Kabul's needy, which was beyond her call of duty. Many of her colleagues rarely ventured further than Kabul's Bond Street, Chicken Street. They always remained close to their air-conditioned limousines and the officially designated United Nations bunker and in twenty-four-hour walkie-talkie contact. This didn't prevent their collecting a hazardous duty allowance of $600 a month which was more than five times the local average yearly salary.

Our house was arguably one of the most pleasant in Kabul, and with Baba the gardener, Bibi the duchess, Mabouba the daily and Nick Jan or Nick Mohammed as I was called after the name given to me by the mujahedeen but now also used by government officials, we became a small community of sorts drawn all the more together by the shared dangers and precarious times in which we lived. Baba was a grandfather without any children or grandchildren. Like countless Afghans he had lost his family to the war; his siblings died when their village was bombarded; one of his two sons had been killed fighting with the mujahedeen, the other, a government soldier, had been blown out of the sky by a Stinger missile. Baba had no home of his own, no possessions and no savings. His village near the Panjshir valley had been destroyed by a combination of government shelling and inter-mujahedeen fighting. His only living relatives were his sisters-in-law and their babies, who remained beneath the head-to-toe burqa and were too tradition-bound to find work. They lived on Baba's generosity.

Baba lived in a room to the side of the garden. He was very devout and regularly said his prayers five times a day. Not once did we know him to miss them. He was a powerful man with leathery skin, steel-hard hands and wounded eyes. He was fiercely proud and the perfect picture of Afghan civility. He wore a brightly-coloured skullcap at all times and had a well-kept beard which he trimmed with a pair of scissors and a dry razor. He had an endearing mischievous grin which I imagined could turn merciless if you crossed him. The love he had lost in his family he invested in the tender loving care he gave to the garden and his flowers. Like all Afghans who came from the countryside one needed to subtract between fifteen and twenty years from his appearance to estimate his age. By this equation Baba looked seventy-five but was probably in his late fifties or early sixties.

Mabouba and her family had so far escaped the ravages of the war. Her parents came to Kabul from the north, and she had the features of the people descended from the armies of Ghenghis Khan. She always arrived at the house covered from head to toe in a ragged corn-coloured burqa, but it was removed once she entered the house. She very quickly became my second mother and I still keep in touch with her and her family. Like other mothers in the capital, it was impossible for her to keep her mind on the job at hand. The suffering and traumatization of the capital's residents was growing daily; that summer a day-care centre, five schools, two cinemas, residential districts and bazaars were hit by salvos of mujahedeen rockets in their stepped-up offensive against the city. The government had been forced to extend the summer holidays and keep the schools closed because of the rocketing and the mujahedeen's newly acquired cluster bombs that sent shards of shrapnel into people. Those children too young to work were free to play in the streets. Some mothers wanted their children to remain indoors for protection against the incoming rockets, but the rockets were just as likely to land on houses as in the street. If Mabouba's two young children weren't with her she spent her day close to the telephone. When the large dry bang of an exploding rocket hit the city, Mabouba, like thousands of mothers, reached for the phone.

The continuing rocketing was beginning to change the social

architecture of the city. Most of the well-to-do residents had already
fled the country. Now those families that could afford the bus fare
to the border with Pakistan or to the peaceful northern city of
Mazar-i-Sharif were leaving in droves, tens of thousands each
month. Every morning families abandoned everything that could
not be carried and made their way through the streets towards
decrepit multi-coloured buses packed with more tired victims of the
war. The passengers stared vacantly out of the buses, trucks and
pickups that lined the roads leading from the city. The smiles had
disappeared from their usually cheerful faces. Their future was in
exile, and they were frightened of the dangers of the roads ahead.
As they poured out of the city, the loud drone of the massive Soviet
transporters, their cascading missile-deflecting flares leaving a trail
across the sky, flew overhead bringing more weapons, ammunition and despair. Ten, twenty, sometimes over fifty a day arrived
from the Soviet Union, their cargoes discharged as quickly as
possible before the increasingly accurate long-range mujahedeen
mortars struck the airport.

The city's poorest residents had nowhere to go. They were too
poor to escape the slaughter. They lived in hillside squats or in the
tumbledown houses in the medieval warren of streets below the
Bala Hissar fort. At sunrise lean young boys dressed in threadbare
clothes and sandals made from recycled car tyres left their homes to
go to work as ironmongers, carpenters and shopkeepers. Their
faces were full of suffering and laughter. The indomitable spirit in
their eyes and their constant smiles were their most distinctive and
contagious traits. The energy they gave to their work and the range
of entrepreneurship seemed to have no bounds. The maze of
market streets that during the winter had been ankle deep in mud
had dried, but the dust was tinged with poverty.

Kabul was still threatened by hunger. Women and children spent
hours in queues, waiting hopefully, patiently, for bread and fuel.
There was never enough. Market prices fluctuated according to the
whims of the besieging mujahedeen. Some groups refused to
negotiate; others had signed protocols with the government and
took money or a percentage of goods in return for the unhindered
passage of commodities into the capital. Everyone and everything
had its price.

The bazaar grew and folded from dawn to dusk like the ebb and flow of maritime tides. At its height everyone was trying to edge their way past pushcarts piled high with pomegranates, soap or raisins, or dodge street-sellers squatting on their haunches, their stock-in-trade placed on the ground in front of them, small pyramids of vegetables on makeshift tarpaulins. Men and children hopped through the streets and across Kabul's bridges on home-made wooden crutches, limbless from the blasts of war. News of the fighting that was raging all around the country was hard to come by. I went to the market on most days of the week to meet regular contacts, glean information and note the fluctuations in the prices of basic commodities, which were finely tuned to the war that surrounded us on all sides. An increase in the price of flour, sugar and cooking oil indicated that the mujahedeen were tighten-ing their noose around the city; fresh supplies of pomegranates might mean the road from Kandahar was open; and any rise of the dollar meant the road to Pakistan was closed. With the lean, wiry merchants arriving from distant villages in travel-stained shalwar camise, tired turban and waistcoat to hawk the carpets slung over their shoulders came news of the fighting as well as of the changing fortunes and allegiances of the numerous groups competing for control of Afghan real estate.

I lost no time renewing my acquaintance with the children I had met on my previous visits. I was anxious to know if they had survived the rockets and keen to discover how they were faring in a city that had been under siege since the Soviet army had left. I had brought copies of European magazines for those who had made the pages from my previous assignment, and for those that hadn't I brought a photograph of themselves. I found most of the children on the same street corners or in the same workshops, like Faizullah the puncture man, whose satisfied clients were bringing him more damaged tyres than ever before. Others plied their wares in the Char Chatta bazaar, the Deh Afghanon or Feroshgah bus stations or worked as waiters and cooks in tea houses and lunch parlours. Some still sold cigarettes, matches and chewing gum in Pashtunistan Square or outside the Ariana Airlines ticket office. They rarely sold a whole pack, but more usually a single stick of chewing gum or one cigarette at a time. The young entrepreneurs no longer just carried heavy buckets of water up the steep mountainsides to their homes; young girls and boys plied the streets bucket and glass in hand in search of thirsty customers. Everyone was trying to make a sale; no one was aggressive. Veiled women weaved around the pushcarts and donkeys laden with fruits and vegetables. Their hands appeared from underneath their pleated burqas to feel the produce for freshness. They bargained with grocers who would never know the identity of the matrons who emerged and disappeared into the rivers of people like ghosts. There was no space in the narrow lanes and yet everyone seemed to find space. Amongst the teeming crowds were soldiers, cadets and university students in sharp shoes and T-shirts with portraits of George Michael or the insignia of the University of Nebraska bought from the secondhand clothes market. Their female counter-parts travelled, like the men, in groups, their dark hair down to their waists and their heads covered with white scarves. They wore pretty dresses, dark stockings with bobbysocks and carried umbrellas to protect them from the fierce sun, and they followed the latest European fashions and music trends in Afghan and Soviet magazines. In sharp contrast were the Kutchis or campers – the nomads. Life had changed little for them since Alexander the Great and Marco Polo crossed what is now Afghanistan. However, their way of life had been completely disrupted by the current civil war. Like every other group the nomads had suffered as a result of the fighting. Their traditional routes had been mined and now, as tens of thousands of citizens were fleeing the capital, the Kutchis had come to Kabul in their thousands to seek a safe haven from mujahedeen and government anti-personnel mines. They also came in the hope of receiving humanitarian assistance. Every day of the week Kutchi women, eyes rimmed with smudged kohl, and dressed in voluminous heavy dresses, came to the market to sell wool and dairy products as well as their jewellery and heirlooms, their eyes caught by the modern colourful plastic bangles imported from India and Pakistan.

The *chai khanas*, tea shops, were almost empty, the kebab stands were busier. The smoke hung low over the charcoal-fired braziers where merchants and hungry-eyed children watched the roasting of succulent skewers of fresh meat. Behind them a butcher with a sharp knife held tightly between his toes sliced thick cuts of meat into small cubed chunks. Close by I could hear the loud noise of hammering, like rain on a tin roof, as the metal workers moulded sheets of aluminium into household objects. On several of the shops' walls hung artificial prostheses – limbs made from recycled metal. No materials were discarded; everything could be recycled: ammunition boxes into door frames, old tyres into sandals, shoes and buckets, spent anti-aircraft bullet shells into handles. Everywhere was the stink of rotting refuse, untreated sewage and raw pollution, the smell and din of old, smoke-belching Volgas and Cadillacs. Everything was symptomatic of poverty.

Beneath the tension of poverty was the underlying fear of the rockets, the invisible terror, the blind victimization of a people struggling to survive. No one and everyone had their name on the rockets. The country was divided into people who confronted the violence, resisted it or – the silent majority – simply endured it. For those that remained alive there was a very narrow margin of hope. They dreamed of peace. For two months a day without rocketing had been rare. When there were no rockets everything seemed normal.

One lazy afternoon I sat in the shade of the central telephone exchange talking to Manoucher and Farid, two ten-year-olds resting against a wall, taking a break from selling confectionery from their portable kiosks. They traded news and exchanged cigarette-card-sized pictures of Rambo and Arnold Schwarzenegger. Manoucher was wearing a pair of oversize dirty overalls hitched at the waist with a shining Soviet army belt embossed with a hammer and sickle. He saw me looking at the belt and told me his father had died in the war. As if reading my mind, he explained, 'We don't have the technology to make belt buckles. We don't even have the technology to make the simplest of things –a needle.' As he finished his sentence the sharp crack of an exploding rocket struck terror in the heart of the city; a dense, black plume rose from the dusty streets. People stopped and stared at the column of thick smoke across the river. Horror and anxiety lined their faces. Rockets often came in twos and threes. When and where would the next one fall? I walked towards the small but crowded market street to find the smouldering wreckage of a building that had collapsed like a pack of cards. Struts and beams hung like torn limbs, imperfectly attached, swaying on the precariously balanced remains of the structure. Rubble, masonry and glass were strewn across the street. The shrapnel from the exploding shell had become bullets decapitating and piercing anyone in its path. There had been no warning, no chance to escape. Loose debris was still falling as shopkeepers and shoppers tried to pull bodies out of the smoke-filled wreckage. Dead and injured lay in the street. A thin young boy bathed in blood writhed in agony. His sister lay motionless beside him; she had been killed by a small piece of shrapnel. The air was filled by the moans of the barely living who were being loaded into cars, taxis and pickups to be taken to the nearby Avicenne emergency hospital. Fire engines could be heard in the distance. Relatives and friends tried to comfort the injured. A middle-aged shopkeeper clutched the body of a man whose life had just slipped away. He turned on me angrily. 'Tell the Americans to stop sending their rockets!' he shouted. Moments later a man came towards me and dropped a fragment of rocket at my feet. 'Made in America,' he said and walked off.

I filed a report for both UPI and Voice of America on the most recent attacks. On the same day a rocket had fallen in the heart of the bazaar and altogether thirty-three people had died in twenty-seven separate rocket attacks. Amongst the dead was the emergency hospital's chief pharmacist, killed as he cycled past a bus stop on his way to work. In another attack a mother had returned to her home in the Karte Parwan district near the Intercontinental Hotel to find that her two daughters who had been playing in the garden and her sixteen-year-old niece who had been ironing had been injured when a rocket crashed into their house. On the second floor of her home a pile of newly pressed sheets stained with blood lay amid the twisted metal fragments of the rocket and the overturned iron. Several older women who had escaped unharmed stood in the hall shaking, cursing the foreigners' intervention, but too shocked to sip the tea neighbours had brought them. 'Why are the United States and the Soviet Union doing this? I think they are trying to divide the world up between themselves. Instead they are dividing Afghan brothers. Afghan is killing Afghan,' said the distraught father of the two young girls. 'Why are they doing this to innocent people? What have we done to deserve this?'

Two rockets fell in Taimani, one of them injuring a baby as his mother breast-fed him. On a Kohte Sangi hillside a twelve-year-old returned home from work in a bicycle workshop to find that his immediate family had been killed when a rocket had slammed into their recently built home. That night a group of children who had been playing in a street in the Microrayan district were injured by the time-delayed bomblets from a cluster shell. Keeping count of the rockets, the dead and injured followed an all too regular pattern that resembled counting fallen skittles. The toll was meaningless unless you were related to the thirty-three people who had died in Kabul today, or the seventy-eight in the past week, or the one hundred in the first week of August. To the editors of foreign newspapers, the numbers of dead and injured, the tally of rocket attacks appeared on their computer screens in the same way as did their local sports results.

The rockets continued to kill indiscriminately. A direct hit on a tram followed one on a bus shelter and a car bomb in the centre of Kabul. No telex or international phone link could describe the depths of the human tragedy. For every rocket attack on Kabul, the government would launch its own powerful weapons of destruction. It was like Newton's Third Law of Motion – for every action there is a reaction. From the city the government launched Soviet-supplied Scud ballistic missiles against the enemy. One ton of explosives roared across the night sky towards enemy positions trailing a huge fireball. They were so inaccurate that they had been known to land in neighbouring Pakistan, but more often they landed in small villages and hamlets, flattening them and killing the residents. People fled villages to the security of the cities, but the rockets followed them. The armed groups who claimed to be defending the people were the same as those who were killing them. There seemed no end to the depth of suffering of the ordinary citizens who wanted an end to the war and demanded to know why the United States and the Soviet Union were fighting by proxy in Afghanistan.

* * *

The Afghan Ministry of Foreign Affairs press office was not always pleased with me. My reports were criticized, as was the way they were being edited by the foreign bureaux of UPI and VOA in New Delhi, London and Washington, which led me to the conclusion that the ministry received copies of my telexes and transcripts of my telephone conversations. The foreign affairs spokesman often tried to pressurize me by threatening to revoke my visa. 'You have seen enough,' he said. 'You must leave on the next plane.' I stayed put and defended my reports and the ministry knew that, as the first stringer based in Kabul for Voice of America, my deportation would cause considerable adverse publicity. Some threats were more serious than others. I was told I would be stopped from filing reports because I didn't have 'a writer's licence', and that I was encouraging a 'mass massacre attitude'. Although I attended the government press briefings regularly they rarely revealed anything that was news in itself. At one I asked a military spokesman from the Supreme Defence Council to comment on a statement issued by the mujahedeen's interim government.

I was told: 'We do not recognize any government which is born in the filthy skirt of an alien people.'

'What about the current military position?' I asked.

'Even the mujahedeen's masters are crying. If the mujahedeen are in such a hurry to go to hell we will help them,' said the general, thumping the table with a clenched fist. I made a note of his statement.

It was never easy to understand how the war was being fought in Afghanistan. A government official took me to see an American-supplied Stinger surface-to-air missile which they had just purchased from a renegade mujahedeen commander. I looked at the American markings. A sticker on the brand-new weapon read, 'Confidential National Security Information. Unauthorized disclosure subject to criminal sanctions.' The Americans had already discovered that the mujahedeen had been selling Stingers to Iranian Revolutionary Guards. Now the CIA, the Pentagon, Iranian revolutionaries and the Afghan government were competing for weapons that had been given to the mujahedeen, some of which, like the one shown to me, had contributed to the arsenal of weapons they were meant to destroy.

THE SUMMER FIGHTING SEASON

I asked the government official if they would consider selling their newly acquired Stinger.

'We would never consider selling, or arming mercenaries or foreign governments. We have a responsibility to see they do not fall into the hands of terrorists,' said the official.

'And if the United States wished to purchase this weapon from you?'

'Well, we would consider . . .' He didn't finish his sentence. The depths of absurdity didn't stop at the resale of weapons to the enemy they were intended to destroy.

While the US Drug Enforcement Agency was using American taxpayers' money to stem the flow of heroin from Helmand in Afghanistan, the CIA were using the same taxpayers' money to finance some mujahedeen leaders in Helmand who were involved in the production and transportation of the drug the DEA were trying to eliminate.

Sitting in Kabul it was difficult to get a clear picture of what was happening elsewhere in Afghanistan. Since the Soviet withdrawal the government had been reluctant to take journalists into the countryside. However, that was about to change, although we were rarely given more than a few hours' notice and even then, for security reasons, the journalists and even the pilots of the planes that were to take us to besieged garrison towns had no idea of our destination until the moment of departure. Within two days of my arrival several journalists and myself would be the first to fly in fixed-winged aircraft to towns that were surrounded on all sides by the mujahedeen. In the next two months I would travel by military troop carriers, helicopter gunships and armoured personnel carriers to Jalalabad, Herat, Kandahar, Chakhcharan, Mazar-i-Sharif, Shindand and Jabal Saraj on the Salang Highway.

Two hours after curfew we climbed into the unlit Soviet-built Antonov-28 commando transport plane.

At the daily press briefing there had been no hint of what was to come later in the evening. As usual I left the Ministry of Foreign Affairs to file my report to UPI on the telex machine in the lobby of the Kabul Hotel. Afterwards I hailed one of Kabul's yellow taxis.

Even though it was still over three hours to curfew, it would soon be impossible to find a taxi as traffic disappeared from the streets as if an encroaching plague was about to sweep the town.

When I got home Masti rushed to the door to greet me. She spoke hurriedly. 'The ministry called. They asked you to be ready in an hour, and to bring an overnight bag.'

I called the ministry for confirmation. There was no answer. They had gone home. I waited with my rucksack packed with the barest essentials, which included a 1967 guide book on Afghanistan and a toilet roll which I knew would be a luxury.

As ten o'clock and curfew arrived the only noises came from the scavenging dogs and the heavy armour that crisscrossed Kabul to take up new positions. I began to lose hope that I would be going anywhere. The infectious excitement of travelling out of the capital that had caught up Masti, Baba and myself had disappeared when the heavy pounding on the house's metal doors echoed across the courtyard. 'They're here!' exclaimed Baba, who always insisted on going to the door.

I climbed into a Russian-built Lada jeep which is often associated with the Afghan secret service. Lyse Doucet, a correspondent for the BBC World Service, and Chris Hooke, a cameraman for BBC television's *Panorama*, were in the back seat with our government escort, Naqib.

'Naqib, where are we going?' I asked nervously.

'You'll see,' he said, giving nothing away.

'The rumour is Jalalabad,' said Lyse.

'But the airport has been closed for five months,' I said to my companions. The mujahedeen rocketing of Jalalabad airport had been so fierce over the last five months that it had knocked out the control tower and the radar, and put the runway out of action. In the first month of the biggest battle in Afghanistan, Soviet officials said that more than 2,000 civilians had been killed or wounded, together with 3,000 government defenders and 8,000 mujahedeen, in the fighting for Jalalabad which had begun in early March. Out of the pre-battle population of about 200,000 around 80,000 remained, with hundreds continuing to flee to either Pakistan or Kabul to escape the fighting. Those who had stayed spent most of their days and nights in basement shelters. That was in April. Recently the mujahedeen had been pushed back, but they were still close enough to bring down government aircraft with their US-supplied Stinger and British Blowpipe ground-to-air missiles. The only supplies to have reached Jalalabad were by helicopter or air-drops.

When we reached the first intersection, a soldier stepped into the beam of our light. '*Drish!*' he yelled, pointing his sub-machine-gun at our driver, who braked to a halt. Another soldier walked towards the car while the young man with the sub-machine-gun kept it trained on our driver. Naqib wound down the window and whispered a password into the soldier's ear. The soldier looked at us. 'Cigarette?' Luckily none of us smoked. We were stopped at every intersection *en route* to the airport; there wouldn't have been enough cigarettes in Kabul to go around.

The darkened airport was a hive of activity. In the moonless night the fully-laden Kamaz trucks driving along the taxiways to waiting rows of unlit Antonov transport planes could only just be made out against the charcoal sky. Teams of soldiers filled the planes with weapons, ammunition and drums of fuel. Groups of civilians waited hopefully along the perimeter fence for a lift home to beleaguered garrison towns.

Earlier in the evening Kabul's garrison had launched half a dozen Scud missiles towards enemy positions around Jalalabad and Khost.

I wondered which of the two destinations we were going to. Jalalabad was less than a hundred miles away, but the mujahedeen had cut the road linking it to Kabul. The same was true of Khost, which was farther from Kabul but even closer than Jalalabad to the border with Pakistan. Both government-held towns had recently repulsed fierce mujahedeen offensives. Both could only be reached by military nightflight. Neither inspired confidence or security.

'Naqib, we're going to Khost, aren't we?' said Lyse.

'No, we are going to Jalalabad,' said Naqib as we waited to board the plane.

'But I thought it was closed?' I questioned Naqib.

'We want to prove to you the mujahedeen are lying. The airport has been open for two weeks.'

Afghan television had joined us to get pictures of the foreign correspondents visiting Jalalabad, a city with a long history as Afghanistan's winter capital and much favoured by Kabul's kings.

The foreign journalists were to be the guinea pigs. Looking on the bright side, it would be a journalistic coup – if we survived.

For Captain Hamid, conditions were as he wanted them: a dark, moonless night. Captain Hamid, his co-pilot and navigator were part of the 12th Hero transport squadron, so named after President Najibullah's decision to bestow on them the accolade 'hero' for their loyalty and daring which had made the government's survival possible – if only just.

I climbed into the cockpit of the Antonov-28, a camouflaged twin-engined plane which, with the Antonovs-12 and -32, were the workhorses of the Afghan air force. Some pilots had defected but the majority had stayed. Few had a story like that of our navigator, who had found himself an unwitting accomplice to a defecting captain and crew some four years before.

'What happened?' I asked the navigator.

'I had no choice. We were flying a regular night sortie to Paktia province when the captain of the aircraft told me to navigate us to the border with Pakistan over Parachinar and on to Islamabad. I did as I was told.'

'And then?'

'I spent two years in Pakistan trying to find a way back to Kabul. I eventually returned through New Delhi.'

'Why did you return?' I didn't want to appear naïve, but it seemed the chances of surviving in the air force were smaller than the chances of evading death by enemy ground fire. Some squadrons had lost half their men in the last eighteen months.

His answer was simple. 'My family are here. Afghanistan is my home.'

'If you will excuse me,' the captain interrupted. He wanted to run through his pre-flight check with the rest of his crew.

We were third in line for take-off. When enemy positions around the besieged towns were reported quiet the Kabul control tower was given the all clear for the waiting planes. As I settled into the cramped cockpit I could hear the control tower clearing each plane in turn. 'Clear to take-off for Khost.' 'Clear for Kandahar.' Every night the drone of the turbo-props landing and taking off could be heard across Kabul.

When the two Antonov-32s had disappeared into the night, Captain Hamid manoeuvred us onto the runway. As we lined up, the pilots had the planes' engines revving at full pitch. 'All clear for Jalalabad,' signalled the military air traffic controller. Captain Hamid extended the wings' flaps, released the brakes and gave the engines full throttle. We roared down the runway bumping across the uneven tarmac. Adrenalin surged through my body and at 110 knots, we were off the ground and immediately began banking sharply to our left. We spiralled upwards in a tight circle over the airport, a narrow corridor that was presumed safe from incoming rockets. The city lights and hurricane lamps beneath us sank away. We were heading for the deepest uninterrupted ink-blue ocean. The world seemingly turned upside down, then the pilot levelled the plane at 22,000 feet. Below us in the distance streaks of lightning crashed into the clouds. The flicker of bright light was an electrical storm, but it made me think of an artillery barrage, or exploding air-fuel bombs.

Above the jagged peaks of the Hindu Kush the war seemed a distant nightmare, but not for long. We seemed to have only just reached our cruising altitude when the captain turned to receive a signal from the navigator. Still at 22,000 feet the captain lowered the landing gear, put the plane into a 45-degree controlled dive descent and extended the air brake foils downwards. This was the moment for which I had steeled myself. I felt the perspiration on my forehead and a bead of sweat trickle down my neck; my stomach was doing somersaults. At 12,000 feet we were in range of the Stinger surface-to-air missiles. As we hurtled towards Jalalabad the Antonov felt like a spaceship re-entering the earth's atmosphere, or a flying coffin. The pilots and navigator peered through the cockpit windows nervously, alert for the tell-tale glow of a Stinger's solid-fuel exhaust. Each time the engine pressure changed, my heart skipped a beat. Captain Hamid glanced at the altimeter that was in near free fall. We were descending at a jet fighter's pace with no hint of an airport below us. At 10,000 feet the blacked-out airport came to life – its lights were switched on for three seconds. At 5,000 feet the pattern was repeated for the pilots to navigate by. We were four hundred feet from the runway when a searchlight on the back of a truck positioned at the end of the runway was illuminated. The runway bore the number 13.

Few words could describe the emotion I felt on landing safely at Jalalabad. Pilots flying to besieged garrisons such as Khost and Jalalabad received one extra dollar a flight to supplement their $30 a month salary, enough to purchase a dozen eggs. The crew of the Antonov that had brought us were hoping to make a further round-trip flight to the city before daybreak.

At the airport's sandbagged and heavily fortified entrance soldiers were using their rifle butts to stop a crowd of would-be passengers with dead and injured relatives from charging the plane. It was their only way out of the encircled city.

We headed along a tree-lined avenue into the city, less than three miles away. As in Kabul, curfew was enforced here, but with one difference: Afghan government troops and militia had orders to shoot curfew breakers on sight.

I searched through the pages of my guide book until I came to the section on Jalalabad.

'Jalalabad', it said, 'is Afghanistan's Côte d'Azur.' I knew our visit would be anything but a picnic.

We checked in to the Spinghar Hotel. According to the guide book advanced reservations were recommended even during the winter months. It was summer. The concierge behaved as though he had spent the last twelve years waiting for our arrival. He had also grown out of his suit, which was several sizes too small.

'Would you like a room?' he asked in perfect English.

The same concierge served us a midnight snack, a piece of chicken so tough that it bounced on our plates, poured tea and showed us to our rooms.

The room's window-panes had shattered as a result of a bomb blast; the air-conditioner was still fixed to the window frame but was not working. It was stiflingly hot and Chris and I decided to take our bedding onto the roof. We scrambled around in the dark searching for some space to place our mattresses. I was exhausted and slept soundly until daybreak when I was woken by a group of young conscripts who had gathered to laugh at us. In the darkness

Chris and I had found a space in the middle of a sandbagged machine-gun nest guarding the entrance to the hotel.

After a light breakfast the Deputy Governor of Nangrahar Province gave us a tour of the city and its surroundings. Jalalabad, a city celebrated for centuries for the beauty of its gardens, orchards and palaces, had suffered the country's fiercest and bloodiest battle of the war. For the five previous months the town centre had been the focus of a cascade of mortar, artillery and rocket fire. The deputy governor compared the city's bombardment to Leningrad in the Second World War. He said that as many as 16,000 shells and rockets had hit the city on some days and that during the 124 days the battle had raged a total of 840,000 shells and rockets had fallen on the city. He took us to a recently reopened high school. What he didn't tell us was that out of a pre-offensive total of over sixty teachers only five remained; the others had been killed or had risked being shot as they fled to Pakistan to join the three million Afghans living in desolate refugee camps.

When Jalaluddin Akbar, Moghul Emperor of India, founded the city of Jalalabad in a fertile plain set against the forbidding Hindu Kush mountains to the east in 1570, he gave it his own name, meaning Abode of Splendour. Now it was a sad skeleton of its former self with many of its palaces destroyed. The bombardment had been so intense that hundreds of craters marked the streets and walls and nearly three-quarters of the city's buildings were damaged. At an olive factory the roof was peppered with gaping holes from mujahedeen rocket fire. None had been powerful enough to destroy buildings but they had been big enough to kill and maim people. The grid of streets lined with one- and two-storey buildings was empty. Most shops were boarded up. Homes had been abandoned, gardens trampled or untended; and the three-wheeled motorized taxi-scooters were few and far between. One gallon of petrol cost the equivalent of five weeks' salary.

We were escorted to the outskirts of the city. Whatever direction we travelled all roads led to the mujahedeen. To the west the road to Kabul was cut at the steep mountain gorge where Afghan tribesmen had sliced a British expeditionary force to pieces in 1842. To the east the mujahedeen controlled the strategic road to Pakistan beyond the garrison town of Samarkhel which had changed hands a number of times over the past six months. Its buildings were smashed and charred beyond recognition. It was impossible to tell whether the damage was caused during the mujahedeen's capture of the hamlet or in a government counter-offensive. On the wall of a destroyed generating station, its turbines buried in rubble, the mujahedeen had scrawled, 'Death to the infidels of the world.'

Everywhere were the scars of modern warfare: cratered roads, burnt trees, scorched fields. Everywhere was the litter of modern warfare, burnt-out tanks, charred armoured personnel carriers and wrecked and abandoned howitzers. The mujahedeen ran a profitable business collecting scrap metal to be used in a Japanese car plant in Pakistan.

Returning from Samarkhel in the deputy governor's jeep we stopped by the side of the airport to wait for an armoured personnel carrier transporting the other journalists. I was busting to relieve myself and walked into a field. As I began to unbutton my trousers the deputy governor screamed at me, 'Stop!' I turned around.

'You're in a minefield,' he explained.

I couldn't tell the exact path I had taken to reach the spot where I was standing, and the deputy governor didn't know where the mines were planted. I gingerly walked back the twenty paces to the side of the road where the jeep was parked.

'Whose mines are they?' I asked.

'Who knows? Some are our mines, the others were planted by the mujahedeen.'

The country was littered with booby-trapped mines left behind by withdrawing Soviet soldiers. Amongst the devices were pens that exploded when the cap was pulled off and mines in the form of tins of *naswar*, a type of snuff that Afghan men place under the tongue.

I remembered speaking to an English friend of mine who had converted to Islam, had taken the name of Karimullah and had fought alongside the mujahedeen for the better part of ten years. He told me how he was in the advance guard of mujahedeen for the battle of Jalalabad. His group of mujahedeen had joined rebels from several parties, had successfully surrounded the city and had cut off the connecting roads and the airfield. They had reached the perimeter of the Jalalabad airport, were less than three miles from the centre of town, but they didn't know what to do. United States, Pakistani and Saudi Arabian political and military advisers had prompted the attack on Jalalabad, but had not prepared the mujahedeen for conventional warfare, the frontal assault on fortified positions. His eyes glazed over as he told me how the guerrilla fighters had been cut down by tank, artillery and automatic rifle fire.

For many years Karimullah had fought with the fundamentalist mujahedeen party of Yunis Khales's Hesbi. 'During the battle for Jalalabad,' he told me in a New York apartment before I left for Washington, 'I became disenchanted with the foreign fundamentalists, the mujahedeen and the tribal militia who are often more intent on fighting one another than against the government.' Karimullah was equally displeased with the Pakistan-based leaders, with the exception of Khales. He attacked foreign Muslim groups from a dozen countries, including the Sudanese, Egyptians, Bahrainis, Kuwaitis and Saudi Wahhabis, as deeply divided politically and called the rebel leadership in their comfortable Peshawar mansions incompetent and corrupt. 'Most of them are detached from the horrors and rigours of the war. They have little contact with the ravaged country they claim to represent,' he said despondently.

He sat on a chair with his legs crossed. The initial euphoria of the Soviet withdrawal had evaporated. The Najibullah regime had failed to crumble as everyone had predicted. Karimullah talked of making a film about a Soviet officer and defector fighting in Afghanistan. A Saudi prince was interested in financing his project and he showed me his screenplay. Listen to this, he said as he pushed a tape recording of a battle into a tape deck. I listened to the high-pitched chatter of long bursts of machine-gun fire, the jarring sound of a helicopter's rotor blade, explosions and blood-curdling screams. Karimullah was in a world of his own, chasing a dragon he couldn't slay. He seemed at the same time both at peace and tormented. He apologized about breaking up our conversation; it was time for him to pray.

The last I heard of him he was trying to set up a deal to recycle glass in the north of England.

* * *

The town's elders emerged from a mosque into the dusty street. They showed little interest in the foreigners: foreigners had helped to destroy their lives. Those that wanted to talk were tense, bitter and angry. Rockets made some people pathological. It was understandable when you were considered lucky if you had only lost an arm, a leg or half your family. The local hospital was guarded by fierce tribal women carrying semi-automatic Kalashnikovs. In my guide book I had read that Jalalabad's gardens 'offer a peaceful haven for an afternoon's stroll'. Not far from the mausoleum of Amir Habibullah who had been assassinated on a hunting trip in 1919 a multiple rocket launcher sent salvos of rockets towards enemy positions.

I attended a press conference given by the Governor of Nangrahar Province, Lieutenant General Manoki Mangal. Dressed in neatly pressed battle fatigues tucked into polished boots, he sat beneath a photograph of President Najibullah in the bricked-up and sandbagged governor's office in the centre of town. He gave us a list of the casualties of the battle for Jalalabad as if he were reading from a shopping list: 933 houses, 155 shops, 8 schools, 46 government establishments, 54 mosques, 2 dharamsalas (hostels for Hindu and Sikh pilgrims), 4 shrines. There were 1,018 civilians dead, 2,041 injured or disabled. He said 800 government soldiers and officers had died and put the mujahedeen losses at 12,821 killed and 12,953 injured, not including 195 dead foreigners and 17 captured during the course of the battle. We were not given a figure for the number of mujahedeen captured.

Forgotten amongst the statistics and not on the journalists' official itinerary was the little-noticed post office. Perhaps more than anything else that post office confirmed my belief that even in war-ravaged Afghanistan everything is possible, nothing impossible. For three Afghanis (a third of a penny) it was still possible to send a letter to Kabul, for thirty-five Afghanis (three pence) you could send a postcard to England or Pakistan.

When I stepped out into the main street, for just one moment the sound of crickets and tropical birds, the sweet smell of eucalyptus trees and orange groves made it almost possible to forget the war. But the illusion was momentary. High-flying fighter bombers soared overhead seeking out targets for their explosive payloads. In

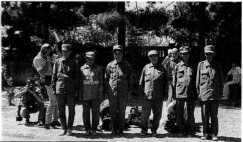

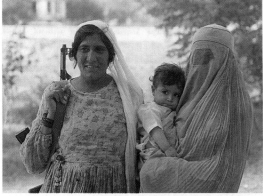

Women in Afghanistan today

Below:
'Madonna versus the veil' highlights the divisions in Afghan society

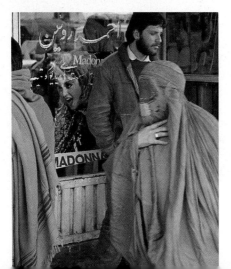

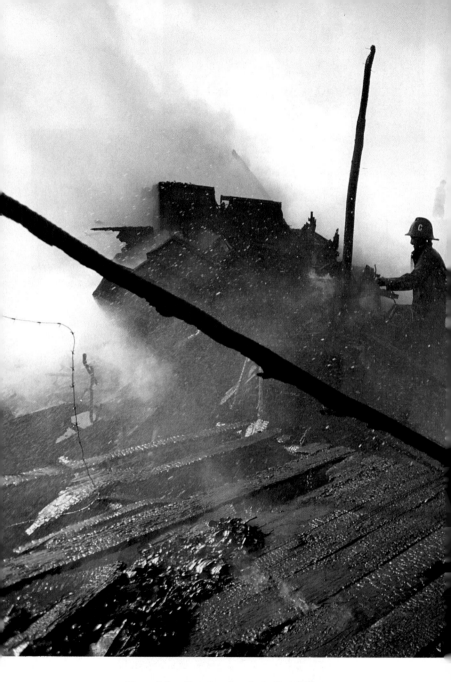

One of the dozens of rockets that fall on
Kabul daily, resulting in the death or
disfigurement of countless civilians

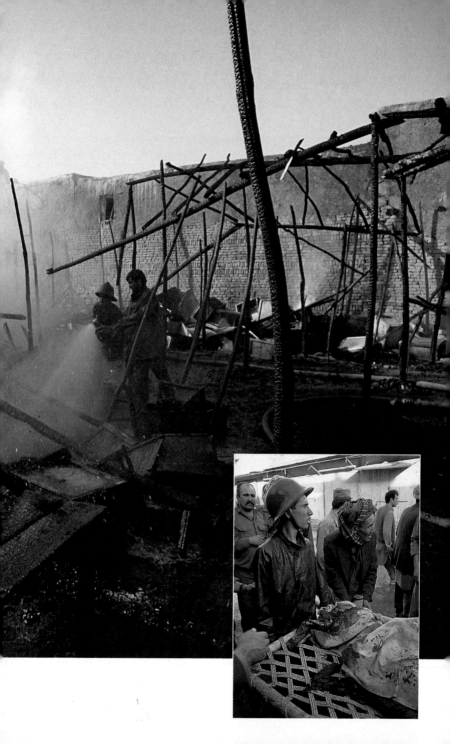

Marastoon, the mental asylum on
the outskirts of Kabul where perfectly
normal orphaned children lived
amongst the insane

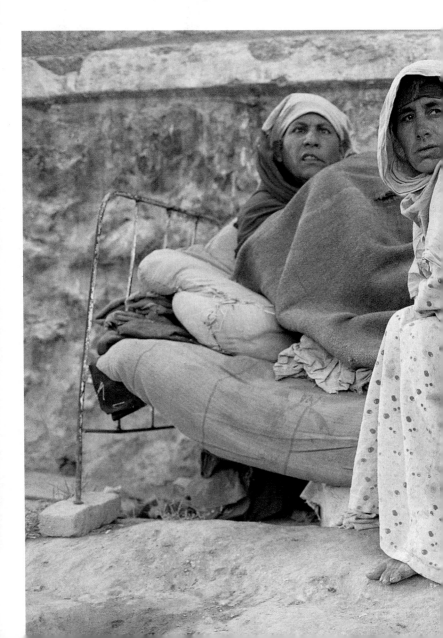

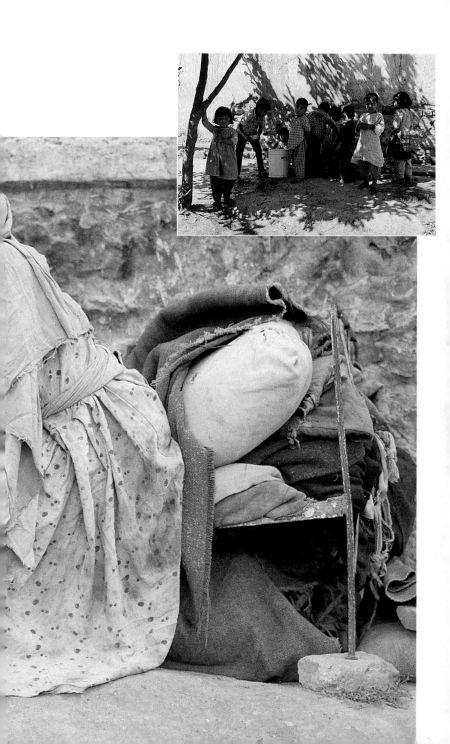

Fun with mermaids on board the
MS Vistafjord

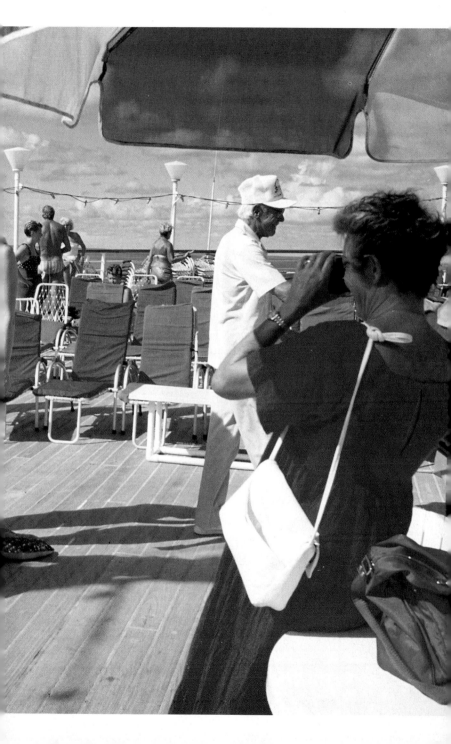

American express

The passengers are looking for sun,
sea and a little something else

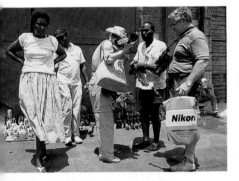

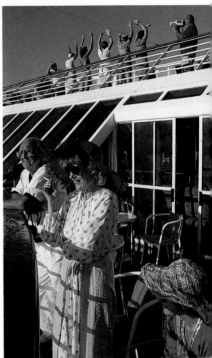

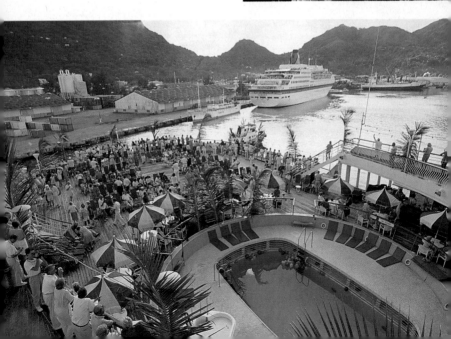

the distance the booms and roars of mortar, artillery and automatic weapons fire rained back and forth between government outposts and mujahedeen positions. By night powerful and inaccurate Scud missiles would land in nearby hamlets, villages and mountains. Over 330 had been fired since the beginning of March nearly five months before. I thought of the words of the US envoy to the mujahedeen: 'The major fighting has yet to come.'

On my return to Kabul I heard through my 'informed' sources that Herat airport had been closed for ten days and that the road from the airport to the city had been cut by the mujahedeen. I wondered whether this was the plan Ismail Khan, the mujahedeen leader with whom I had once travelled, was referring to in a letter I had received from him six months before in London, in which he wrote, 'We expect our latest plans for the war will result in the downfall of the government in this area.'

Abdul Haq Olumi, a general on the government's Supreme Defence Council and a member of the Armed Forces Department of the Central Committee, vigorously denied the reports.

'Lies!' chuckled the general in feigned lightheartedness. 'Who told you the airport is closed? These are scurrilous rumours spread by the Western media. I will show you. When do you want to go?' he asked.

'Tomorrow.'

The general seemed taken aback. The flight to Jalalabad had dented my nerves, but not enough to stop me from going to Herat which, because of my previous connection with the mujahedeen of that city, was the one I most wanted to visit. The general recovered his composure and agreed to take me.

Three days later I was on a flight to Herat. When I got away from my government escort and tried to make contact with Ismail Khan's representatives in the city, my movements were closely shadowed by a man, presumably a local agent of the KHAD secret police. Even if I could slip away I knew the government would not look favourably on my meeting Ismail Khan. He was still battling with the government and they had offered a huge bounty for his death or capture.

* * *

When Mina, a local Herati woman, got married under a brilliant Afghan sun, it was a different kind of shotgun wedding. The bride, dressed in a sequined gown and veil, was pressed against a heavy machine-gun as her wedding truck careered through the potholed streets, leaving a trail of dust – Afghan confetti. Her giggling retinue rumbled behind in other lorries, escorted by young men clutching Kalashnikovs, eyes peeled for a stray bullet or incoming rockets.

It was an ordinary day for Herat. Five years before, I had come to the city with the mujahedeen under the command of Ismail Khan, a former officer in the Afghan army and a popular mujahedeen commander who distinguished himself by leading the first significant uprising against Soviet interference in 1979. That was in Herat, some nine months before the Red Army crossed the frontier. Now eleven years of war and little prospect of real peace had created an American-style Wild West in Herat where guns and money ruled. Like Afghanistan's other historic cities, Jalalabad and Kandahar, Herat had been smashed by years of fighting.

I arrived at the Park Hotel from Herat's airport on the local airport bus service – an armoured personnel carrier with an infantry fighting vehicle as an escort. The loud roar from the APC's powerful engines was deafening as we crashed over a road damaged by tanks, mines and mortar shells. On each side outposts manned by regular army units and tribal militiamen loyal to the government stood vigil against mujahedeen attacks. As we careered along the APC kicked up suffocating clouds of dust that sent donkey trains laden with produce and the local taxi, a horse and trap decorated with screaming red woollen balls and silver bells, scurrying for cover. Overhead the jarring sound of helicopters signalled the approach of two MiG-24 gunships skimming the treetops to avoid Stinger missiles.

Much of Herat was in ruins. Tanks were as common as taxis and charged through the city's streets carrying armed militiamen. Many of the province's 35,000 militiamen had once fought for the mujahedeen but had joined the militia for guns, money and food. We were stopped at a checkpoint manned by teenage militiamen, some barely old enough to shave. They halted old men with flowing beards and thin, rather fine, ravaged faces as they rode to market, searching their turbans, animals and carts for hidden weapons. Many of the young militiamen roamed the streets rifle-butting anyone who got in their way; others lazed on chairs and bed frames with Russian-made RPGs, rocket-propelled grenade launchers, at their side. In 1933 the traveller and writer Robert Byron observed on a visit to Herat that 'the loose-knit men swing through the dark bazaar with a devil-may-care self-confidence. They carry rifles to go shopping as Londoners carry umbrellas.' Little had changed, only now they carried Kalashnikovs and rocket-propelled grenades.

I travelled south with my government escort across the Pul-i-Malan bridge to a village held by the militia. The last time I had crossed the Pul-i-Malan bridge over the Hari Rud river had been with the mujahedeen. In five years of visits to Afghanistan I had travelled over the same section of road on separate occasions with government troops, the local militia and the mujahedeen. Each claimed they alone were in control. The complexities of the allegiances are beyond the grasp of most foreigners.

I had been to the militia-held village once before with Ismail Khan, in August 1984 when the village was mujahedeen-controlled and had in large part been destroyed by relentless bombing raids. The advantages of collaboration were great. Bombing raids had ceased as had government retaliatory operations. The village had also received weapons and economic aid. I recognized one of the militiamen and struck up a conversation with him. It was unlikely he would recognize me. On my previous visit to the village I had been disguised as a mujahedeen, dressed in turban and robes. Incredibly, the militiaman was to be married to a daughter of a mujahedeen commander with whom I had once stayed.

'Is Abdul Sattar still with the mujahedeen?' I asked.

'Yes. When he is not in Iran he is based in Zindijan. He still commands a group of Ismail Khan's men.'

Like many militiamen this man's loyalties were divided. He confided to me that he was still a mujahedeen supporter. But that was in the street when I was away from my government guide. Once reunited with my guide the militiaman declared his support for the government.

Another militiaman's revolver had been given to him by the mujahedeen, his semi-automatic Kalashnikov by the government. As in many guerrilla campaigns, by day the villages belonged to the government, by night to the mujahedeen; only in Herat the different forces were often one and the same people.

Some of Ismail Khan's mujahedeen groups were ordered to join the government militia in order to penetrate government structures. Other militia groups had come to an arrangement with the mujahedeen. How else could Ismail Khan, the government's most wanted man, with a bounty on his head that could make a millionaire out of any Afghan who betrayed him, drive through the heart of the government-controlled city in broad daylight in a government jeep?

Double-dealing was part and parcel of militia practice. However, in Herat, as elsewhere, infighting was rife both among the mujahedeen and the militia; and between the mujahedeen and the militia. The government was content to keep its troops in fixed positions and to portray its members as good Muslims and true nationalists.

On the way back to the city, I tried to prompt our government guide from Kabul, whom I had met on my first visit to the capital and who had at the time spoken of his fondness for whisky, women and Latoya Jackson, to tell me about his own political allegiances. Like the government, he claimed to be a good Muslim, but I suspected he still believed in the Marxist revolution.

'Sadiqi,' I said teasingly, 'you're like a watermelon.'

'A watermelon?'

'Yes, green on the outside and red on the inside.'

Returning to the city our bus stopped near the Pul-i-Malan bridge. Sadiqi got out and headed for the river. I jumped out and called to him to stop. He continued on his way to the riverbank, so I chased after him and tackled him from behind. We both fell to the ground.

'Sadiqi, there are mines,' I explained.

'I was only going to drink some water.'

We looked up and there in the water at the river's edge were the tripwires to submerged mines.

Looking west from Herat's 1,300-year-old citadel all I could see was village after village laid waste by Soviet and Afghan carpet bombing. To the horizon stretched a deserted no-man's-land with no trace of life. Herat's governor conceded that eighty villages and 14,000 houses had been razed. Thousands had died, many buried under the rubble or asphyxiated by the implosion of the bombs.

The Soviets, like Genghis Khan and Tamerlane before them, had fought beneath the citadel's walls. Heratis had once again been sacrificial lambs to personal and foreign ambition. In 1984, when I had stayed with the mujahedeen in the free fire zone to the west of the citadel, we came under repeated helicopter gunship attack, aerial bombardment and artillery fire. Anything that moved was attacked; anything that provided protection was bombed; any sign of life, the telltale smoke rising from a hearth, and the area would be shelled. To the pilots, in every house there was a potential nest of guerrillas. To the tank commanders, every house provided cover for the enemy, restricted his vision and prevented him from firing accurately at his target. Never in my life had I been so shocked and afraid than when I was walking through this landscape which for fifteen miles was far worse than any picture I had seen of the bombing of Dresden or London, and called to mind the total destruction of Hiroshima and Nagasaki.

To the Afghan and Soviet pilots flying at twelve thousand feet one mud-walled village had resembled another and at the flick of a switch the bomber's payload would level three-hundred-year-old trees and centuries-old houses, their ancient carpets, wardrobes and heirlooms, their vineyards and gardens turned to dust.

Mosques, homes and windmills were reduced to thick columns of black smoke. The helicopter pilots couldn't tell whether the dots beneath them were mujahedeen or refugees. They were killed regardless. Countless unmarked graves lined the roads I had travelled with the mujahedeen. The carcasses of rusting tanks lay on their sides. Thousand-pound unexploded bombs projected from the ground like pumpkins. For a hundred square miles nothing was left standing. In 1984 the battle for Herat and the surrounding countryside was at its height and the Soviets and Afghan government forces needed to plug the gaps. Long wide belts of minefields were laid around the city. At night, the mujahedeen moved forward inch by inch prodding the ground for mines which, when discovered, were unearthed with knives. One de-mining operation close to the city had cost the mujahedeen a total of 180 lives and amputations.

The causes of the Afghan civil war remained. Society was as polarized as ever. The Kabul government's representative in Herat, like many members of the ruling People's Democratic Party, was dedicated to the goals of the Socialist Revolution. In his office, lined with books on the lives of Marx, Engels and Lenin and works such as *Dialectical Materialism in Popular Language* and *The Difficult Problems Encountered in Building a Socialist Society*, he talked about the Islamic nature of the government. Senior members of the party spoke of bringing the country out of its backwardness.

At the other end of the political spectrum was Ismail Khan who commands respect among all who once fought for him, and many who fought against him. His dislike of Communism is so great that his goal is to purge the Kremlin's influence in the Soviet Central Asian Republics, the home of 40 million Muslims. He told a friend of mine: 'The war will not end here until the Central Asian Republics are liberated.'

Ismail Khan's anti-Marxist views had considerable support within Afghanistan. Under President Hafizullah Amin 1,000 metres of red cloth had been imported to fly as banners when the people couldn't afford to buy enough cloth to clothe themselves. Many of the red flags that had once flown on government buildings had been lowered and the country's tricolour including the green for Islam had been restored.

With the government bunkered down in the cities and the mujahedeen controlling much of the countryside, the government was offering autonomy and assistance to local commanders. The countryside, like the province and city of Herat, was a mosaic of political, military and tribal fiefdoms where tenuous ceasefires were arranged by local chieftains – warlords in effect – and near-autonomous representatives of the government or militia commanders who were often known as Pashas.

Hasaudin's territory included the part of Herat city where the Park Hotel was situated. In the evening I sat with him and some of his men under the hotel's fir trees while the sound of machine-gun and mortar fire echoed around us like a dull drumbeat. During our conversation at least half a dozen rockets slammed into the city and shook Herat's fifteenth-century Musalla complex. Before the war UNESCO designated the city of Herat a historic monument. The Musalla complex, designed and built in 1417 under Queen Gawhar Shad, wife of Shad Rukh, Tamerlane's son, is now largely destroyed and seeded with mines. Robert Byron described it as 'the most beautiful example of colour in architecture ever devised by man to the glory of his God and himself'.

Hasaudin claimed to be the commander of 1,300 men. 'What is more important,' he said, 'before I joined the government I only had 400 guns. Now the government has given me enough to arm all my men.

'What would you like to drink? Vodka or Johnnie Walker?' Hasaudin asked.

'Nothing thanks.'

'Hashish?'

'No thanks.' Some of his armed teenagers were smoking a joint as they lounged around the tiny pond in the hotel forecourt.

Hasaudin had joined the rebellion against the government at the beginning of the war, which in Herat was considered to be in March 1979, when Soviet advisers and Afghan party members were beheaded in the streets nine months prior to the Soviet invasion. Hasaudin was twenty-two years old then. I asked him why he now sided with the government.

'The Soviets are gone. I don't want to kill soldiers any more; they are Afghans.'

'But what do you think of the government?'

'Taraki, Amin, Karmal, they all came and went, so will Najibullah.'

'And the mujahedeen leaders?'

'Gulbuddin, Rabbani, they're there for now, but for how long?'

He was more interested in drinking his Scotch and talking about Western women than in politics.

'I like blonde American women. My father used to work at this hotel when the tourists were still here. I still live with him, but he would not approve of my drinking, smoking and chasing women.'

His teenage mercenaries wore rag-tag outfits, broken plimsolls or plastic sandals with cheap teacloths for turbans. Those who had already fought battles talked about their adventures much as the youths in Poplar used to talk about skateboarding. For many, killing was a game. War seemed to hold no fears for them. They talked about death in battle with a mixture of bravado and fatalistic resignation, as you or I might discuss the risk of a sporting injury.

They were athletic with tall but scrawny bodies, anything but solid. When they picked up pebbles and turned their heads in my direction to flick them into the pond, I was struck by how much they looked like boys; few had grown up. Only one knew how to write his name; he had recently returned from Iran. One of the boys asked me how many lessons it took to learn to read and write. He must have thought it was like learning to use a gun, which had probably only required a few demonstrations. Sooner or later he would use his weapon to kill, if he had not already.

For the most part they had inherited Hasaudin's lethargy. The only time they became really excited was when they spoke about the beatings they had given their enemies (some of whom had once been their friends). Their minds were on the next battle, like the gangs that roamed the Bronx, Central Los Angeles and Poplar. Like the Inter City Firm, the gang that used to hang out next to my local fish-and-chip shop in East London, Hasaudin's gang was looking to pick a fight with a rival Pashtun tribe, the Nurzai. They were cocksure and waiting for the order from their leader for the next bit of action, when they would become intoxicated on a potent concoction of menace, evil and destruction; for this was the law of the jungle where only the ruthless and the strong survived.

The morning sun rose through the plume of smoke and ash, plunging the province into more despair and hatred. The civil war had touched everyone. Farmers who tilled fields in mujahedeen-controlled territory risked being bombed by the government air force; farmers who were under the militia's jurisdiction risked the wrath of the mujahedeen. The old men who brought their produce to town travelled through a succession of mujahedeen, militia and government military lines and levelled villages and neighbour-hoods. Women were never seen in Herat's streets without their lavender or lilac veils, scurrying like frightened pigeons across the road or shopping in a district where not a single building had escaped being cratered by shells or pockmarked by bullets. In the shadow of a rocketed building a young boy, the son of a mujahed, government soldier or militiaman, or perhaps an orphan, sold tomatoes. The catastrophe that had so quickly wiped out half of Herat will take decades to mend. Nature had survived. Between the rubble and bomb craters weeds and new plants had begun to spring to life. But the civilization beneath them is buried forever.

I returned from Herat with a forty-nine-kilogram bag of sugar to distribute amongst friends. Sugar was a luxury in the capital and my gift was readily accepted. Sadly Masti was returning to Geneva where she was based. She had become frustrated by the slow pace of humanitarian assistance to the capital's needy and the arguments between different United Nations agencies.

There was as much arguing and rivalry between international aid agencies and between ecumenical and evangelical groups as there was goodwill. However, whilst there are over 12,000 non-governmental organizations (groups of specialists and aid charities) in the world, only a handful had a base in the capital of one of the world's most impoverished nations.

But the relief agencies were not always responsible for the failure of assistance to reach areas of need. Humanitarian supplies were hijacked by rival mujahedeen groups who were not prepared to allow help to reach people under the control of a rival group. Both the promise of food and its denial were used by commanders to control and intimidate the population. The man-made disaster of the war was in some cases compounded by international aid which was determined by criteria that were often a complex mix of political, military, strategic, geographical and commercial concerns. Indeed the current political stalemate was likely to be reinforced by the small amounts of humanitarian aid that reached the country, for it was subject to political pressures from both the donors and the recipients controlling it. Whilst international staff argued about inflated *per diems*, travel expenses and allowances, the people most in need of assistance remained the victims of international and local politics far beyond their control.

A local driver took Masti to the airport. He vented his anger at the impending chaos: 'Every week at great expense the United Nations brings a new consultant to Kabul. There are bigger offices, more consultants, more meetings, more reports, but nothing in the warehouses!'

'It's what they call advance planning,' said Masti, who had suggested to me that if all United Nations paperwork was written on rice paper, with water there would probably be enough rice pudding to feed everyone on the planet.

A week after Masti left Kabul the United Nations plane that had carried her to Islamabad was punctured by shrapnel from salvos of long-range cluster rockets as it waited on the tarmac at Kabul to take UN officials back to Pakistan. Passengers who had been waiting for the regular flight to Delhi had been queuing at a ship's container which was used as a security entrance to the airport. As the first rockets fell in and around the airport, the passengers abandoned their suitcases, took shelter under the terminal's staircase or ran to the nearest vehicles to take them back into the centre of town, which was marginally safer. An Antonov-12 transport carrier and a mobile radar unit were destroyed. Rockets also hit the cargo terminal and damaged an Ariana Tupolev. At least one soldier and a fireman were killed. Considering the severity of the attack, the damage to material and human lives was remarkably light.

Mabouba and Baba continued to work at the house after Masti left at the beginning of August. The rent was paid until the end of September, when I was scheduled to return to Europe or the United States. I struck up a relationship with a woman who, like Masti, was exiled from her homeland. Our moments together had to be stolen on the Sabbath when Baba left the house to go to the Pul-i-Khishti central mosque. At all other times if Baba wasn't tending his flowers he was sure to chaperone any woman invited to the house.

By the Sabbath everyone was exhausted from the constant rocketing of the city, so the streets were empty at weekends except for those on their way to prayers. Before leaving for the mosque Baba always prayed for a rocket-free day. 'May Satan's ears be deaf,' he used to say as he left the house. New weapons had been added to the government arsenal and the peace-shattering bangs could no longer be so clearly distinguished as had once been the case. Incoming and outgoing became 'ingoing' and 'outcoming' in the confusion of whose rockets were doing what to whom.

On the first Sabbath in September Mabouba invited Baba and me to dinner. It was a rare honour given the current political climate. Ordinary Afghans were frightened to become too closely associated with foreigners, particularly journalists, and visits to their homes could only be made in great secrecy. But Mabouba would not listen to the risks. Baba and I were expected for dinner and her ten-year-old son Selim would come and fetch us. It would not have been appropriate for Baba and me to be seen with her in the street even if she was hidden behind the burqa.

Baba wore the shalwar camise and neatly pressed turban he reserved for his Friday visits to the mosque. He had a grin that stretched from one side of his face to the other, revealing his few remaining teeth. He picked a healthy bouquet of flowers from the garden and a bunch of grapes that grew from a trellis of vines for Mabouba's household. As he did so he reprimanded me for never having time to admire his flowers. It was true I was often too busy chasing stories and in the process I had hurt his feelings. In future I would pay more attention to his garden.

Mabouba lived in Qalai Fatullah, a quiet residential neighbourhood not far from the centre of town. Dinner had been planned well in advance, for electricity was only available on alternate nights and then just for a few hours at a time. As we waited for it to be switched on Mabouba's husband and Baba unfurled prayer mats in the spartan living-cum-dining-cum-bedroom and prayed towards Mecca.

We sat on thin sponge mattresses covered in stretch nylon, laid around the walls of the room. Like the curtains, they were printed with garish floral patterns. In the corner next to a tall refrigerator was the home's proudest possession, an old pre-Daoud Philips television set. At precisely eight o'clock Qalai Fatullah's mains supply sprang to life and the room's bare lightbulb played to the beat of the fluctuating current which made the shadows dance as if the bulb were being blown by a gentle breeze. Mabouba and her eldest daughter made *ashak*, my favourite Afghan dish, tiny dumplings filled with leeks. We also had *bolani*, a type of pancake filled with spinach or greens.

Conversation always returned to the war. When we talked about local seasonal fruits Mabouba's youngest daughter Mina mentioned the country's destroyed orchards. When Baba regaled us with tales of his childhood travels, Mabouba's husband sighed at the country's paths and mountain passes littered with anti-personnel mines. We watched a Yugoslavian promotional programme on the 'green and white' television set. Everyone marvelled at Belgrade and Zagreb's beautiful skyscrapers and highways, at Sarajevo's arenas and Dubrovnik's jewel of a port and scenic coastland. For one hour Mabouba's family, Baba and I were transported to a remote and distant Disneyland.

At nine o'clock Baba and I walked home. Baba handed me a letter and asked me to deliver it to the doctor. Maybe I had lost something in the translation. I asked Baba why he couldn't go himself.

'I don't know the doctor,' said Baba.

'Neither do I,' but Baba didn't look convinced. I suggested he take his letter to the hospital. Baba looked at me as if I were mad. Only later, after my visit to Chakhcharan, did Baba's letter to the doctor make any sense.

WELCOME TO CHAKHCHARAN said the sign in front of the broken carcass of an Antonov-28. We had just landed in the capital of Afghanistan's most remote and poorest province.

For centuries Chakhcharan had been at the crossroads of nomadic life. In summer caravans of Pashtun nomads came from Pakistan, but also from Maimana in the north, Kabul and Kandahar, to sell camels, horses, donkeys and sheep and to purchase provisions. For the remaining six months of the year snow cuts the province off from the rest of the country. Chakhcharan was no more than a village. Ghor province didn't possess a single paved road, and the province's only car, an old rusting government-owned yellow Volga, stood neglected in the quiet main street.

The lonely paths that cut across valleys and barren mountains remained empty. The Soviet infantry battalion and helicopter squadron that had been stationed in Chakhcharan were gone. They had left not a single trace to mark their ten-year occupation, but for years the nomads did not return and this year was no exception.

I had come to the centre of Afghanistan to witness a mujahedeen group endorse President Najibullah's policy of national reconciliation – autonomy and assistance to the local commander and village elders in return for a peaceful co-existence. Our group consisted of a handful of high-ranking Afghan army officers and government officials and half a dozen journalists, two from the Soviet Union, the rest from Western news agencies. The small convoy of armoured personnel carriers and jeeps crossed the barren plain towards the village of Tagai Timur, kicking up huge clouds of dust. A week before and the government vehicles would have been attacked had they attempted to move out of the provincial capital.

The ceremony had been planned in advance. As the army generals and journalists climbed out of the jeeps and off the armoured personnel carriers, the town's elders moved forward to greet us and hundreds of mujahedeen came striding over the hills in billowing trousers and turbans, guns slung over their shoulders. Sheep were ritually slaughtered in front of us as we walked up the narrow path into the town, the blood that poured from their throats claimed immediately by the parched earth.

The mujahedeen lined up behind a display of their weapons: two anti-aircraft guns, a 75mm cannon, Egyptian-made rockets, Chinese-made recoilless rifles and rocket-propelled grenades, Italian mines, captured Soviet machine-guns and grenades, still packed like eggs in their boxes, and an American heat-seeking Stinger missile.

Slowly the army officers and government representatives made their way down the line of mujahedeen, respectfully bowing, clasping hands and hugging the guerrillas and each of the tribal elders. A few women had ventured out of their homes, but clung sheepishly to their front doors. Most stood like frightened kittens ready to scurry back into their houses either at the command of the head of the family or simply by force of tradition. Some stood transfixed by the scene before them; it was unlikely that any of them had ever seen a foreigner. But the Afghan general who pressed crisp one-thousand–Afghani notes into the women's hands was as foreign to them as the visiting correspondents.

The tribal chieftain, Ibrahim Beg, claimed to be the head of 21,000 followers. None of them had seen a government official in ten years. Many had come from the surrounding villages out of curiosity, to gawp as one would if Martians had landed, but more importantly they wanted to see what peace looked like. Peace for a few lucky villagers was a one-thousand–Afghani note handed out like a stick of bubble gum. But for the few who had won the Afghan pools, there was nothing to spend it on. Tagai Timur had no shops. More importantly, there was no electricity, running water, road or doctor. The villagers and children were just as likely to die from diarrhoea as from a bullet wound.

The weatherbeaten faces, lined foreheads, fierce eyes and scraggly beards spoke chapters about their harsh lives and medieval living conditions. The twentieth century had reached Tagai Timur only in the form of a pair of 1970s metal-rimmed sunglasses, Japanese watches, a wireless and, of course, as in every other Afghan village, the sophisticated armoury that was medieval only in its inhumanity.

Our government interpreter introduced our hosts as the mujahedeen group belonging to Harakat-i-Islami. I knew from a previous visit to the region that in fact the group wasn't the Shiite Harakat of Sheik Asef Mohseni, as he had said, but the Sunni Harakat-i-Engelab-i-Islami of Maulawi Mohammed Nabi Mohammedi. With such a confusing array of groups the interpreter could be forgiven for the mistake, but within this error stood the deep divide between the educated urbanized elite and the tribal elders who ruled the countryside and inhabited a different world. The Marxist revolution grew out of a frustrated desire for progress in a country where strict social customs are enforced by a clergy with wide secular influence. Villages like Tagai Timur exist in the time warp of remote Afghan valleys and have little or no contact with the outside world. Islamic time regulates life by the call to prayers, and with every sentence Allah and the Prophet Mohammed are invoked. Under the ultra-radical and hardline President Amin, who thrust his Marxist ideology on his people at the point of a gun, alienation grew and open hostility spread until men such as Ibrahim Beg took up arms against the imposed revolution. When I asked Beg how he had chosen Harakat-i-Engelab-i-Islami in preference to one of the other mujahedeen parties he told me they had been the first mujahedeen group to offer him weapons.

Recently, however, supplies had dried up and his decision to support the government's policy of national reconciliation was made without consulting mujahedeen leaders in Pakistan.

Sitting down to lunch in the local mosque, government officers and tribal elders rested their guns against the mud brick walls. Local agreements camouflaged, for the time being at least, the alienation that had been the cause of the uprising. The generals and officials were unlikely to consider the rotten odour of the village as indicative of anything but its backwardness. Ibrahim Beg looked at the government Vice-Minister for State Security and announced to the attendant audience, 'Under the Soviets our government was an infidel government, but with the Soviets gone, President Naji-bullah's government is serving the people and Islam.' It was not very convincing. Beg and his supporters faced acute shortages of food and weapons and only the government was in a position to provide them.

Under the agreement Ibrahim Beg got both weapons and food, and the government relinquished central authority in return for a ceasefire. Neither side had to accept the other's ideology and both were free to sit side by side as they tucked into a hearty lunch of steaming pilau, freshly cooked mutton and yoghurt. After lunch some government officers and local tribal elders exchanged pistols and revolvers as if trading stamps.

Through an interpreter I questioned Ibrahim Beg about his request for a school.

'Will girls be allowed to attend the school?' I asked.

'We will think about that later,' said Beg. My interpreter swallowed hard with indignation as he translated. All the tribal elders believed that women should remain covered, but nothing was going to dampen the spirits of the army officers as we all marched out of the mosque into the bright daylight for the peace ceremony in the local square.

To one side the government had placed ten tons of Soviet wheat, warm winter coats, boots, wide-brimmed washing bowls, galvanized iron pails and five new Kalashnikovs, with promises of more to come. To the other side of the square officials, peasants and village elders gathered in a large circle waiting for the ceremony to begin.

Tribal elders put their signature, a thumbprint, to an agreement that amongst other things exempted local men from military service. Everyone held their hands out to find communion with God, and the local mullah offered prayers. But at the very moment the message of peace from President Najibullah was about to be read an incoming artillery shell exploded on the hillside 500 metres from where we stood. There was a moment of consternation, but the ceremony continued.

As the familiar plume of black smoke rose, Hayatullah, Ibrahim Beg's eldest son, cursed the rival Jamiat-i-Islami group for the rocket attack. Beg's men were predominantly Aimaq. The Jamiat group that had fired the rocket were Tajik. And the Hesbi, who were also at odds with both Beg and Jamiat, were Pashtun. Over the years Ibrahim Beg had lost nearly 250 men in clashes with Jamiat and Hesbi, but only twelve in past battles with the government.

Mujahedeen groups, who only months before were fighting the Soviets, were now accepting arms and money provided by the Soviet Union and scorning weapons from the United States and the Pakistan influence they had once so readily accepted. The two Soviet journalists didn't seem surprised by what was taking place, but they questioned aloud how much longer the Afghan government could continue the costly exercise of buying villages.

'Gorbachev once called Afghanistan a bleeding wound,' said one of the Soviets named Anatol. 'Financially we are haemorrhaging still.'

There was unlikely to be peace without economic prosperity, but equally there was no hope of economic prosperity without peace. The mountains and valleys of Afghanistan were fighting religious and cultural battles that were centuries old. The civil war was more about tribal and sexual apartheid than about the defeat of a foreign invader. Suspicion of foreigners was dwarfed by a continuing suspicion of anyone outside one's own immediate clan.

Leaving Tagai Timur better armed with its heat-seeking missile and arsenal of anti-aircraft guns intact we headed back to Chakhcharan's gravel airstrip. As we taxied for take-off, I nervously eyed the Antonov's cabin, which was equipped with a parachute harness. The Vice-Minister for State Security, Lieutenant-

General Jalal Razminda,* reassured me, 'The region around Chakhcharan is now in our hands.' I breathed a sigh of relief.

Once in the air the firing of magnesium flares to foil heat-seeking missiles began. The pilot wasn't taking any chances.

If the Antonovs were the Afghan air force's workhorses, helicopters were their taxis. I travelled in several helicopter gunships (one riddled with bullet holes) once to watch a convoy of armaments and trucks arriving from the Soviet Union and on another occasion to visit a small garrison. They flew in single file or in packs at tremendous speed, just above the ground, hugging the terrain, scattering flocks of terrified sheep in every direction and sending villagers diving for cover. At one time the helicopters flew at several thousand feet but the introduction of Stinger and Blowpipe missiles changed that. They dropped altitude to fifteen or thirty feet and raced above the ground at 140 miles an hour. A pilot's blink, a moment of lapsed concentration, and all aboard would be history.

During the course of the summer I had had enough terror to last a lifetime, but I knew that the terror I had faced was nothing compared to the terror confronting all Afghans. At the beginning of September I travelled along the Salang Highway, Kabul's umbilical cord to the Soviet Union, on an armoured personnel carrier decorated with plastic flowers and postcards of Indian film stars which danced to the damaged road's corrugations. On either side of us village after village had been obliterated by savage shelling and carpet bombing. In a replay of Vietnam's Mi Lai, men, women and children had been massacred by withdrawing Soviet troops. The torn and twisted wreckages of crumpled hamlets clung to the

*Eight months after the Tagai Timur peace ceremony, in April 1990, Lieutenant-General Razminda and Fazle Haq Khaleqyar, the governor of Herat province, joined thousands of mujahedeen and civilians in a plain twenty-five miles east of Herat to mark the laying down of arms by the latest mujahedeen group to join Afghanistan's national reconciliation policy. As the governor and the lieutenant-general embraced the resistance leaders, three armed men opened fire. The ceremony turned into a massacre, Lieutenant-General Razminda was killed, the governor seriously wounded. The governor's guard killed the assassins and the open plain erupted in a hail of gunfire from all sides. Several high-ranking officers were killed and wounded in the firefight and hand-to-hand combat with knives and pistols. Dozens of civilians, children, soldiers and mujahedeen died in the intense crossfire before tanks moved in with bursts of gunfire to halt the carnage. At least two mujahedeen groups claimed responsibility for the assassination attempt.

hillsides and hilltops as testimony to man's barbarity. Along the road and in the river bed were the carcasses of Soviet and Afghan armour silenced in ambushes, and the charred remains of convoys of tankers and trucks lay upturned.

The fields were untended, the civilians and animals gone. The intermittent sound of the river and the convoys of trucks and military vehicles carrying fuel, food and ammunition to the capital echoed against the mountains.

We stopped at one military post where government soldiers were busy repositioning their tank and reinforcing their bunkers. Above us along the mountain ridges the army were building new security posts to protect the highway from mujahedeen and bandit attack.

I pressed the local commandant about the reports which said hundreds of villagers had been massacred.

'The mujahedeen used these villages to launch their ambushes,' said the colonel.

'But what about civilian casualties?'

'They were warned about the impending attacks,' he insisted. 'Most were evacuated from the area. Only a few were killed or injured,' he added.

There were no civilians to ask.

In Kandahar, where I went to watch the arrival of a government convoy of weapons and foodstuffs, Lieutenant-General Nur Ul-Haq Olumi, the local government army commander and governor, a graduate of both US and Soviet military training schools, had struck a deal with local mujahedeen commanders. In return for allowing food into the city the government garrisons permitted the mujahedeen to enter the city to go shopping providing their guns were deposited at government checkpoints. On leaving the city they could return to the checkpoint to collect their weapons. I discussed these arrangements with an officer who seemed as confused by the shifting alliances as he was by the first Western journalists he had seen since the beginning of the war. He told me that the Soviet Union was the enemy and the United States their friend. The afternoon calm was shattered by a rocket that smashed into the airport. I looked to the soldier. He shrugged his shoulders. 'The mujahedeen still fire shells at us, if only to maintain their self-respect.' Self-respect came in the shape of coffins, mourning relatives and injured passengers on the Antonov that took us back to Kabul.

Every foreigner's visit to a beleaguered city was filmed by an Afghan TV crew. By the end of the summer I had become a familiar figure on Afghan television. Afterwards I was stopped in the streets of Kabul and asked for an eyewitness account of the situation around the country. Baba, like the soldiers in the street outside my house, was anxious for news and hopeful that the killing was near an end. Government soldiers were gaining in confidence daily and many of Kabul's residents who, like Baba, had once been mujahedeen sympathizers were now angry and bitter at the mujahedeen rocketing of the city. With each casualty the mujahedeen were losing support.

'Have you given my letter to the doctor?' asked Baba the day after I returned from Kandahar. I had kept Baba's letter, not knowing quite what to do with it.

'I'm sorry Baba, I haven't.' Baba looked hurt. 'Can I get you some medicine?'

'Medicine?' repeated Baba, surprised. 'Who said anything about medicine?'

'Baba, are you ill? I don't know any doctors.'

'I've seen you on television with him.'

'Who?'

'Dr Najibullah.'

Baba had seen me at a televised presidential press conference and had paid a scribe to write his letter asking *the* doctor, who also happened to be *the* President, for assistance. Amongst the requests was a plea for a government–subsidized apartment.

Both the government and the mujahedeen received more in weapons from the superpowers than the country's total gross national product. Since my first visit to Kabul in March the government had received over 500 Scud missiles (which according to some reports cost a million dollars apiece), 200 new tanks and 615 armoured personnel carriers, and still each day was punctuated by the roar of the massive Soviet Ilyushin transporters overhead. There had been approximately 1,200 flights in the last month.

By September the weather was beginning to change, the nights were decidedly cool. Winter was fast approaching, and the government was making frantic efforts to fill its silos with grain; hundreds of trucks that had made it along the Salang waited in long lines to discharge their loads. As in the previous winter the children had begun stripping the city's trees of their bark for fuel. Each day prices edged upwards and the local currency grew weaker. The previous winter no one had died of hunger, but cases were reported of children dying from exposure and pneumonia. I was told of a brother and sister who had frozen to death because they were afraid to go home to their parents from the bakery empty-handed. Squatters and the displaced living in the hillside shanty towns faced temperatures of minus twenty degrees with little or no fuel or electricity, and hours and days standing in lines for rations of bread and fuel. And still the rocketing of the cities and countryside continued. Internal refugees who had earlier fled to the north were now heading southwards after an unusual amount of rocketing in and around the northern city of Mazar-i-Sharif. There seemed no end to the ordinary people's suffering. As I stepped out of the mayor's office, a truck carrying fuel for the Scud missiles veered out of control as it rounded a corner, in the process discharging its four canisters of rocket fuel. One of them hit the ground and exploded, sending a huge noxious cloud of red fuming nitric acid into the air.

Lost amongst the war's casualties were the many civilians who had been permanently scarred by the effects of eleven years of civil strife. On the outskirts of Kabul I visited Marastoon, a mental asylum where for two years thirteen children of imprisoned parents aged from two-and-a-half to twelve shared a crumbling compound with the mentally disturbed, crippled and blind, as well as lepers who remained untreated for lack of medicine. One of the children had been molested by an insane inmate, another beaten. Most of the inmates roamed freely across the compound of dilapidated mud-walled shacks. They lived in almost pitch-dark rooms with bars on the windows and slept on bare metal bunks.

Amongst the stink of excrement and dried sweat a ten-year-old girl squatted in the corner of a room silently tearing at her filthy clothes until she was naked. No one knew her name. She had been found wandering in the bazaar five years before. Shakila, a woman of around twenty, approached me. She suffered from epilepsy and told me she wanted to escape because she was beaten regularly. An older woman with the ends of a baby milk powder tin cut away to make an improvised bracelet sat crouched on a table. She had been driven mad by trying to find her husband who had been killed in the war. Many of the inmates stared vacantly into space, some sat together on beds, aimless in unison. Men in pairs, their heads shaved, dressed in filthy rags, carried flat barrows of coal under the watchful eye of an attendant with a stave. Some inmates sat against a mud wall with their torn clothes pushed around their feet to hide the manacles around their ankles. There were no doctors, no treatment, no rehabilitation. And amongst the insane and demented inmates roamed the children.

I thought I had seen everything. But the children's circumstances seemed somehow more disturbing than any of the atrocities I had witnessed. For lack of money these small children were being socialized into the madness that surrounded them. There was no hope or future for them under their present circumstances. The oldest of them told me he dreamed of biscuits.

When I said goodbye to Mabouba I found myself almost crying. I wondered what would happen to her and her children. Soon snow would blanket the Hindu Kush and the fighting season would end, but the spring thaw would inevitably herald another cycle of violence. I thought of the appalling chaos, the wretched state of the country and the incalculable number of wrecked lives: a whole generation lost to the imported technology of destruction. Afghanistan was as heavily armed as it was poor. Mabouba's children faced an uncertain future haunted by the spectre of death, disfigurement and destitution. What did Mabouba or other mothers know about the tribal and ethnic tensions, the growing in-fighting between the numerous warlords and between the mujahedeen, the militia and the government? What did they care about the competing interests of India and Pakistan, Iran and Saudi Arabia, the fight for supremacy between the United States and the Soviet Union?

The scale of the tragedy was so great that it is impossible to speak of Afghanistan without thinking of a nation soaked in blood and devastated by war. There was little an individual could do, but I felt I could try to do something about the children in Marastoon. I was haunted by the shackled men, the convulsing inmates, the pleading women, and the sane children amongst them who might end up like the naked ten-year-old. But my project would have to wait until I could return because my two-month stay had reached its end.

On the day I left Kabul for New York more mujahedeen-fired rockets struck Kabul. One struck a bus shelter on the airport road. The scene resembled an abattoir. Pedestrians and shopkeepers calmly gathered human remains. One shopkeeper made a make-shift grave in a ditch next to a field. Another placed a torn leather shoe on top of a twisted metal fragment from the rocket to mark the site. It was a forlorn memorial to the continuing war in the middle of a dusty street. The shopkeepers who had survived were dragging what remained of a pushcart out of the way so that they could get back to business. Twelve people were killed and seventeen injured. But rockets or no rockets, in Kabul stalls reopen and life continues.

According to a UN official, in the first nine months after the Soviet withdrawal there had been 557 attacks, 403 bombing incidents and 201,000 rockets, heavy artillery and mortar shells had fallen on Afghan soil. The Afghan government claimed to be talking to nearly six hundred groups representing 45,000 guerrillas.

I landed in New York minutes before a plane crashed at La Guardia airport. Two passengers were killed and seven admitted to hospital. The crash made the front pages of the *New York Times* and late-night and early-morning television news shows. The mujahedeen rockets that killed twelve people and wounded seventeen were relegated to three paragraphs in the *New York Times*, at the bottom of an inside page, and weren't mentioned in the British press. When I left Kabul at the end of September there were five international correspondents in the capital. By the end of the year there were two, and outside the city there was no one to report the destruction wrought by the government-fired Scud missiles. Since the departure of the Soviet army Afghanistan was no longer news, the abandoned children in Marastoon forgotten people in a forgotten country.

Meanwhile the US State Department was making slow progress with its scheme to render President Najibullah the last party member in Afghanistan. An Afghan general with a senior position in the President's office had recently defected. He had been brought to the States and, from a special government fund, given a salary which was progressively reduced each month. The former general found it increasingly difficult to live on this diminishing stipend and now earns money delivering pizzas in Washington DC.

11

THE QE2 AND THE
NEW AGE THERAPIST

Your companion to travel, leisure and
the Good Life.

Cunard's *Lifestyle* magazine

Queen Elizabeth 2, *Southampton–New York, September–October 1989*

The *QE2* is the largest consumer of caviar in the world. As a guest
lecturer travelling in a first-class cabin I found it hard to believe that
less than ten days before I had been flying in a bullet-ridden
helicopter over a country decimated by war. In today's era of jet air
travel it is possible to switch continents in a day. In one week I had
left Kabul, travelled to New York and then, at the invitation of
Cunard, flown to England to join the *Queen Elizabeth 2* at
Southampton for her voyage to the States. The *QE2*, I discovered,
was for people who wanted to slow down from Concorde.

My travelling companion was a New Age therapist who claimed
to be able to communicate with the dolphins and whales. We
arrived at the quayside where the band of the 1st Battalion Royal
Regiment of Wales played 'Land of Hope and Glory'. I looked up at
the floating cathedral and worried about how I would occupy my
time once on the ship. Passengers dressed in furs arrived in
chauffeur-driven limousines and Rolls-Royces with sets of
designer-label suitcases. I lifted Melissa's two heavy suitcases from
my stepfather's Toyota. 'Don't you think you should make two
trips?' she asked affectionately. Before I considered the option, a
smartly uniformed man was on hand to take care of our luggage.

I wasn't sure of Melissa's age. I can't even remember how old I
was when I first met her: I might have been eight or nine; but I do
remember she was the first girl I fancied. Even though we were

introduced to each other by our respective parents, I doubt she even registered my presence on that first occasion. I was young and timid and had only a vague idea about what happened between men and women whereas Melissa was already of an age to take a serious interest in boys and vice versa. My present lifestyle made it virtually impossible to have a serious relationship, for that matter any relationship at all. This year I had been at home for a total of three weeks since January, and that was on eleven separate occasions. On the other hand, I had no wish to 'settle down', as my mother euphemistically calls a steady relationship, so as not to mention marriage; and in my case she suggested – for she would never do more than suggest – 'It was also time to grow up.' This meant time to buy some furniture, i.e. a bed.

Even though I had recently had a series of affairs I still thought of Melissa. We had become friends and she remained one of the most beautiful women I had ever seen. Her hair was black and long and smooth and moved gracefully as did her supple body. She had a fiery spirit and everything was black or white for her; she was either incredibly high or very low, there was no in between. When she had something on her mind nothing and no one could stop her. Over the years we had come to recognize that there was more than just friendship between us, but we were both too strong-willed; it had been like two trains heading towards each other at full speed. She had a temper that you couldn't extinguish and accused me of being a typical Taurean – 'stubborn'. When she agreed to join me for the crossing I knew it would be either dynamite or fireworks: never simply all right.

Melissa had recently taken up the study of alternative medicine, in fact was teaching it, and her mind was set on intergalactic travel. She had just finished a course in cranial sacral work on the flow of the cerebral spinal fluids. 'They work the autonomic nervous system,' she explained. 'When the head becomes totally compacted the fluids can't work, or repump, and the system can no longer operate.'

We checked into our cabin. We had two portholes, a fridge, a television set, a telephone and a bottle of champagne. Before we occupied the cabin Melissa waved a magical joss stick around to purify it. People, she explained, are electrical frequencies and they leave their energy and thoughts in blankets, paintings and clothes.

We sailed out of Southampton into the darkness. The water was perfectly still, the murmur from the engine room so quiet I might have mistaken it for the noise of the air-conditioning, the motion so smooth that at times it seemed the mother of all ships was the mother of all hotels, likely to sink only from the financial wealth of the passengers. If you weren't into bridge, bingo or jigsaw puzzles, golf, deck quoits or dance competitions, you could always do some serious power shopping on Boat Deck where the most prestigious fashion, designer and jewellery collections were for sale. There was even a mini-Harrods.

I ate in the Princess Grill. The dress code was like the decor and furnishings, expensive. There were three options: formal meant tuxedo or dinner jacket for men and evening/cocktail dress for ladies. Informal meant suit or jacket and tie for gentlemen and afternoon/cocktail dress for ladies. Optional meant either formal or informal wear. In the Princess Grill I discovered that if you didn't want to eat from the menu, you could order something you had dreamed up in advance and, providing the cooks had the ingredients, it would be served with vintage wines.

The awesome choice of foods only became truly apparent when I visited the ship's stores. Belowdecks a vast network of storerooms and cold stores held a treasure trove of edible delicacies. I looked at the shelves: almonds ground, almonds flaked, essence of almonds . . . food for diabetics, food for low-calorie diets, and kosher and halal meat. The ship's three butchers were kept busy ten hours a day. A computer gave an up-to-the-minute inventory: Day One 10,000 eggs consumed with 70,000 eggs still in store. (The store could hold 170,000 eggs.) One of the storerooms contained a padlocked metal cage and within the cage a locked trunk. Inside the trunk was the most prized of all the ship's delicacies: caviar. In the first nine months of the year the ship's passengers had eaten $74,348.25 worth of caviar. Some passengers were never happy; the more they had paid for their passage, the more they consumed. The more they consumed, the more they complained. Apart from the pair on the cover of the ship's glossy brochure, Melissa and I seemed to be the only young couple on board.

At the dinner table Melissa could see through the passengers, giving me on-the-spot diagnoses of their problems. 'You see the greyish couple sitting in the corner,' she would say. 'He has a thyroid and cholesterol problem and she is in love with him.'

'How can you tell?' I asked.

'She has the same throat energy.'

When the wine waiter had finished pouring our wine, she whispered to me, 'He has a jarred nervous system.'

'They're caught up in total insecurity . . . operating below their navels. They haven't learnt to bring themselves through their personalities and consciousness,' she said of the passengers. Which couldn't be said of Melissa. Whether she was meditating on deck, doing her yoga in the gym or changing passengers' electrical frequencies, her presence was always felt.

The first of my two lectures was announced in the ship's daily newsletter as part of the Festival of Life Programme. It fell on Oscar de la Renta fragrance day and was sandwiched between a Louis Feraud fashion show and Holy Mass. My brief was to give a talk designed to help the passengers discover new interests, learn something of value or rekindle old interests. But I had to compete with Steiners of London who were giving a hairdressing and beauty demonstration at the same time. Facials and fat-loss treatments were indeed BIG competition. Many of the passengers had had their faces lifted so many times that they were unlikely to know where their ears and chins might be from one day to the next.

Once I had given the lecture I became acquainted with some of the passengers. Many had been born into money or had married it. One of the younger passengers from Palm Beach and New York was going home having spent the summer touring Europe. He thought Melissa and I were on our honeymoon and kept sending us bottles of champagne. He seemed lonely. Melissa thought he had a twisted neck polarity problem. One day I joined him on the Promenade Deck and he confided to me that the less he worked the more he earned – at present he worked fifteen minutes a day. He'd committed himself to reducing his workload to fifteen minutes a week the following year.

It was difficult to keep up with the jet-set gossip, the 'in' restaurants and the 'smart' resorts. One passenger claimed that the best Bellini's were at Cipriani's, the best sandwiches at Pierre's. 'I don't exist without a sandwich from the Pierre,' he was apt to

repeat, and the only decent service was at the Plaza Athenée. I
made a mental note. Amongst the passengers' European trophies
being shipped across the Atlantic were classic cars, items from the
Duchess of Windsor's jewellery box and a $15 million art collection
whose owner complained that he had had to pay $80,000 to insure
it. When the passengers weren't showing off the latest in designer
wear and making new social contacts they were planning their
winter holidays.

I never asked Melissa if she had made contact with the dolphins
and whales, but when I went to the ship's bridge the captain and
his officers didn't seem to be in contact with their ship either. There
were no crew members at the wheel; we were sailing on auto-pilot.
There was no play with a sextant; we were being directed by a
satellite we couldn't see and the ship seemed to navigate itself. In
Afghanistan you were lucky if you knew which valley you were in.
On the QE2 with a satellite navigation system you could tell your
position to a few yards; you could walk the deck and work out your
speed and the distance you had travelled either across the ocean or
relative to the ship. Even in the middle of the Atlantic the QE2 was
linked to the rest of the world by telephone, telex or fax, unless you
wanted to reach Afghanistan, which didn't yet possess a single fax
and which would take six weeks to reach by telephone. In one
day the QE2 could earn almost as much as Afghanistan's gross
national product.

On the third night I was sitting on the edge of my bed in my best
white dress shirt, in fact my only white shirt, bow tie, dinner jacket
and black dress shoes. I thought I looked like one of the guests at an
awards ceremony. I was waiting for Melissa so that I could help her
with her zip. She appeared out of the bathroom radiant, with a
sparkling pair of earrings and a dress that would turn anyone's
head even if they had a thyroid or twisted neck polarity problem.
As we walked to the restaurant she told me that I must begin to
unlearn the differences, the illusory differences between men and
women, day and night, hot and cold. Looking at Melissa that
seemed hard to do.

At the restaurant we had to follow a particular form of etiquette.
Even though Melissa and I sat at our own table there was the polite
nod to other guests and the reciprocation of cordial greetings with

the *maître d'hôtel*, the wine waiter, waiter and busboy. Costumes were carefully noted before the guests resumed their conversations in discreet tones. *Coq au vin* and *pommes de terre alumettes* might have been chicken and chips elsewhere, but the food like the service was unrivalled.

Melissa asked for a bit of space after dinner. She had missed her daily yoga session and wanted our cabin to herself for a while. I went to the casino where people fed the slot machines with the same passion that television couch potatoes devour crisps and salted cashew nuts. The roulette tables were managed by mini-skirted croupiers. Gamblers lost their stake several times over on a single number, stakes which were more than some people could earn in a week, for others a lifetime's savings.

After what I considered a reasonable delay, and $27 richer, I returned to the cabin to find Melissa quite pale and excited. I attributed this to her standing on her head and her pallor was emphasized by the fact that she had wiped her lipstick from her lips. Melissa believed in previous lives, reincarnation. That evening she had entered other realities, spheres where there were Bodhisattvas, by stimulating and activating the seven centres in the body called chakras – which she explained to me once I had climbed into bed. 'To reach spontaneous experiences you must concentrate on energy centres or chakra points. The most closely connected to the heart is known as "anahata". It is sensitive and powerful . . . Or you can use breathing, mantric sound or visualization. When you concentrate on these centres you move into higher states of energy that take you beyond three-dimensional reality and are thus gateways into other dimensions that normally remain elusive to man's everyday reality.' I placed my hand gently on Melissa's shoulder. She went on speaking. 'You must understand the original source – light, but before light there is darkness, before darkness . . .' My mind wandered over the activities listed in the *QE2*'s brochure: reminiscing, resting, sleeping, watching, physical fitness, theme nights. There was one activity missing from the list, I thought to myself. I moved closer to Melissa.

In the morning I felt that I might possibly be able to settle down – a bit. Of course Melissa and I still didn't see eye to eye on everything. After my second lecture, at which passengers saw pictures of the atrocities being committed against Afghan civilians, Kurdish refugees and disenfranchised Iranians, I had an argument with her on the nature of the violence they had seen. I saw soldiers as brutes who killed, tortured and beat people; Melissa, on the other hand, saw soldiers as a consequence of man's viciousness. There was always an aura of truth about what she had to say.

Time and reality were suspended during the crossing. For the five days I had been as happy as a pig. On the eve of our arrival I decided to go swimming. It was early October and we were sailing down the eastern seabord along the coast of New Brunswick, past Maine, New England and Long Island. In Cleveland I had had the choice of an indoor swimming pool or an outdoor swimming pool. On the QE2 there were two of each. I took one last swim before we sailed into New York harbour. It was an experience I shall never forget: Manhattan's towering skyscrapers rising out of the Hudson River sheathed in the sun's morning rays. The richest city in the world loomed nearer with no hint of the grime and violence of its streets.

Disembarking in New York, one senior citizen approached me with a porter in tow, wheeling a trolley of Louis Vuitton suitcases to a waiting stretch limousine. She paused in front of me to say, 'I enjoyed your talks. However, after the second one I was unable to eat my lunch.'

The QE2 would soon be heading for Yokohama in Japan. If the previous year's trip was anything to go by, the QE2's boutiques would have to increase their staff fivefold from twenty people to 110 or more and stay open until midnight to cope with the rush of business. Thousands of Japanese had joined the QE2 for eating and shopping tours, to get married and to sleep in the cabins. H. Stern, the jeweller, had trouble keeping its $3,600 sapphire, gold and diamond watches in stock and one shop manager had placed an emergency order for an air-freight delivery of 1½ tons of Swiss chocolates. Cabins had cost up to $2,658 a night. The trip for the throngs of Japanese tourists was extraordinary for another reason. The ship went nowhere, and seven hundred guests paying $350 a night had no view at all.

Melissa and I went our separate ways. I had to stay in New York to see my picture agent, Melissa had to return to her practice in

London. I took her to Kennedy Airport and hugged her fondly. As I did she whispered in my ear, 'I'm a catalyst for you to grow whether it takes six hours or six thousand years.'

Four months later I was surprised to receive another invitation, this time to lecture on MS *Vistafjord*, another Cunard ship, smaller than the *QE2* but more elegant and intimate. If the *QE2* was for people who wanted to slow down from Concorde, the *Vistafjord* was for those who needed to slow down from *everything*.

12

LIBYA:
REVOLUTIONIZING
THE LONG WEEKEND

It is an undisputed fact that both man
and woman are human beings. It follows as a
self-evident fact that woman and man are
equal as human beings. Discrimination between man and woman is a flagrant act of
oppression without any justification. For
woman eats and drinks as man eats and
drinks . . . Woman loves and hates as man
loves and hates . . . Woman, like man, needs
shelter, clothing and vehicles . . . Woman
lives and dies as man lives and dies.

But why are there man and woman?
Human society is composed neither of man
alone nor of woman alone.

Woman is a female and man is a male.
According to a gynaecologist, woman men-
struates or suffers feebleness every month,
while man, being a male, does not menstruate.

Muammar Al Qadhafi,
The Green Book, Part Three,
'The Social Basis of the
Third Universal Theory'

From the halls of Montezuma
To the shores of Tripoli,
We will fight our country's battles
On land and sea.

US Marine song

Kiss the hand you cannot sever.

Tuareg saying

I think the *Daily Telegraph* expected me to say Rome or Venice when they asked me where I would like to spend a long weekend. But after four months in Iran and Afghanistan, I was looking for beaches free of tourists and untrampled Roman ruins, and I also needed to recover from my *QE2* hangover.

I wanted to visit Libya or, more precisely, Tripoli-sur-mer, better known as the terrorist capital of the world and, according to the country's leader Muammar Al Qadhafi, possible birthplace of the sixteenth-century Arab playwright, Sheik Zbir.

Tourism in Libya? Although Libya hadn't thrown open its borders to Western tourists, the Colonel had recently abolished most Libyan border checkpoints and customs houses. The new Libyan Board of Tourism was expecting an invasion of inebriated foreigners keen to spend a couple of weeks in one of dozens of Betty Ford clinics it hoped to set up. But for the moment detoxification was not sufficient reason for a visa unless you also had a proven track record of denouncing worldwide imperialist aggression.

I flew to Rome to meet the connecting flight to Tripoli. My revolutionary credentials didn't extend beyond a lapsed membership of the Chelsea Football Supporters' Club, but the sunglassed Libyan secret service agent seemed happy to take my boarding pass for the Libyan Arab Airlines flight, 'The People's Choice'. In accordance with revolutionary principles the airline allows no separate classes and no seat allocations, and the fight for seats was worse than a game of musical chairs. I was more concerned that I hadn't received a letter of invitation from the Libyan People's Bureau who had suggested that I combine my visit to this once much-favoured holiday spot with 'Mourning Day' during the Month of Revenge. Mourning Day commemorated the 77th Anniversary of the Most Massive Deportation Suffered by the Arab Population of Libya, which began on 26 October 1911, when thousands of civilians including women and children were shipped out of Libya to Italian prisons on remote islands. Libya's colonial rulers attempted to rid the country of its native population and clear the way for a complete 'Italianization' programme. In fact the Bureau had called the *Daily Telegraph* the day before my departure to tell them that my visit should be postponed. I had told my editor to inform them I had already left, and now, as I unwrapped The People's Choice in-flight sweets provided by the Libyan Firm of Liberated Industrial Products I contemplated my arrival *sans invitation*.

The overweight German oil driller sitting next to me on the flight downed miniature liqueur bottles in anticipation of the coming months: Libya was dry. He lectured me on the recent wild fluctuations of the world's stock markets: 'It's like last year's October crash – the Jews, they're responsible,' he said with ill-concealed venom. What made him think I wasn't Jewish, I wondered. Maybe he thought I was, or maybe it was the alcohol.

I felt all the more unnerved on landing at Tripoli's international airport. Planes from Swissair, Austrian Airlines, Alitalia and one with German markings, an Iron Cross on each wing and 'Luftwaffe' written on the side, stood on the tarmac. There was obviously money to be made here. They were joined by airlines from the pariahs of the international community who had formed a loose confederation of the oppressed; the departure board's lights flashing Damascus, Tehran and Baghdad.

At the immigration counter I was greeted by a sign in English: 'No Democracy With People's Congresses and Committees Every-where'. I imagined the continuing renaissance of the Barbary spirit; the smell of gunpowder in streets full of gun-toting, home-brewed revolutionaries and secret policemen hostile to any foreigner, especially one carrying a valid passport from a democratically elected government; and all this superimposed on a country whose deserts were dotted with the nomadic Bedouin culture and the camel-mounted Tuareg. But these images were quickly dispelled. A man from the Foreign Information Bureau had been sent to facilitate my arrival. He greeted me in English: 'Don't worry, be happy.' We cleared customs without any hiccups. My driver, a keen BBC World Service listener, and I sped along an immaculately surfaced highway to the city centre, passing row upon row of electricity pylons rising above palms, olive groves and Roman ruins.

The pace of construction was furious. New houses in an eclectic style combining Berber with Bauhaus were being built on every street. Most of the nomadic Tuareg had moved into heavily subsidized council estates which resounded to the strains of Heavy Metal music. The Libyan Tuareg no longer ride camels but drive BMWs and Toyota pickups with their camels in the back.

If it were not for the mounds of foetid rubbish everywhere, Libya could claim to be the Switzerland of Africa, with a small, wealthy population of about the same size who want to go abroad to spend their money because at home everything shuts at 9 P.M. It is a capital which at first sight appears immaculately clean, the result of a decree to paint everything a dazzling green and white in readiness for the twentieth anniversary of the revolution on 1 September 1989. This not only included green kerbsides and the vast expanse of newly painted green tarmac appropriately named Green Square but, as I was later to discover in an empty seaside tourist bungalow, freshly painted toilet seats, revolutionary green, of course. I drove along Al Fat'h (Victory of the Revolution) Avenue lined with the Leader's portrait, which for that matter appeared everywhere in the city, everywhere in Libya. In London a Libyan exile had told me there were 8 million Libyans: 4 million people and 4 million pictures of Qadhafi. These I found painted on hillsides, on buildings with his smiling benevolent image twenty times life size, on billboards, on posters in every public place, in shops and offices, in photographs riding horseback, on stamps as an admiral, army general and fighter pilot or dressed in designer dictator nomad outfits, on postcards juggling a football, on a gigantic hot air balloon, on T-shirts, wristwatches, plates and even ashtrays.

I checked into the El Kabir, Tripoli's main hotel, where staff and guests greeted me with 'brother', 'comrade' or '*citoyen*'. Above the receptionist's head a commemorative plaque was engraved with 'The party system aborts democracy'. In the lobby the editor of a British newspaper published in the London borough of Wandsworth was hawking his paper *Friday* with the headline, 'Torture MAGGIE THE BITCH'. As a correspondent for the *Daily Telegraph* I felt deeply out of place.

The hotel was host to a panoply of revolutionary, counter-revolutionary and quasi-revolutionary groups invited to denounce all forms of imperialist and colonialist actions during Mourning Day. Joining them were members of the Scottish TUC and an Australian journalist who had come to ask the Colonel why the Libyan government would no longer buy Australian sheep. I had been warned in advance by a friend that the El Kabir was often patronized by a wide range of groups. The previous year a West German ice hockey coach had come to seek sponsorship for his team and an American preacher with a large wooden cross had stopped here on his way around the world.

In addition to New Caledonian separatists from the South Pacific, Chadian rebels, American Indians and Black Muslims, Kurdish peshmergas from Iraq, Flemish separatists, Communist guerrillas from the Philippines and Maoists from South America, it was rumoured that Abu Nidal, the leader of the Fat'h Revolutionary Council which was responsible for an attack on a Jewish synagogue in Istanbul and attacks on the Rome and Vienna airports, was in residence at the hotel. However, I later heard guests speculate in hushed conversations that Abu Nidal's actions, once praised by Libya as 'heroic', were out of favour and that Abu Mousa, a rival Palestinian leader, as well as Ahmad Jebril and his Popular Front for the Liberation of Palestine which was believed to be responsible for blowing up the Pan Am jet over Lockerbie, were in.

The hotel's green and white façade of Islamic arches was draped in black cloth for the victims of Italian colonization. From my room with a seafront view I could see a large parking lot where a brisk cash trade in European cars was taking place. There was a blue Peugeot with French licence plates from Lyon, a silver Mercedes 200 from Dortmund and a bright burgundy BMW from the Canton of Vaud in Switzerland. I slipped my shoes off, lounged on the bed and took a look at the book in the drawer of the bedside table. It was not the Koran or the Bible but Muammar Al Qadhafi's *Green Book* in three parts: 'The Solution of the Problem of Democracy: The Authority of the People', 'The Solution of the Economic Problem: Socialism', and 'The Social Basis of the Third Universal Theory'. Within the *Green Book* the Great Leader of the Revolution, who had toppled King Idris in a coup twenty years before, addresses everything from spectator sports and horsemanship to the needs and the role of the masses in his new society: 'Representation is a falsification of democracy . . . The most tyrannical dictatorships the world has known have existed under the shadow of parliaments.' I looked elsewhere for entertainment but the streets were deserted, the restaurants were closed and there were no nightclubs or bars. It was as I imagined Bournemouth out of season. I returned to the hotel and switched on the television. The news was in English and the newscaster began with a quote that seemed to encapsulate Qadhafi's Green Revolution for the complete dismantling of the authority of the government, its ministries and most of the bureaucracy, and for their replacement by committees: 'The struggle will end with the destruction of all traditional govern-mental configurations once power, wealth and arms are in the hands of the people.' The news was followed by songs on the merits of Qadhafi's Universal Theory and the sixteenth and final part of a series on the *Green Book* setting out the social, economic and political structure of Qadhafi's revolution. I fell asleep.

Breakfast was served in a nondescript air-conditioned banquet room. The fine print on the label for 'Quality Jam' read glucose and pectin; the label on the butter warned, 'Do not eat 12 months after date of manufacture' – there was still a day to run. I ordered fresh orange juice. The Tunisian waiter politely informed me, 'We don't serve anything fresh here.' I drank powdered orange juice crush. It was only slightly less disgusting than the salt water served in jugs from an aquifer beneath the streets of Tripoli that is so depleted that sea water has seeped into it.

To smooth my visit, the Foreign Information Bureau assigned Saleh as my guide. He told me his sister was a revolutionary nun, but wasn't a member of Qadhafi's crack team of female bodyguards known as The Green Nuns of the Revolution. Saleh's older brother was also in the armed forces; he was a 'human frog', which I later discovered was a deep-sea diver. Saleh suggested a tour that would include Popular Congresses, Revolutionary Committees, the Green Book Centre and possibly the minefields of Tripolitania. I explained I was a tourist and wished to visit the beaches, museums and Roman ruins and to make a short trip to the desert to meet the Tuareg.

While my request was being considered I set off for Tripoli's

Medina, which isn't exactly the bustling market more commonly associated with African and Middle Eastern bazaars. I've seen more street vendors outside Selfridges than in downtown Tripoli and there were no hordes descending on the souk determined to trade or die. In fact, the only time I saw anything approaching a free-for-all was when one of the locally employed Bulgarian nurses was spotted, causing the kind of stampede you would expect on the first day of the Harrods sale.

Most of the shops and offices only opened for a few hours in the morning; many never opened at all. A few butchers were selling some baby camel meat, and certain traditional handicrafts were still in evidence, just. A coppersmith was beating out an intricate Arabic pattern but with sayings from the *Green Book* rather than the Koran. The traditional weavers making lengths of expensive striped silk used for weddings were being replaced by cheap imported wedding dresses from South Korea. From somewhere in the bazaar a tape recorder played reggae music and the sounds of Africa. I heard a taped band from the Ivory Coast sing 'America break the neck of apartheid'. The only poverty I saw was amongst the immigrants from the Maghreb and beyond. Libyans don't work. Virtually all labour was imported from Tunisia, Algeria, Morocco, Mali, Ghana, Chad, the Philippines, Thailand and China.

Back at the hotel delegates who had been pouring in from all over the world to attend Mourning Day were still waiting for the phonecall summoning them to meet with the Colonel. So too was the Australian journalist, who looked bored. He stared into his chemically flavoured orange juice; he had spent two weeks waiting by the phone. When the Foreign Information Bureau told us we were to attend the International Symposium on Libyan Exiles in Italy the delegates thought this would be the moment that the Great Leader had chosen for his appearance. A fleet of limousines and Revolutionary Green Chevrolets whisked us to the conference centre. There was no Leader but we all received a book of the speech to be given by the 'Brother Colonel' on the 77th Anniversary of the Most Massive Deportation Suffered by the Arab Population of Libya, in which he expressed 'the sacred fire of vengeance that burns in the deepest of our sentiments and fires them up'. It was a speech condemning 'the criminal imperialists . . . the crawling

Europeans . . . the colonialist dogs . . .' As he explained, 'The damned fire of colonialism began when Julius Caesar fooled Cleopatra,' and it continued until 'the American Sixth Fleet crossed the Strait of Messina on 14 April 1986 under another rabid dog, Reagan'. Forthwith we were told that the two months of the calendar named after Julius Caesar and Augustus would be changed to Nasser and Hannibal.

At the symposium I sat between Tony Gilbert from Liberation, a left-wing British movement which incorporates the Movement for Colonial Freedom, and one of the Scottish members of the TUC. I was careful when I introduced myself to other groups for in this setting Britain was often referred to as 'Little Britain' or 'the Britain of Thatcher the Baby Killer'. In between calls from the Independent Peace Movement of Greece for an end to the occupation of Cyprus and calls from the Lebanese Communist Party for the removal of foreign forces from Lebanon, one of the members of the Scottish TUC expressed the idea of twinning Tripoli with Stornoway in the Outer Hebrides.

During the break the World Centre for Researches and Studies on the *Green Book* offered copies in 84 languages including Thai, Japanese, Chinese, a new edition in Russian and one in Serbo-Croat. I thought even Jackie Collins's agent could learn a few tips from The Great Leader. The New Jewel Movement from Grenada and the Caribbean Labour Solidarity asked me to write about the difficulties faced by the Grenadan revolutionaries, but before the former head of one of that Caribbean island's youth assemblies had finished lecturing me on the genesis, evolution and significance of the Grenada revolution a Central American group interjected. They said they needed British help to fight against repression in Central America. I asked the Nicaraguan delegation if they had received any support for their campaign. 'Yes, from ASLEF,' said their spokesman, referring to the British train drivers' union. They had at least found more support than either the Scottish TUC – who had come to Libya to seek links with Libyan workers only to be told 'there are no workers here, only partners' – or the Kurds, who were berated by one delegate for not organizing their working classes.

I travelled back to the El Kabir with a feisty Finnish woman. I was curious.

'Where are you from?' I asked.

'Beverly Hills.'

She described herself as an 'international vagabond'. I asked her to lunch but she had decided to go with the group on a tour to the minefields of Tripolitania. I had no desire to disturb mines that had lain in the desert since 1939. Instead I would renew my search for the Tuareg.

I did find one Tuareg family, not in tents in the desert but on the twelfth floor of a council estate. Our conversation was drowned out by the children's boom box that reverberated to the sounds of the rock group Iron Maiden. The parents suggested I try looking for the desert Tuareg in Ghadames, an oasis in the Sahara.

Tripoli has several 'museums', including Qadhafi's former house mangled by United States bombing. Plaster dangled from the ceiling and glass from the shattered windows littered the floor. Souvenir hunters will go away disappointed; the rubble that fell on the furniture and beds is encased in Perspex viewing boxes. The shrine's visitors' book, which was held open by a piece of shrapnel from one of the bombs that fell on the house, read like a *Who's Who* of the CIA's most wanted list: Presidents Daniel Ortega of Nicaragua and Hafez Assad of Syria, Isabel Peron, Yasser Arafat . . . I looked at the comment from the Organization of Islamic States: 'Interestingly barbaric and awful'. Muammar Al Qadhafi had survived an attempt on his life which the CIA would have called 'termination with extreme prejudice'. However, unlike plots against Fidel Castro, the CIA hadn't hired Mafia hit men, concocted exotic poisons or made exploding cigars. Instead Ronald Reagan launched a squadron of fighter-bombers against Qadhafi in April 1986 in a clear violation of both international and US law banning the assassination of foreign leaders. Not only did not one of the Pentagon's smart bombs have Qadhafi's name on it but a large number of innocent civilians were killed and maimed in the attack, including a baby girl whom Qadhafi later called his adopted daughter.

Qadhafi's close brush with martyrdom gave him added prestige. Before the US bombing raid Libya was called the Socialist People's Libyan Arab Jamahiriya. After the attack, in honour of the great victory over the forces of American imperialism, Qadhafi renamed his country the Great Socialist People's Libyan Arab Jamahiriya and a monument marking the victory is an added tourist attraction. It is an immense sculpture of a golden fist clutching a model of a US F-111, the one US plane they managed to shoot down during the bombing raid.

The only time I saw gun-toting revolutionaries was on Mourning Day. It had been planned for all communications to cease for the day. There would be no flights in and out of the country, telephones and telexes would be suspended and there would be no television. Even the street lights were to be extinguished and traffic was supposed to come to a halt. In reality the mourning did not seem to be universally observed by the people of Tripoli. Traffic jams were as much in evidence as usual and I didn't see many people wearing black mourning clothes or armbands. At the secondary school where we had gathered, everyone was again kept waiting. A military band, not dressed in revolutionary green but in sky blue, played several awkward tunes while dozens of members of the People's Militia swathed in bright green turbans and tunics with Pierre Cardin belts stood to attention. The groupies, anti-imperialists and journalists milled around waiting . . . They would have to wait a while longer. The Colonel didn't show up.

I eventually made it into the desert, or so to speak; it had been like waiting for Chelsea to score a hat-trick, only thankfully I didn't have to wait as long. There was no need for a four-wheel-drive vehicle as every major Libyan town is linked by a magnificent network of roads. There was also no chance of getting lost – you just follow the trail of rubbish. In fact, Libya is a social anthropologist's dream: he could decipher and date everything eaten since non-biodegradable packaging was introduced.

I travelled to Ghadames to meet the former head of the Ifarous Tuareg. Ghadames had once been an important trading centre whose influence extended from Niger to the Mediterranean. It had been a major crossroad where Tuareg, Roman legionnaires, Carthaginians, North African traders and sub-Saharan travellers met. In its bustling market African pottery had been bartered for salt, Spanish copper, Etruscan vases, Phoenician glass and painted fabrics. The Tuareg had also run a profitable trade selling black slaves from the south to Neapolitan and Berber traders.

Today the magnificent old town with its covered streets which provided the correct amount of shade to give natural air-conditioning but enough light to see one's way, and above the passageways the traditional houses which provided a perfect mixture of function with decoration, has been abandoned. The heart of the town has moved to ultra-modern housing estates and a network of wide open streets that provide no privacy but a large degree of anonymity. Schools and a hospital had brought hope for the future, unlike the under-stocked People's Supermarket which had replaced the souk. I looked at the almost empty shelves: Turkish laundry powder, boxes of Italian rice and tomato paste, Cuban cigars, Algerian washing-up powder, Indian tea and soap from Casablanca. The town's residents might be clean but they would be hungry.

Today's travellers were like Ahmed whom I met walking along the verge of the road that crossed the desert from the Algerian border. He had no belongings other than a blanket to wrap up in at night. He was unemployed with a family to support back in Algiers, and he had come to Libya in search of work. I gave him a lift and dropped him in town where heavy-turbaned Tuareg lounged in their smart sedans listening to Heavy Metal music broadcast from a coffee shop.

I met the former chief of the Ifarous tribe, Shawi Agh Lala, at my hotel. Indiscreetly I asked him his age. 'I've never spent a night in a hospital,' he answered. Then I asked him whether he preferred travelling by jet or camel. 'I prefer to travel by jet because it's quick and comfortable, but I like travelling by camel because you don't have so far to fall and when you do fall you don't hurt yourself.' Shawi Agh Lala had an honorary doctorate from Al Fat'h University and he liked life in the town; it was comfortable and his children were receiving an education. What he missed about the desert was the feeling of 'being tired'. Later, he told me his plan to solve the world's population crisis, and as part of the package of measures he was offering to take two British old-age pensioners into the desert with him.

Even in the remotest corners of Libya, the Colonel was omnipresent in the form of portraits and slogans. A sign in the desert read, 'Democracy means people's rule, not people's expression.' However, my driver for this excursion, Omar Azogi, had done more for Pan-Arabism than his revered leader. He had taken two wives: a Tunisian and an Egyptian. When I pressed him about the marital arrangements he sighed despairingly at my ignorance. 'Look, if you have two cars and one breaks down or has a puncture, you use the other car.'

There is much to see in Libya. I spent four days visiting magnificent Roman ruins, seaside villas with some of the finest mosaics in the world. All the sights had remained relatively untouched since the Vandals marched across Libya thirteen centuries ago.

When I returned to Tripoli and the El Kabir, I found the Australian journalist staring disconsolately into a half-empty glass of orange crush. I didn't have to ask; I already knew what had happened, or, more precisely, hadn't happened. The anti-imperialists, the international vagabond, the journalists had all stuck together in the lobby of the hotel, in a state of readiness waiting for the call from the Leader like firemen waiting for a fire. They had all trooped out together, expecting to see the Colonel at the opening of a new school, a new supermarket and a ceremony to mark the anniversary of the Battle of Hani. They had sometimes waited for hours, sometimes at night, sometimes during the day, but always in vain.

Qadhafi and his cohorts had more than one thing in common with SPECTRE in James Bond; in the lobby of the Kabir the Mass Democratic Movement handed me their manifesto signed 'The Struggle Continues, Victory is Certain'. Not only did they seek world domination through Machiavellian schemes, their leaders were equally elusive.

On the eve of Mourning Day the body of an Italian technician was found on the road leading from the city to the airport. He had been shot to death and his body set alight. A man from the Foreign Information Bureau called the killing an 'ordinary, criminal crime'. But suspicions lingered that the killing might have been carried out in a frenzy of anti-Italian feeling for the thousands of Libyans massacred and executed during the Italian occupation of Libya and for the thousands of prisoners who died on Italian soil from malnutrition, disease and freezing temperatures. The graves of many of the victims, like the ultimate fate of the Italian technician, remain unknown even today. Some speculated that the Italian was murdered to sabotage Qadhafi's campaign to pressure Italy for compensation. 'I'm sorry it happened,' said Qadhafi, who had finally agreed to give an interview to an Italian journalist. 'I hope he had life insurance.'

I found no hostility to foreigners and many Libyans remain Anglophiles. I met Libyans who quoted Charles Dickens or supported Watford Football Club, and on the eve of my departure I met a Tripolitan who commented whimsically in a Geordie accent on the similarities between Tripoli's street lighting and Regent Street's at Christmas. 'It's the same, only we don't have that woman from *Dynasty*, Joan Collins, to switch the lights on.'

The following morning as the plane climbed out across the shores of Tripolitania and over the Mediterranean, I asked the passenger seated next to me whether Qadhafi was likely to remain in power. He quoted Qadhafi: 'The last twenty years was merely an introduction to the revolution.' I thought how ironical that without oil, Western expertise, technology and finance, and without the British and American companies who continue to drill it, there would be no Qadhafi, no Green Revolution, no aiding and abetting of revolutionary and rebel movements which, like the IRA, often work against the interests of the very countries that help Qadhafi to finance his revolution.

13

THE TORTILLA
CURTAIN

> If you travel the world, it's full of people
> whose dream is to end up in the United
> States. There is no other country which
> captures to such an extent the imagina-
> tion of ordinary people.
>
> Sir Ralph Dahrendorf

Tijuana, January 1990

After fourteen months and more than a hundred flights I set myself
a New Year resolution: I would not travel anywhere until I had
completed writing the sequel to my first book. I would write it in the
seclusion of the tiny, remote Wiltshire hamlet of Upper Upham
where there would be few distractions. First, I had some loose ends
to tie up; I needed to go to the *Daily Telegraph* to chase up payment
for my Libyan article. Bernice, the *Telegraph*'s travel editor, suggested I join her for lunch on Friday at the end of the first week in
January 1990.

'Where would you like to go this year?' asked Bernice. It was a
fantastic offer that set my mind in motion, but I explained that I had
decided to stay in Wiltshire in order to write. 'How about three
weeks in Chile and Argentina – Patagonia in February?' she
offered. It was like showing a red cape to a bull. I had always
wanted to go to Patagonia, but I could also think of other places I
had dreamed of travelling to: Burundi, Angola and Cuba . . . It
wasn't that I no longer wished to see the dramatic glaciers of
Patagonia tumbling into the sea, but I was now more interested in
the human landscape – the downturn in the Argentinian economy.
I wanted to know how people coped with soaring unemployment

and monthly inflation in excess of one thousand per cent. At lunch we were joined by another editor, Marsha. She too was looking for a piece, 3,000 words for the front page of the Review section of the paper.

I told Bernice and Marsha about my friends like Cormac – whose family were originally from Ireland but who held British passports – from whom I had rented a council flat in Poplar and who were working illegally in the United States, and others like Qadir in Washington whose fourteen-year-old nephew had been smuggled from Kabul to Pakistan where he was now languishing in a refugee camp to avoid being conscripted into the Afghan army. Like millions of others, Cormac, Qadir and his nephew had something in common: they had dreamed of going to America. Cormac was in Los Angeles finding it increasingly difficult to get work without papers. Qadir and his family were desperately saving every penny in order to collect the $5,000 needed to pay smugglers to have the boy taken first to Germany and then from Germany to Mexico, where he would be smuggled across the border into the United States. For hundreds of thousands of would-be immigrants, the point of entry into the land of opportunity was no longer New York City's Ellis Island but Tijuana.

'When do you want to go?' asked Marsha.

'Sorry?'

'Can you leave tomorrow? I want you to file the story in two weeks' time.' It seemed too good an offer to miss. I thought of my resolution. I hesitated, but two days later I was on a plane bound for Los Angeles.

I had heard much about Tijuana; you could buy $21 Rolex watches, $18 Gucci watches; a friend of a friend had got married in a brothel one evening and divorced the next; and I was told that Tijuana had the world's largest floating population: two million in the day and one million at night, with the missing one million all trying to cross into the United States.

However, I had joined a different invasion, one which heads south every weekend in search of thrills and Margarita cocktails.

I rented a car from the Alamo agency and drove down Interstate 5 to San Diego and Tijuana. I joined thousands of youngsters in RVs –

recreation vehicles: four-wheelers, convertibles and compact sedans – who, unable to drink alcohol in the United States because the minimum legal age requirement in most states is twenty-one, were intent on getting 'primitive' in Tijuana where the minimum drinking age is eighteen.

As we approached the border, an enormous highway sign with flashing lights and bold letters warned us 'CAUTION: WATCH FOR PEOPLE CROSSING ROAD' – the only reference to the thousands of Mexicans and other nationals who try to enter the United States illegally every night. Many of them are desperate and, in a bid to avoid capture, run across eight lanes of sixty-five-mile-an-hour traffic. For anyone heading south into Tijuana there are no formalities at the border, but I had to leave my rental car in the US. I had been warned by the Alamo that under no circumstances was I to take the rented car into Mexico.

A hundred yards in, huge billboards gave advance notice of the good times and cheap drinks available in Tijuana. I shouldered my pack and headed for the centre of town along a route littered with empty tequila and beer bottles. Many youngsters I passed would not even make it to their Mecca, Avenida Revolucion; for they were already cradling enormous Margaritas in glasses the size of soup bowls.

Over 36 million people were checked across the border in both directions at Tijuana in 1988, and more than 50 million in 1989 – these figures only included the 'legals', which makes this not only the world's busiest land border crossing but, according to Tijuana's Chamber of Commerce, the world's most visited city. Few stay overnight; most spend three or four hours on 'El Main Street' – between meals, relying on bottled drinks. Even so, the problem of hotel accommodation was acute, and after several failed attempts to find a room in the centre of town I eventually obtained one in a flophouse in Tijuana's flea-and-cockroach infested Zona Norte, a crowded section of town next to the tourist district. In the event I didn't see my room or get to bed for the first two days. La Coahuila, the immediate area surrounding my flophouse, was home to the infamous coyotes or smugglers of *pollos*, literally chickens, migrant workers without visas wishing to cross into the United States. It has come to be known as 'the largest consulate in the world' because so many unofficial crossings are arranged here.

As dusk approached I went for a stroll along the Tortilla Curtain, the chain-link fence that separates Mexico from the United States. This part of the border, like much of the rest of California, Texas and New Mexico, once belonged to Mexico. The first reaction from the would-be immigrants, mistaking me for an American or possibly an agent for La Migra, the dreaded Border Patrol, was hostile. I explained I was from England. They now understood that maybe I too was joining them in search of the Promised Land. '¿Los Angeles?' they asked, the most popular destination for those crossing la frontera. One pollo equated England with Adolf Hitler. The right war but the wrong side, I explained, to which he answered in the only English he knew: 'Ay cabron, crazy mother-fucker.'

As night fell they came in their hundreds from every part of Mexico: mothers carrying their babies under their arms, parents holding their children's hands, young girls and young men on their own or in groups, many still in their teens. Chatting and joking they walked along the embankment of the Rio Tijuana Canal in preparation for crossing into the United States. Mexican hot dog stands selling tamales and tacos lined the route at intervals; street-sellers sold cigarettes and dustbin liners, which at first I thought were for the pollos' possessions, but most visitors to this Mexican Riviera had come empty-handed, with only the clothes they wore; the waterproof plastic dustbin liners were to tie around your feet and legs to protect you from the raw sewage and toxic wastes when wading across the knee-deep Tijuana River Canal.

One small group sat huddled together. They offered me the last few drags of a joint they were passing around. I declined; they laughed: '¿WHHass up, man?' They couldn't speak English but many had adopted the lingua franca of American inner cities. 'No shit man,' said an adolescent, holding a can of Coca-Cola up to me. As I passed another group squatting by a campfire they shouted, '¿WHHass happenin', man?'

Whilst they were limbering up to warm themselves against the night chill I noticed that most were dressed in similar fashion. They wore two pairs of trousers one over the other, trainers, sweatshirts and jackets and all had donned Gimme hats – baseball caps emblazoned with the embroidered designs of Gringolandia.

Roberto was typical of the army of undocumented migrants on this thin stretch of land that separates the most powerful nation in the world from one of the most indebted. Roberto was nineteen and had just arrived at the border after travelling for three and a half days by bus and truck from Hidalgo, south of Mexico City. He could not afford a coyote who, for $350–$400, would not only smuggle him across the border but arrange for his safe passage to his final destination – Los Angeles. Very few had jobs already arranged; those who did usually worked in the construction or service industries as labourers or cleaners, jobs arranged through friends or family already installed in El Norte or possibly held over from a previous visit. Roberto had no job to go to. I asked him if he knew it would be difficult to find work. He told me, 'I'll do anything. I'll wash dishes.'

Getting caught by La Migra wasn't much of a deterrent. Even though the Border Patrol had helicopters and light aircraft, horse and scooter patrols and a fleet of jeeps at their disposal as well as sophisticated surveillance equipment including a variety of pressure, magnetic and infra-red sensors and nightscopes that could pick out clusters of illegal aliens. Roberto, like others, told me that if he got caught, once he had been returned to the Mexican side of the border he couldn't afford to return home. He would try and try again until he succeeded. Two brothers, a twenty-five- and a twenty-eight-year-old, were proof of this; they had returned to the embankment to make a second attempt. The previous night they had made it as far as the glamorous lights of San Diego half an hour north of the border before being caught.

Increasingly many undocumented migrants turn to coyotes who will take them north on credit. Other coyotes will take them for nothing and sell them in turn to *polleros*, 'chicken sellers', who have arranged jobs for the pollos. So enslaved, the pollo will forfeit half his weekly salary to the pollero.

Every day as more and more people congregated here to flee underemployment and overpopulation, more holes appeared in the chain-link fence. Other sections were torn down either by sheer weight of numbers trying to cross or by accomplices.

The tens of thousands of Mexicans who had congregated along the border were joined by large numbers of Central Americans as well as South Americans and those from other depressed economies of the world in their bid to flee poverty, persecution, civil strife and war.

It seemed no one takes notice of two large signs installed on the border by the Mexican Baja California government that warned: 'BE CAREFUL. DANGER. THINK OF YOUR FAMILY'. This referred to the treacherous routes through Deadman's Canyon and Washerwoman Flats. The terrain was not dissimilar to that at border crossings I have made between Iran, Pakistan and Afghanistan where after sundown border bandits prey on the would-be immigrants knowing that they carry with them most of their worldly possessions. Large numbers of migrants are robbed, knifed, raped and murdered; most victims won't report attacks for fear of being deported.

The installation of new high-powered floodlights to illuminate a key swathe of the border (this followed the failure to build a controversial ditch) has made it more difficult for the undocumented immigrants to cross, but it has also made it more difficult for the bandits who prey on the migrants under cover of darkness.

Leaving the immediate border area for the heart of the tourist centre a different type of light was meant to attract rather than deter. On Friday and Saturday nights there are even more people on Avenida Revolucion than waiting in the shadow of the border. The sidewalks overflow with hawkers, gawkers, beggars and stalkers, while neon and syncopated flashbulb wizardry heralds an alcoholic nirvana.

The street is one twenty-four-hour fiesta with no siesta; its superhero and unofficial mascot is Captain Condom, a condom-headed caped crusader with the caption 'The World Has Never Needed Him More'. At the bottom end of Revolucion pimps beckon passers-by into the striptease clubs: 'Check it out! Check it out! Have a look! Pussy Galore!' Every block has its full quota of street-sellers: a cigarette seller who shouts, 'American cancer! American cancer!' and the ubiquitous Indians from Oaxaca in southern Mexico, descendants of the Mixtecas who speak not Spanish but their native tongue, and enough commercial English to make a sale – 'Three for one dollar!' I overheard a college-age kid ask one of the pimps for 'Spanish fly', which for centuries has had a reputation as an aphrodisiac that produces insatiable lust. As the name implies, it is an extract prepared from the dried body of a small insect and its reputation is based on the fact that it is a strong irritant of the urinary tract. I was later told that not only does Spanish fly not work, it can kill. Presumably the man dies with a hard-on.

From every building flags, banners and tequila touts spread the word: FREE TEQUILA WITH ANY BEER OR MARGARITA, TWO TEQUILAS FOR THE PRICE OF ONE, BEER FOR 50 CENTS. I began my tequila tour at Margarita Village. Two Corona beers later it was on to Viva Zapata! A Tecate and Dos Equis beer later I found myself at Escape. Here the young Americans had taken to Tequila Poppers, a shot of tequila mixed with a small dose of 7-Up. The potent potion is slammed down one's throat by a specialized bartender who proceeds to place the customer's jaw in an armlock. The bartender then tries to pry the young customer's head off his neck through rapid, jerking lateral movements. The effect has been described as somewhere between drowning, feeling very drunk very rapidly and whiplash. To remain conscious beyond three Tequila Poppers is something of a miracle. The customers, often very young and unaccustomed to alcohol, complained of being drugged.

Tijuana, or TeeJay as it is known affectionately by Americans, grew out of its northern neighbour's desire for entertainment and debauchery. If you were not intending to break someone's law, you were in the wrong town. During Prohibition Americans came here to drink. Al Capone, Douglas Fairbanks Jr, Clark Gable, Jean Harlow and the Aga Khan all patronized the lavish Agua Caliente resort and casino complex. During the Second World War nearly half the female adult population was employed in prostitution to service the large military bases at San Diego, and it was in Tijuana that Margarita Cansino became Rita Hayworth.

At that time the town could not boast more than 45,000 inhabitants; it has now grown dramatically to nearly 1.5 million. The population has doubled and then sextupled in recent decades and continues to grow at over double the national population growth figure for Mexico. However, the gold Louis XV chandeliers at the Agua Caliente resort have disappeared, as has the casino; their modern counterpart – television sets – hang from the ceilings of every bar and discotheque and many restaurants. During the night they are tuned to American MTV with its steady diet of pop videos, and during the day they show American wrestling.

Today, although casino gambling is forbidden, you can place a bet at Tijuana's racetrack (which was closed during my visit owing to a strike) or alternatively you can go to the Jai Alai stadium on Revolucion to have a flutter on this fast-moving game that has its origins in Spain. It was at the Jai Alai stadium during a break from the fifty-two discotheques and bars on Revolucion that I met an insurers' convention down from San Diego for a night of action. For Joe Bains and Fred Christian from the Raisin Bargaining Association, the couple from the Fremont Pickle and Tomato Growers and Janet Little from the Peach Canning Association it was probably an evening unlike any other.

Above all, the evenings were for young Mexicans and US high school and college students as well as for US sailors and Marines from nearby bases. They flocked to places like Las Pulgas (The Fleas) where they danced the Lambada and listened to Rock, Cumbia, Ranchero, the Merengue, Salsa and Gypsy music. Most of the Latin songs were about the guy who betrayed his best friend or the woman who left him. The variety of music was matched by the variety of African–American brothers' haircuts: Flat Top, Mohawk, Kwame. The owner told me that between 4,000 and 7,000 kids pass through the club every weekend night. The club was more rigorous about security than many European airports. 'We take care of the people; we confiscate knives and guns,' said the owner. He sold 300,000 beers a month and called his place 'the most democratic, cheapest disco for people who don't have money'. But Las Pulgas was also the place where for two dollars you could buy a *sexo in la playa* – sex on the beach – not the real thing, or maybe that as well, but a tequila mix. I could not but help admiring the beautiful blonde blue-eyed Mexican girls like Paty, a laboratory technician from Sonora, but at thirty-one I felt like a relic from the dinosaur age. At Baby Rock, a new club in Zona Rio, I entered a three-storey artificial cave with interior tropical vegetation and waterfalls that Fred and Wilma of the Flintstones might have commissioned had they won the pools. Tammy from Minnesota, who kept running her hands through her blonde locks, told me, 'It's fast; you can have a wild time for twenty dollars and I luuuv the chaos!'

By the end of the evening I had drunk so much tequila my breath would have distilled water. No one was ugly at 4 A.M.

I arranged to spend an evening on patrol with the Mexican Municipal Police. In the duty sergeant's office loud Mariachi music hollered from a radio set. I was mesmerized by a beautiful policewoman who wore a pair of Ray Bans, a leather jacket and bright red lipstick. She sat at an old typewriter. Behind her a sub-machine-gun hung from the wall and in the opposite corner of the room a television set on top of a filing cabinet played *Hooperman*, a US cop soap opera.

I went on patrol with Miguel Angel. He spoke good English and wore a miniature pair of handcuffs as a tie-pin. His ambition was to join the California Highway Patrol. By 2 A.M. the Mexican Municipal Police had their hands full. Revolucion echoed to the constant wail of police sirens as six patrol cars began to pick up the drunks. The cars had to weave in and out of four lanes of traffic to avoid drunks who staggered aimlessly across the middle of the road. Our squad car pulled up in front of three American teenagers who were kissing a young girl. She, or rather, to the Americans' embarrassment, he, proved to be a transvestite and was taken into custody by Miguel for abusive language – he turned out to be a minor. By the end of the evening the cops had detained 105 drunks. For our 3 A.M. coffee break Miguel double parked his squad car outside New York, a nightclub in La Cahuila, a bright neon oasis amongst dark, unlit streets of low-level buildings with peeling paint and crumbling plaster, home to bandits, thieves, smugglers, murderers, pimps and prostitutes. A barman showed us to a private cubicle on the first floor with curtains that opened to give an unobstructed view of the stage where '*bailarinas*' from Mexico and the Philippines performed from a manual of provocative dances that were meant to stiffen the parts other beers can't reach. We ordered several drinks. I went to pay for them. They were on the house.

Miguel had once worked for the feared Federales, the Mexican equivalent of the FBI. Here in Tijuana the Federales drove expensive American cars with Californian licence plates. The US consular officials in Tijuana didn't want to discuss this matter on the record. Miguel was more forthcoming: the Federales put in orders for specific models and car thieves delivered them within weeks. The Federales, although in theory undercover agents, could be spotted a mile away; they wore cowboy boots, sunglasses and the telltale sign was a bulge in the trousers where they kept their pistol. At the local Federal station they were less helpful than the Municipales. The desk officer was engrossed in a picture-book novella called *Sensación de Terror*; another lay on his desk, *Adulterio Satánico*. I waited to see an inspector who would show me a recent cache of arms that had been captured on the border; the haul included grenades, machine-guns and explosives. As I waited in the reception room several posters next to a crucifix caught my attention; below a picture of a young boy the caption read: $500 reward if found, Victor Cervantes Lopez, lost and mentally retarded, Sacramento, California. There was also a poster of a man wanted by the FBI, the Drug Enforcement Agency and the New York City Police. From what I had understood the Federales were a law unto themselves interested mainly in collecting extempore fines and 'physical measures to encourage talking'.

The rivalry between the Federales, Municipales and the Policia del Estado extended to Baja Californians and Mexicans from the capital, Mexico City. Miguel was openly distrustful of these last. 'Don't kill a man from Mexico City,' he advised, 'because if you do, five more will come to the funeral.'

In the early hours of the morning the route back to the border was littered with youngsters, their path lined with street-sellers and beggars. Unbridled debauchery exists side by side with destitution. Some Americans too drunk to walk to the border crossing might find a young Mexican to wheel them back in a supermarket trolley. Others, in a drunken haze, scavenged for souvenirs. One of the more popular trophies was a lifesize plastic piggybank of a human skull wearing a Second World War German helmet with a swastika; another was a larger than lifesize Big Mac piggybank. As they reached the border a six-year-old Indian boy played 'La Bamba' on a guitar as big as himself. A group of Americans gathered around him and joined in the singing; they tried to teach him to play 'Twist and Shout'. Another group began to throw dollar bills up in the air; there was a mad scramble as the beggar children fought over the unexpected windfall. One college kid told the Mexican children, 'My watch is more expensive than your wardrobe.'

A second wave of Americans followed the departure of the high school and college students. The naval servicemen from San Diego and the Marines from Camp Pendelton have a curfew, so only when it is lifted at 5 A.M. were they able to return Stateside.

It seems that everyone who goes to Tijuana has a desperate need to be someone else. Mexicans wishing to reach the US try to adopt the persona of a Hispanic American through a Green Card, asylum card or social security number. Guatemalans and Salvadoreans migrate to Tijuana in search of work (there is almost zero unemployment in Tijuana) but they must lose their Central American accents and buy false Mexican papers in order to do so. It is said that no one from the large Chinese–Mexican community in Baja California has ever died. A steady wave of Mainland Chinese is quick to assume the identity of anyone recently deceased so that, as with their Central American counterparts who have assumed a Mexican identity, any subsequent capture on entering the United States illegally won't mean deportation back to their homeland, just voluntary repatriation to neighbouring Mexico. And then there are the fourteen- to seventeen-year-old Americans who, providing they are tall enough to reach above the bar, present false IDs to enable them to get a drink.

An older group of Americans come to TeeJay for miracle AIDS and cancer cures; drugs that are unavailable in the United States can be bought freely over the counter including steroids and antibiotics. More than six million pills were confiscated on the US side of the border during 1989. Others descend on Tijuana for quickie divorces or to have their teeth or cars fixed; and childless couples from as far away as Oregon arrive on day trips in the hope of buying a child. 'It's quite incredible,' said a US consular official. 'A couple arrives here at the consulate and expects us to believe that they've come from Michigan on a day trip and the wife has given birth in Tijuana and they need papers for the child so that they can take the baby back into the States.'

But Tijuana is like no other town. Where else can you find an Islamic minaret, a Castilian tower, Chinese roofs, Spanish colonial,

Art Deco and French provincial architecture as well as a cocktail bar whose roof is a gigantic sombrero? Shanty towns where abandoned and rusting cars are embedded in a foot of dried mud continue to grow; every day a new hill is colonized and homes built of crude cardboard, tin and wood planks are reached by stairs of old stacked tyres alongside gullies which quickly become rivers of refuse and human faeces. When the children weren't performing Ranchero music on the local buses for a few pesos they played in the middle of what passes as a road but was also a stagnant pond of untreated sewage. But here, unlike any other shanty town I have visited, money from the north has helped towards the purchase of satellite dishes which have begun to appear on the corrugated tin and asbestos roofs of dilapidated shacks, bringing HBO – a US movie channel – and *I Love Lucy* into their homes with electricity often hijacked from the local grid.

The economic miracle that has taken place in Tijuana as multi-national companies have set up state-of-the-art factories (one in ten television sets in the world is now made in Tijuana) is due, like everything else, to its close proximity to the United States. But even in a city where numerous Help Wanted signs offer regular employment, it seems nothing can stop the tidal wave of undocumented migrants bent on entering the United States, and as each new dawn breaks, buses and planes disgorge more passengers who have travelled on a one-way ticket.

Every day a few miles from the border in southern California's San Ysidro US Border Patrol communications room a bank of computer monitors lights up as unidentified objects trigger sensors out in the field. Each new 'hit' sets off a flashing band of light, but within seconds a dozen bands begin to flash alternately; the computers looked like a video arcade; the operator alerts the nearest field agent to the immediate breakthrough: 'Sector 5 – we have one hit.' Within seconds that became two and then three and four hits. It could be a car or several pollos on foot. Meanwhile, another field agent called headquarters for assistance. He was alone and a group of ten or twelve pollos was heading his way. But the control room couldn't offer immediate help. 'We're swamped,' came the despairing reply from the control room operator.

When I went out in the late afternoon with Border Patrol supervisor Paul Franco, the scale of the influx became immediately apparent. On one hill just on the US side of the border nearly a hundred undocumented migrants were waiting to make their move north. Within hours the Border Patrol was chasing unidentified cars that had rendezvoused with their loads of pollos. On foot the Border Patrol gave chase through the local housing estates of San Ysidro and Chula Vista, and in jeeps they roared up and down the hard shoulders of the highway. The army of undocumented immigrants had become a locust, every which way you turned elderly couples, adolescents and middle-aged men and women were making their bid to cross the fine line that separated their dream from unmitigated poverty. When a hovering helicopter or jeep searchlight was turned on them a few young athletic ones made a frantic effort to escape. This often involved scrambling over high fences lizard fashion and, more dangerously, running across the dense fast-moving traffic on the freeway.

The horse patrol had apprehended a group of youngsters including two transvestites. In a housing estate Paul Franco spotted three young men who immediately made a run for it. He caught one of them, but lost the other two, or so I thought; it wasn't long before his well-trained eye spotted two sets of sneakers barely visible between the perimeter wall of a house and a bush. In an impossible space two youths were sandwiched one on top of the other. This led to a further arrest of a group of seven sitting in the back of a stolen car. Amongst the group was twelve-year-old Sonya from Mexico City *en route* to Los Angeles with her twenty-three-year-old brother. Her hair was matted and tangled from sleeping rough during the seven days it had taken them to reach the United States. Her voice was soft and rich with fatigue. They told me how they had set out from their home to reach Los Angeles to find work to send money home to their impoverished family. Sonya had hoped to work as a maid. Physically she was still a girl and it seemed incredible that an American family would employ her. But without questioning her further, for I didn't want to compromise her in front of the Border Patrol, I was sure she saw her present incarceration as only a temporary setback; she spoke with the determination of someone two or three times her age. Ten minutes later in a nearby parking lot thirty-five-year-old Jorge was looking for a ride north when he was spotted. He tried to escape between parked cars, but was apprehended and his wrists bound behind his back with soft plastic handcuffs. He was no stranger to the United States, he told me he was returning from the southern state of Oaxaca having spent his Christmas holidays with his family. He described the home that awaited him near the luxury residences and manicured lawns of the southern Californian town of Laguna Niguel. For the past three years Jorge had lived with a community of Mexican migrant workers in shacks made of felt paper, rubbish bags and scrap wood. He had earned a modest living as a construction worker, window washer and gardener. He didn't know if he would find work when he eventually made it back to his squalid camp near Laguna Niguel, and was equally concerned by rising racism and the violence of stabbings and shootings by US private citizens, law enforcement agencies and local non-Hispanic and Hispanic gangs that were increasingly threatening the lives of immigrant workers. Later as we cruised the highway towards San Ysidro, Paul Franco caught a couple wandering in the darkness. They looked lost and dazed in the jeep's headlights as he went to arrest them.

Herman and Luisa were grandparents several years beyond European or North American retirement age, but penniless with no savings, pension or medical insurance, and since their children and grandchildren were too poor to support them they planned to start life all over again. Confused and bewildered, they climbed into a Border Patrol jeep that would take them back to the control centre where they would be processed conveyor-belt fashion. Their names and ages, home addresses and marital status would be noted and filed and they would spend the rest of the night in one of several huge concrete cells with dozens of others who were neither among the 700,000 legal Mexican immigrants, the 1.2 million amnestied under special legislation or the 1 million agricultural workers legalized by the US between 1980 and 1989. It didn't matter how far the illegal immigrant had penetrated within the United States or how long he or she had stayed – and there are fines for employing immigrants without a Green Card permitting the holder to work in the United States – the apprehended Mexican illegals would be returned 'voluntarily' to Mexico the following morning. Other nationalities would face the lengthier process of deportation to their home country. Sonya and her brother, Jorge; Herman and Luisa would become statistics, evidence of the underlying trend of massed illegal immigration to the States; but I was also sure they were united in the desire and determination to try once more to reach their common goal and the distant dream of full employment.

By the end of the evening shift from 3 to 11 P.M. the Border Patrol had apprehended 1,300 illegal aliens (47% up on the same day from the previous year). Included amongst them were twenty-two OTMs (other than Mexicans) from thirteen different countries (including seven from Guatemala, one Honduran, a Brazilian and a West German).

During 1989 this Border Patrol apprehended would-be immigrants of seventy-two nationalities on the San Diego sector, including nationals from Portugal, Ecuador, Poland, Egypt, Ivory Coast, Guyana, China, Pakistan, India, West Germany, Australia and Great Britain. In all nearly 370,000 Mexicans and OTMs were apprehended, slightly down on the previous year, and, incredible as these figures seem, the Border Patrol estimates that for every illegal immigrant arrested, up to six avoid apprehension.

While walls that separated people were coming down around the world this was one wall that no one, least of all American officials, wanted to discuss, even if, in the words of Paul Franco, there were holes large enough to 'drive the *Queen Mary* through'.

In addition to the arrests of illegals, there were enormous seizures of narcotics, firearms, large quantities of cash and stolen vehicles, the figures on which were carefully reported to me as I was being driven back to the car that I had rented in Los Angeles. The lists were fascinating, increasingly so as we spent some time looking for my Mitsubishi Mirage. The name was purely coincidental, but I never did find it: the Mirage had become another statistic as it too joined the ever growing list of stolen cars.

After my evening with the US Border Patrol I returned to my hotel on the Mexican side of the border. When I left TeeJay I was stopped by a streethawker who had cursed me – '*Hijo de chingada!* [Son of a bitch!]' – the previous day for taking his photograph. Seeing I was leaving, he spoke to me in English. He behaved like an oversized version of Grumpy in *Snow White and the Seven Dwarfs* and wore a Corona (beer) University sweatshirt. He sold jewellery that was displayed on a velvet mat across his forearm like a *maître d'hôtel*'s napkin. '*¿Que pasa carnal?* Man, you gonna send me my picture?' – 'How can I send it to a street corner?' I asked, surprised by his sudden affability.

'I just come down here to sell jewellery to the tourists. In the evening I go home to Chula Vista on the US side of the border for cushi cushi with my woman and do the San Diego clubs where I play jazz.'

I agreed to send him his picture. As I walked to the border a beggar approached me. 'Can you spare some change?'

'I don't have any.'

'That's what they all say.'

Beyond him was a man on his knees burrowing a channel like a badger with his hands under the chain-link fence near a section of disused railway line. Over the past ten days I had watched people tunnel, squeeze and climb across the border fence and have their bodies squashed into car boots in a variety of positions known previously only to the *Kama Sutra* and the Spanish Inquisition. I photographed the burrowing man. He stopped for a moment to consider his predicament. Without a trace of self-pity he said, '*La pobreza de la humanidad* [the poverty of mankind]'.

A small group of demonstrators, amongst them Americans from north of the border, carried placards and shouted well-versed mantras: GRINGOS OUT OF PANAMA! YANKEES OUT OF EL SALVADOR! ¡VIVA F.M.L.N.! ¡MUERA EL IMPERIALISMO! (Death to Imperialism!) ¡VIVA LA HEROICA LUCHA DEL PANAMENO! (Long Live the Heroic Panamanian Struggle!) A group of local shopkeepers had gathered to watch the protesters pass. One of them turned to me: 'We used to shout "Yankee, go home!" Now they should be shouting "Yankee, go home and take me with you."'

I returned to LA by coach. Well, East LA or, as the bus conductor told the passengers, *Este Los Angeles*. I was the only 'Anglo' and during the journey we were treated to nothing but Mariachi music. We were dropped *entre la calle San Pedro e la calle San Julian* in East LA. In fact, it was some minutes, past mobile taco stands and bilingual shops, before I reached my first all-Anglo sign, 'Freddie's

Beer and Girls', by which time I had been offered a bus transfer ticket at half price and for $2 a phone access code that would enable me to call anywhere in the United States. But this was not the Promised Land that the undocumented migrants had envisaged.

Every day hundreds of undocumented Mexicans like Ruben stand on the sunbaked streets of Los Angeles waiting for work. He had spent three years in Los Angeles as an illegal alien. He had two children, one he had never seen. He told me he would work for $35 a day; sometimes he would work for nothing if he was given a meal. In Mexico he worked as a cook for between $25 and $28 dollars a week. Here, he told me, he was lucky if he got two days' work a week, but he had no intention of returning to Mexico even though, living in squalor in a room with ten men, he had virtually no hope of regular employment.

There were more fortunate ones, like Estella who worked as a maid in Beverly Hills. She was smuggled across the US/Mexican border in the boot of a car with five others. When she first arrived she spoke no English and her employer spoke no Spanish. But Beverly Hills bookshops do a brisk business in 'indispensable guides for those who speak little or no Spanish and must communicate with the Spanish-speaking household help'. *Home Maid Spanish* contains simplified instructions in Spanish for cleaning the house and child care: This is the automatic dishwasher; Polish the silver; Have you ever shopped in a supermarket? This is very valuable, please be careful when you handle it. Estella had, however, quickly learnt the words give, put, clean, scrub, wash, polish, fold, store, empty, starch, wax, dust, rinse and vacuum.

Sadly, many had crossed one frontier, an international boundary, only to face another frontier – those that exist within our own society, neighbourhood and even household.

Once Mexicans reach the United States some become acronyms, such as SAWs (seasonal agricultural workers) and RAWs (replacement agricultural workers). Foreigners caught on the wrong side of the border and unable to return to the States are called beached whales. The gap in time and distance across a short stretch of borderland is immeasurable. Tijuana's vibrant unchecked growth is replaced by California's post-industrial high-tech organization. There is an ambivalence in America's attitude to the influx of

Mexicans, and talk of California becoming the first high-tech Third World country. One Californian woman asked, 'Why don't we just buy Mexico? It could become the fifty-first state.' Mexicans, on the other hand, point out that some 3.5 million Mexicans, or about five per cent of Mexico's 1980 population, had come permanently to the States over the last decade, and they have a wry smile and a glint in their eye when they tell you that in this new era of national uprisings and secessionist movements, 'Many countries have come to dominate areas that once upon a time didn't belong to them.' For the moment the reality seemed to belong to the young child on the Tijuana bus to the Central Camionera, the coach station, who sang:

> I dreamed of money in the bank,
> And of driving a Cadillac.
> I married a blonde, hoping I'd become a US citizen
> – but she turned out to be a pollo, too,
> And now I'm back home, driving my burro.

The owner of Las Pulgas has his own solution: 'Tijuana needs more bars, so that more people can get drunk and forget reality.'

A year later revellers heading south to Mexico would have spotted a new highway sign as they approached the border: a triangle with three figures in black. The road sign, depicting a family of three sprinting in different directions, is to warn drivers of the increasing number of illegal immigrants so overwhelmed by the traffic that they promptly get run over. In fact, in the year since my visit more than 127 were killed near San Clemente alone. A helpful local highway patrolman was quoted as saying, 'People are so confused they run in all directions. It's like a pinball machine, you just don't know which way they're darting.'

14

HEAVEN'S WAITING
ROOM

> If the rich could hire other people to die
> for them, the poor could make a won-
> derful living.
>
> Yiddish proverb

MS Vistafjord, *the Arab and Indian Oceans, March 1990*

After Mexico -- well, more accurately, after Mexico, Belgium and
two visits to the United States in the first two months of 1990 – I
knew I would have to settle down if I was going to finish my book. I
collected my notes from my studio, a former Salvation Army
meeting hall in Brixton, rather grandly called the Citadel, even if it
had no heating and a leaking loof – and prepared to return to the
seclusion of my parents' house in the Wiltshire hamlet of Upper
Upham.

As I zipped up a heavy holdall full of notes written on everything
from boarding cards, airline tickets and postcards to scraps of loose
paper, the telephone rang. I was in two minds as to whether to
answer it. It continued to ring. I hesitated while my mind conjured
up some of the possibilities: an accident in the family, an Afghan
who had made it to London, an assignment. I answered the phone.

I heard the click of an international telephone connection. 'May I
speak to Nick Danziger, please?' The 'Danziger' was drawn out and
I guessed the gentle voice was American.

'Joanne O . . .'

'Joanne,' I interrupted rather abruptly, but I didn't know any
other Joannes and I immediately recognized the voice as that of the
woman who had hired me for the QE2 lectures.

'What are your plans for the next month?' By now I should have recognized the first symptoms of my fatal addiction to offers of travel. Maybe I should have hung up, at least made an excuse that I had a plane to catch, was late for a family funeral or for the wedding of my best friend.

'I'm hoping to get on with writing my book,' I said, sincerely but without much conviction.

'Will you be free for the last two weeks in March?' I had a premonition and it didn't have me sitting at a desk deep in the Wiltshire countryside. 'For a world cruise,' she added.

'Sorry?' I said lamely, wishing this was a bad dream that would go away.

'Part of a world cruise – you would join the *Vistafjord* in Bombay,' said Joanne.

'Bombay,' I repeated dreamily, my head beginning to fill with images of the city. I looked out of the damp studio's misted windows.

'Bombay, the Seychelles, Mombasa, Durban,' said Joanne. I felt myself sinking. I was already high on place names; travel ran like blood through my veins.

'First-class cabin?' I asked firmly, knowing that if they wanted me badly enough this wasn't an unreasonable request. After all, I had been spoilt on the *QE2* and, chuckling to myself, I reasoned that I now had standards to maintain.

'First-class cabin, sailing from Bombay on 14 March 1990, and you can collect your airline tickets from British Airways,' said Joanne, 'I'll send you the details in a fax.'

My publishers were expecting twelve chapters by September, and I had barely begun. The two chapters I had finished were written between trips to Libya, the United States and Mexico. Mexico made it thirteen chapters and, according to this routine, if I was to include the world cruise the book would never be completed.

Bombay, I thought to myself. The name conjured up images of suffocating humidity, streets a whirlpool of slender dark bodies, the notorious cages for prostitutes, a rich tapestry of languages, religions, temples and mystics. I also knew that joining a ship would allow no more than the most cursory of glances at the teeming metropolis.

* * *

I met two other guest lecturers at Heathrow Airport, Sally Ann Howes, the singer and actress and star of the film *Chitty Chitty Bang Bang*, and Martin Smith who had recently finished starring as the phantom in Andrew Lloyd Webber's musical *Phantom of the Opera*. We left London after lunch and reached Bombay in time for breakfast.

As we emerged from the customs hall we were besieged by a group of scrawny, hungry-eyed boys and young men.

'Mister! Mister! English! American!' They were tugging at Sally Ann's jacket sleeve. 'Bags? Hotel? Taxi?' they beseeched.

They had closed in on us. They took charge of our trolley. They took charge of procuring a taxi, of loading the bags. We tried to keep count of our bags: one, two, three . . . one, two, three, four, five . . . Had they all been loaded into the boot of the taxi? One, two, three, four . . . How many bags were on the front seat? Where were our carry-on bags? Was this some elaborate sting operation?

The scrawny boys didn't want Indian rupees, they wanted US dollars, but they would take pounds sterling.

Bombay hit me like no other city; at night the sandy beaches of Rio turn into dormitories, the New York subway turns into a dormitory, but the whole of Bombay turns into one massive dormitory – 2½ million people are said to find their home on the pavements of a city that is half as big again as London. Our taxi driver informed us that even amongst this seeming chaos, there was order, everyone's sleeping place was strictly assigned.

Our driver kept his hand on the shrill honking horn as our old Viscount automobile weaved in and out of gaunt men naked to the midriff with sleep still in their eyes as they crossed the road. Cantonment after cantonment passed by in a haze of brittle tumbledown shacks, groups of street sleepers huddled together under a single sheet. Cooking fires, kerosene lamps, buckets and bullocks all merged into one massive campsite. And each new dawn the legions of immigrant families continued to arrive.

I don't know whether Arthur Koestler entered Bombay by the same route thirty years before but as he got out of his chauffeur-driven car a wall of heat and dust hit him. He described the stench of sewers as akin to 'a wet, smelly diaper being wrapped around my head'. Sally Ann, Martin and I stepped out of our taxi into the air-conditioned Taj Mahal Hotel opposite the Gateway to India, an enormous arch commemorating George V's visit to the city in 1911.

As the three of us stood at the reception counter in the Taj's lobby I was struck by its reassuring pre-First World War atmosphere.

'How can I help you, Madam?' said the receptionist to Sally Ann.

'I would like a room, please.' It was not yet six o'clock and the sun had still to break through the early-morning mist.

I could tell the receptionist was beginning to feel awkward. Martin and I were clearly with Sally Ann. She looked too young to be our mother, but too mature to be our sister. Did she want a single room, a double room or separate rooms? He hesitated. 'One room, Madam?'

'Yes.'

'A double?'

'If you haven't got a double room, we will share a single,' said Sally Ann, turning towards Martin and then me with theatrical innuendo.

'Hhuh-h.' The receptionist tried to clear his dry throat. A bead of sweat trickled from his neatly cropped sideburn. 'How long will you be staying?'

'Just for the day.'

The key to room 716 jingled as he nervously handed it to the bellboy.

The bellboy led the way. Sally Ann followed with Martin, myself and a porter, a train of suitcases and suit bags in tow.

We had to join the MS *Vistafjord* in the evening. There was not much time, but we had the whole day ahead of us and Martin suggested we visit exotic Elephanta Island with its Hindu caves. We crossed Bombay Harbour by motor launch from the Gateway of India.

'You will not be able to see the island because of the mist,' our guide explained. 'Nor,' she continued, 'should you expect to see any elephants. There aren't any.'

'What about the stone elephant at the pier?' asked a fellow tourist looking up from his guide book.

'It was smashed by the Portuguese many years ago.'

It wasn't an auspicious start.

* * *

Like the Gateway to India, Elephanta expected tourists. The locals were waiting for the arrival of fair-skinned travellers, like vultures hovering over carrion. Grown men followed you like abandoned animals who would not go away until distracted by a few morsels of charity. Their wretched lives were so tied to foreigners' largesse that the sale of one picture postcard meant a stay of execution from the virulent pain of a hungry stomach.

There were many steps leading up to the hilltop caves. For 40 rupees bearers would carry you to the top in a palanquin. Sally Ann elected to be carried. At the entrance to the caves the bearers asked her for 100 rupees.

'We agreed 40 rupees!' Sally Ann protested.

'Double weight – 100 rupees.' It wasn't so much the hurt of being double-crossed as the injured pride.

'What was it like?' asked Martin.

'It was like riding a camel,' said Sally Ann. I thought it was more like being taken for a ride.

The most impressive statue was the three-headed Trimurti, depicting the triple aspect of Hindu divinity (Brahma, Vishnu and Shiva). Our group stood in front of the spectacular figure hewn from the cave's natural stone. 'Twelve hundred years ago,' the guide's voice rippled against the wall carvings, 'the followers of the Hindu God Shiva carved this temple out of the solid rock.'

'Sounds like a fairy tale to me,' said an American tourist. His wife elbowed him in the stomach.

The guide continued without further interruptions. She pointed to the decay, which she blamed on changing global weather patterns. She also told us that the scientist who planned the nuclear reactor opposite Elephanta Island had done so to contrast artificial energy – the reactor – with pure energy – the captivating sculptural reliefs and columns of the caves. The material world seemed all too aptly captured in the sign for tourists above a nearby snack stand that read BREAD, BUTTER AND JAM.

We spent the rest of the day touring Bombay in a taxi. Our driver pointed to a row of tall, modern, concrete tenements. 'They're so small compared to your apartments,' he sighed.

'What's the population of Bombay?' I asked.

'Too many people, too much pollution, too little sanitation,' he answered.

We ate the most delicious meal at the hotel: fresh shrimps, sizzling lamb and delicacies wrapped in vine leaves. For a moment I forgot the beggars outside.

As we drove to the quayside to join the pristine ship we passed the masses, like pigeons, already homing in on their stone beds as if they were invisibly marked with each person's name. Untended monuments, alleyways, roofs, shopfronts, alcoves – no nook or cranny was too poor or too ghastly to rest one's head.

The *Vistafjord* was much smaller and more intimate than the *QE2*. There were two pools instead of four and fewer restaurants and shops. But if you didn't have a bank account with savings that ran to as many digits as an international telephone number this was no place to be unless you were one of the Scandinavian pursers, German cabin stewardesses, Honduran waiters, Polish musicians, or one of the three Chinese brothers in the laundry room called Number One, Number Two and Number Three. Forty-two different nationalities worked on the ship. Amongst the passengers were Miss New Jersey 1932 as well as a family of ten: a mother-in-law, two aunts, an uncle, three children and their tutor, and of course the parents. The four-and-a-half-month, five-continent world cruise, without extras – tips and tours – would not have left the family much change out of a million dollars. The passengers were mainly American or German with a smattering of British and South African. Most had retired. The ship also had a Bishop, a Father and a Rabbi on board, plus four caskets and a mortuary in case of the last of life's eventualities. One passenger had already passed away since the *Vistafjord* left New York three months before.

If you were a passenger and not old enough to qualify for a London Transport bus pass, you were treated as a drug dealer, pimp or money launderer, or thought to have connections with the Mafia. Apart from the three children, there was only one young passenger on board. He was a twenty-two-year-old self-made German tycoon – an industrialist.

Dinner was not always Formal Dress, but it was always a ceremony. Unofficially a formal evening was known as a red, green or blue day. Red was for rubies, blue for sapphires and green for emeralds and St Patrick's Day. The ladies spent their days having their hair re-gilded, their nails manicured and polished to a flawless sheen. Just thinking about how much time it took them to get ready for dinner made me tired. They stood in the dining-room doorway waiting for the admiring glances. When their presence had been noted they would advance slowly and gracefully between the tables with the *maître d'hôtel* as escort. With the barest royal nod of the head they would acknowledge those who noted their presence. This was the visual cross-fire of brand names: Jean Muir and Yves Saint Laurent, Giorgio Armani and Gucci, Hermès and Christian Dior, Gianni Versace and Chanel, Cartier and Van Clef and Arpels. They already wore the only prizes: strings of shimmering pearls, sparkling diamonds and precious stones the size of pigeons' eggs.

Suggested dress for our first night at sea was something 'Raj' – tailored dresses from Hong Kong, Thai silk from Bangkok and Singapore, saris and Indian silk from Bombay. Sally Ann wore a crimson dress with arm-length gloves that were likely to give some of the older men cardiac arrest, but she knew how to take the muted applause from her admiring audience. Sally Ann always looked quite splendid, elegant and controlled.

At our table the other men would stand to attention as Sally Ann was helped into her chair by Martin or myself. Once seated they returned to their seafood salads. Emanuel, our Portuguese waiter, darted forward brandishing a gigantic menu the size of an atlas's endpapers; the wine waiter produced a bottle of our favourite wine for inspection; and light conversation was exchanged. The waiters moved with elasticity to carry out our orders. Then once we were served, they hovered with second helpings of meat, fish, vegetables and salads. You never had to raise your hand. The waiters were always there, hovering, and there were always seconds and thirds and fourths. You could dream yourself into a heavy cholesterol problem just by looking at the rich food.

Passengers called on one another to catch up on the latest gossip. A regular caller at our table was a loud and confident woman from Boca Raton, Florida, called Mary Lou. She was of indeterminate age and her hair was of no real colour. She must have been blonde once and extraordinarily beautiful. Her companion was introduced to us as Harold. Mary Lou held Harold on her arm; he was thickset with a mop of brown hair and a large paunch. He never spoke and he wasn't wearing 'Raj'; Harold was a cuddly toy gorilla. 'It's Harold's turn tonight,' Mary Lou explained. 'He gets awfully jealous if Mildred is seen in the dining room too often.' I wondered who Mildred was. Was she a red evening friend or a blue evening friend? Mildred turned out to be a companion for Harold. Mary Lou explained that Harold had been lonely ever since her father had bought him as a present for her. Mildred and Harold, at Mary Lou's expense, later adopted a Tasmanian Devil called Fluffy.

Mary Lou lived in a $96,000 cabin with a private balcony. Harold, Mildred, Fluffy and her wardrobe had an adjoining cabin for the same price. It crossed my mind that I could do worse than become a cuddly toy for four and a half months a year. Mary Lou, Harold and Mildred had joined the ship in Fort Lauderdale and had sailed through the Caribbean, the Panama Canal, across the Pacific to Honolulu and the South Pacific to the Gilbert Islands, the Solomon Islands, New Caledonia, Australia, Papua New Guinea, the Philippines, Hong Kong, Singapore, Phuket off Thailand, the Maldives and Goa. We were now heading across the Arabian Sea to our next destination, Mahé in the Seychelles.

Most of the passengers were glad to have left Bombay and India behind. The Harrisons from Palm Springs, California, told me that they had overdosed on temples. 'I thought I was going to be ill if I had to look at another goddamn temple,' said Phyllis Harrison. Rose Madison had seen a photograph of the Taj Mahal. The real thing wasn't an improvement, she said, regretting the $1,800 she had spent on a two-night tour to the imperial city of Agra. On St Patrick's Day, forty-eight hours after we had sailed out of Bombay, a comedian jollied the passengers along. We all knew what they had thought of the stench of poverty in Bombay. The comedian announced to an audience bedecked in emeralds, 'After we left Bombay an atom bomb was dropped on the city.'

The audience fell silent in horror.

'It caused $10 worth of damage!' They roared with laughter.

I wanted to cry, but then the passengers had raised a total of $8,651.64 in cash plus 319 rupees and three large boxes of clothing for Sister Leonie and Sister Janette of the Missionaries of Charity in Bombay.

An émigré virtuoso violinist followed the comedian. He spoke in heavily accented English.

'Is easy,' he said, introducing himself. 'Just remember my name is LOVE.' He repeated, 'My name is: THAT IS LOVE – my name is VLADISLAV.' He continued, 'Tonight I play for you; I play request for eighty-year-old woman who has request for her one-hundred-and-four-year-old mother!' The eighty-year-old great-grandmother and the one-hundred-and-four-year-old great-great-grandmother took to the dance floor like ducks to water. I hoped I would have as much energy when I reached their age.

As I walked to my cabin after a nightcap, I overheard a query outside one of the ship's lifts: 'Is this to protect your millions or to invest your millions?'

The *Vistafjord*'s newsletter informed us that the Seychelles had been variously called the 'Forgotten Islands', 'Lost Eden' and 'Forgotten Paradise' but they were anything but forgotten. Since the first settlers, '*les grands blancs*', arrived with slaves in 1770, little had changed. Two centuries later *les grands blancs* were the passengers from three enormous cruise ships. I joined the ship's American Express tour to Moyenne Island.

American Express took on a new but appropriate meaning. We left Mahé at ten o'clock and would have to be back at the quayside by four, a total of six hours. 'Above all, relax!' said our guide. 'This is not a tour for those in a hurry.'

The sun burned out of a cloudless blue sky. I squinted in the clear light. The sea was like glass, at once translucent and reflective. The coral islands hovered in the heat haze.

For the sail-away party from the Seychelles Tony and Roman's Polish musicians became Tony and Roman's Beach Boys. I had been on board the ship for four days. So far Tony and Roman had been billed as an orchestra, a Leprechaun trio, a brass band and an ensemble. Mary Lou's friend Edith wore a special hat for the occasion: an enormous shocking-pink floppy-brimmed hat that made a cowboy's ten-gallon look like a pimple on an elephant's bottom. Passengers searched for souvenirs during their port visits like junkies looking for a fix. Mr Harrison had bought himself a T-shirt with the slogan MAHÉ IS PARADISE. He told me he was collecting T-shirts. The next day I saw him wearing another This is Paradise T-shirt – GRAND CAYMAN IS PARADISE said the slogan, and later still there were others: Tarawa, Noumea, Phuket and Male in the Maldives all belonged to the same club. One of the pursers who hadn't been able to go ashore because she had helped supervise the loading of palm fronds for the sail-away party commented, 'Another shitty day in paradise.' The day's film *Mutiny on the Bounty* reflected wishful thinking.

I slipped into a pattern: some swimming and a stroll on deck past passengers asleep in deckchairs with a copy of a John le Carré or Len Deighton spy thriller resting on their noses for protection against the sun. I gave up trying to seduce one of the ship's 'hot tickets' – dancers Zizi, Joni, Julee and Dianna; they already had boyfriends or relationships with the crew. At dinner I waffled about a good Australian Chardonnay. Wine was a safer topic than pearls unless the wine came from South Africa; Martin and I were asked why we wouldn't order South African wine, but our answer fell on deaf ears.

I tried to stay away from controversial topics as much as was humanly possible. As usual during my lectures I showed slides. While I waited for the passengers to settle into their seats I heard Mr Wilson who sat at our dining table tell his wife not to wake him if he fell asleep. There were several coughs during the lecture and three passengers left to go to the toilet, but they returned. Mr Wilson didn't fall asleep, but an elderly gentleman in the front row was snoring before I began. He slept soundly through the whole lecture, but was woken by the applause at the end and joined in enthusiastically. During question time after the second of my four lectures, the ship's Rabbi asked me if I had been approached by Western intelligence agencies. I hadn't. I added that I didn't always agree with the West's attitude towards the developing world. After the lecture I was approached by an extremely angry woman whose delicately sculpted hair was the colour of stainless steel. She told me proudly she could trace her ancestry back to the early years of the American Republic. Her narrow-mindedness made me think that the last time a member of her family had travelled outside the continental USA must have been in the bridal suite on the *Mayflower*.

'What's so great about the East?' She was gathering her rage. 'Don't you think religion is keeping these countries backward?'

'Excuse me, Madam,' I said politely, 'I think you misunderstood me. I wasn't making comparisons.'

'Let me tell you something. Immigrants are ruining our country, and what's left of it the Japanese are buying.' Had her family not once been immigrants, and what about overseas American investments, which are substantially higher than the holdings of foreigners in the US? Besides, the British and the Dutch had much bigger investments in the States than the Japanese, but I wanted no part in this argument.

'And,' she pointed a finger at me accusingly, 'name me one religion that has built more hospitals than Christianity?'

I found Martin at the bar.

'I have this wonderful beach house in Laguna Niguel. Something mine and not daddy's or mummy's.' The man speaking to Martin was seventy.

I repeated my conversation with the woman who traced her ancestry back to the founding of the Republic and had a profound dislike of immigrants.

The man from Laguna Niguel didn't give Martin a chance to speak. 'I can't help being anti-Semitic, that's the way I was brought up,' he told us happily.

I had always thought that sex was the greatest leveller. But on board the *Vistafjord* the greatest equalizer was the ship's self-service laundry room. Here, the Bishop, the Rabbi and the anti-Semite, in probably the only launderette in the world where you will find millionaires (who had paid tens of thousands of dollars for a cabin but wouldn't spend extra money on the laundry service) made their peace amongst the tumble-dryers and washing machines. The wives were quite happy to leave their husbands in charge of the washing, but they had to be coached through the loading and unloading.

'Now Marvin,' said a wife patiently to her husband, 'when the clothes are dry take them out of the dryer.'

'When will that be, dear?' asked Marvin.

'When it's dry.' Marvin's wife was already into the ship's corridor.

'Are we talking one minute or one hour?' cried Marvin after his wife.

Martin had an altogether unexpected reason for calling in the laundry service. He had put his back out and his cabin stewardess told him Number Two in the laundry room gave a great massage. Number Two arrived in Martin's room with his two brothers: Number One, the eldest of the three, and Number Three, the youngest. Number Two had until recently been one of the senior physicians in a Shanghai hospital, but he earned more working in the *Vistafjord*'s laundry room than as a top doctor in Shanghai. He stretched Martin out on the floor and asked him to point out where and how the pain hurt him. Then Number Two set to work, pressing the tips of his fingers into Martin's back and neck. 'Relax!' said Number Two. Martin's muscles eased and Number Two's fingers began to waltz across his shoulders. 'Ahhh! That feels good,' sighed Martin.

'Ahhh! That feels good,' sighed Numbers One, Two and Three in unison. They were a match for Tony and Roman's Polish Leprechaun Trio.

I returned to my cabin to find a plate of assorted tea cakes and a note from one of the German cabin stewardesses. 'You hardly had any time for lunch, so I thought you might like some cake for the afternoon. Don't work too hard.' It was signed Christine.

Every day the stewardesses emptied the cabin's wastepaper baskets and ashtrays. Every day they vacuumed the carpet, dusted the artists' prints, desk and furniture. They scrubbed and polished the bathroom and the living-room-cum-bedroom. Finally they sprayed air freshener on everything and replenished the bowl of tropical fruit next to the television set. Their salaries were pitifully low and they counted on passengers' tips. The stewardesses were unanimous that the British were the least generous.

I began to make plans for Mombasa. We would dock in Mombasa at 8 A.M. on 23 March and sail the following day at 2 P.M. That left one and a half days for sightseeing. I looked through the *Vistafjord*'s

American Express excursions; tours 130, 131 and 132 were to Kenya's game reserves. Starting prices began at $1,274 – a snip compared to the 3½-day $3,398 tour of Noumea and New Zealand and the 4-day $2,502 plane and motor coach tour of Kathmandu and Bangkok. My eye was caught by tour number 139 to Mombasa's old Arab Quarter, Dhow Harbour and Fort Jesus, and to watch the Akamba wood carvers at work; at $36 it was within my price range. However, the tour was marked with a red dot. Red dot tours, it was explained in the brochure, were recommended for seasoned travellers only: 'Coaches and/or accommodation may be poor, local guides may be inadequate, aspects of the itinerary could prove difficult, and weather conditions may be uncomfortable.' Tour 139 came with an additional warning: the motor coaches were 'not air-conditioned and usually sub-standard; they might not have loudspeakers, and few trained guides are available.' Not surprisingly, there were still places on tour 139. Tours 130, 131 and 132 were fully booked. The family of ten could add $12,740 to the $17,290 they spent in India and the $29,980 in the South Pacific.

For those going on safari there was a lecture on the dos and don'ts of the tour. 'Please, one piece of luggage only,' explained the travel agent. It was the closest we ever came to a mutiny. Some passengers didn't see how they could manage without two suitcases, a carry-on bag and a vanity case. They were gently reminded it was an overnight excursion. 'What time is the cocktail hour?' asked Mr Wilson.

Passengers remaining in Mombasa were reminded not to wear gold necklaces or impressive jewellery ashore and to avoid walking the streets after dark.

The passengers were up early in anticipation of our arrival in Mombasa. As we entered the natural deep-water bay a hundred couples leaned over the railings of the Promenade Deck. Many were dressed for the safari in pith helmets and dun-coloured shirts and shorts. The husbands held their video cameras to the eye – a hundred Alan Whickers in search of sun, sea and a little something else. A chorus of men talked to their camcorders: 'Here we are arriving in Mombasa,' then turned to their wives and said, 'Say "Hi!"' ' A chorus of wives dutifully said, 'Hi! Here we are arriving in Mombasa.'

As the grand ship manoeuvred towards the quayside, dozens of Kenyan street vendors crowded the quay in anticipation of *les grands blancs*. Improvised stalls were being set up the length of the boat. Precious heirlooms and last week's factory-produced, hand-made antiques vied for the contents of the tourists' wallets.

'Look!' said a passenger aiming his camcorder at the quayside. 'They're wearing shoes on their feet.' Another equally astonished passenger pointed to two people near the gangway that was being lowered into place: 'There's a white couple!'

The Filipino deckhands struggled down the gangway under the weight of the passengers' luggage, bottled water and boxes of biscuits. Within two hours a specially chartered plane would land in the middle of a game reserve from where they would set out in search of elephants, hippos and giraffes. I headed into the centre of Mombasa on the local bus with Christine, the German cabin stewardess, who had the day off.

The West's latest exports were in evidence even in Mombasa's old quarter; children had scrawled 'Welcome Bayern Munich' on a wall and youngsters wore the bright red shirts of Liverpool Football Club. A newer invasion was heralded by posters advertising the services of American evangelists; through worship and a donation, the evangelists promised to cure AIDS and other diseases. We were told when the US Navy's Sixth Fleet had sailed into Mombasa the previous year the city was full to overflowing with women who had come from all over Kenya and as far as Uganda, Tanzania and Central East Africa to trade sex for dollars. However, because of the risk of contracting AIDS, any sailor seen with a local girl would have been punished by court-martial and this had successfully deterred them from the pleasures of the flesh. Many of the women and girls who had dreamed of making their fortunes were left without the worries of an unwanted pregnancy, but also without the cash to feed their undernourished families. Many hadn't been able to afford the fare home and, as night descended over Mombasa, clubs like Istanbul and the Florida were packed with women whose sole purpose was to sell their bodies to any man who would pay. The prostitutes hovered around the crew like bees around flowers in full bloom, dancing with each other and offering themselves like different dishes at a buffet; obsidian, basalt, amber – mothers, sisters, matrons and schoolgirls – you could take them alone or in any combination to suit your pleasure and wallet. Christine and I left the Florida in the early hours of the morning after a floor show where two young semi-naked Filipino women had danced a suggestive Lambada. I thought of the god-forsaken bars in Tijuana, and the Filipino women who performed the same routine seven days a week, 365 days a year on different continents, desperately scratching enough money to send back to their families. If it were not for their remittances to their homes the welfare of their families and country would be in even greater jeopardy.

With only four hours left before the ship sailed for Durban, the next stop on our odyssey, the passengers stormed into Mombasa for another shopping marathon. They bought malachite boxes for their daughters, kaftans for their granddaughters and kitangis for their great-granddaughters. Edith, whom I had last seen wearing a pink floppy-brimmed hat, screamed to Mary Lou across Moi Avenue, 'Darling! It's marvellous: come and look.'

Curious, I followed Mary Lou into the shop. Edith had placed an unusual conical shape on her head. 'Do you have a mirror?' she asked the salesman.

He was dark and young enough to be Edith's great-grandson. He looked embarrassed. 'Excuse me, lady, it's a lampshade,' he said hesitatingly, pointing to the conical shape that rested on the crown of her head.

'Mary Lou, isn't it divine?'

I looked the other way. I could hear the salesman repeating himself: 'Excuse me, lady, these are lampshades.'

Edith returned to the ship with a lampshade on her head and two others in a shopping bag.

In Poplar the salesman would have called the social services. In New York the salesman wouldn't have batted an eyelid.

The Stanleys and Livingstones had returned from their safaris. They had bought bundles of carvings of game animals from the quayside stalls. It was the closest I had got to a giraffe or an elephant. One of the ship's two nurses had bought a wicker chair. The street vendor looked perplexed. 'They don't have chairs in America?' he asked. Ours was the last cruise ship to call on Mombasa that season, and as the *Vistafjord* blew its horn signalling our imminent departure, a quayside vendor frantically screamed, 'Everything half price, closing down sale!'

Mr Harrison, on Promenade Deck with his camcorder, filmed his wife hurrying up the gangway with a small carved lion tucked under her arm. 'As usual Phyllis is the last one on board,' he said to no one in particular, but kept for posterity in the family video collection.

The *Vistafjord*'s in-port movie had been *The Gods Must Be Crazy*. The cruise director had a sense of humour.

Dinner conversation was full of the thrills and spills of observing animals from the safe sanctuary of a thatched lodge. Martin and I were told how at night one of the game reserves was floodlit, 'So we had a better chance of observing the animals as they went to their watering holes,' said Mrs Wilson. It sounded as if the only things missing had been popcorn and programmes. 'We watched elephants mating. It only lasted ten seconds.' Mrs Wilson sounded disappointed.

'If you had one and a half tons on your back you wouldn't want it to last more than ten seconds,' said Sally Ann.

Mrs Wilson was not very well, or no one was taking much notice of her and she was looking for sympathy. Either way, if she took any more pills I worried that she would rattle like maracas each time she moved.

The ship was seductive, but destructive to catching up on my writing. I spent long hours on deck, sometimes in the company of two women from New Jersey.

Floris had befriended Martha who had recently lost her husband. Floris had spent her last thirty winters on world cruises. She joked half-humorously, half-seriously, 'For many of us who have been widowed the cruise is like God's waiting room. We are just waiting for the call.'

Martha was on her first cruise. Her friends in Princeton, New Jersey, had thought it would be good for her to get away from her house and the depressing, damp New Jersey winter. Both Floris and Martha spent the time from sunrise to sunset broiling on the sun deck. Since Bombay they had had to share their dinner table with two suave men who had been sent by their Rio de Janeiro-based shops to sell precious stones and gold jewellery to the passengers. Martha told me it had been a nightmare; both the men fought for their attention but neither Floris nor Martha was interested in them or their brochures. They were not allowed to sell jewellery on board ship, but could do so only when the passengers disembarked in Rio. Both men had promised a grand tour of Rio. They both looked as though they had stepped out of an advertisement for a car or an aftershave. They dressed immaculately, and not a single hair was out of place, like Rudolph Valentino with slicked-back black hair, Ralph Lauren shirts and designer tans and sunglasses.

Martha told me about her gorgeous granddaughter. 'She would love you, but I don't think she'd like the idea of travelling to Afghanistan.'

'Oh?' I said interestedly.

'She's very rich.'

'How rich?' I joked.

'*Very* rich.'

'Rich enough to support a young man?'

Martha, like the cruise director, had a sense of humour; she gave me her granddaughter's New York telephone number. It was the third proposal from a loving grandmother. They described three visions of heaven – a blonde Virginian, a New Jersey undergraduate and a New York dancer. I was in danger of becoming a rich trigamist – or a *very* rich trigamist.

We took our seats in the Garden Lounge. The men sat rigid in their black ties and frilly white dress shirts; the women looked like mermaids in shimmering dresses with sparkling jewels for gills. The audience had gathered with the strict solemnity of a court waiting for the arrival of a crown prince or king. The tension was palpable; we were waiting for the concert pianist to make his entrance. If we waited much longer moths were likely to gather on our clothes. A few intrepid passengers had the courage to ask a waiter for a second glass of cognac or champagne – enough to cause some raised eyebrows amongst the intimate audience. When the pianist finally made his entrance they gave him a handsome round of applause. Then, when it was quiet enough to hear the faint murmur from the air-conditioning, the pianist's hands rose as if ready to strangle someone. They remained hovering above the keys as his face was seized by trancelike concentration. Suddenly the fingers plunged with great delicacy to the keyboard as if some imaginary starting gun had been fired. The audience's faces were consumed by surprise and then horror. Their expressions could have turned butter rancid: the pianist had chosen to play Chopin's Funeral March.

After the concert, when the passengers had recovered their composure with a stiff nightcap, I returned to my cabin to change before meeting Christine on the D aft deck where the crew were allowed to gather. Christine, if caught in my cabin after working hours, would have suffered the modern version of the gangplank: dismissal at the next port of call. Nowadays that was perhaps an equivalent punishment, as most of the sharks seemed to be ashore.

My absence from the cabin did not go unnoticed. 'Where were you last night?' Martin asked the following morning. He knew my interest in Christine had been growing daily. I confessed I had spent the night on the aft deck. 'What?' he said incredulously. 'People pay tens of thousands of dollars for these cabins and you sleep outside on deck!'

'Martin . . .' I was about to explain, but he cut me off.

'It must be love.'

It became a ritual to spend the late afternoons on deck in the fading light of the beautiful days. The sea was nearly perfectly still and stretched out uninterrupted all around us. On our port side mountains of clouds veiled some tropical storm that would bring unfriendly weather to Mozambique and to the vast continent beyond the horizon. The ship cut through the water like a knife slicing through silk. Minutes later there would be no trace of our fleeting passage except for a few hungry birds swooping for food. I leaned against the ship's railings and watched the afternoon twilight fade imperceptibly into dusk until all was dark except for the Promenade Deck's lights and the cracks of light through the cabins' curtains.

The storm hit us without any warning. Those passengers who made it to the dining room ate grimly. Mind over matter was the philosophy of the great-grandmothers and great-grandfathers but their bodies failed them. They were not alone; even the younger passengers had difficulty rising from their seats; everyone's face was pale to the point of translucency.

I went to join the crew in the bowels of the ship. Gary, the shopkeeper, was having a party. He was one of the lucky staff members: he didn't have a bunk bed and he had a porthole.

The sea lapped and crashed against Gary's porthole. From inside the cabin the raging sea was contained in a circular piece of glass which made the Indian Ocean look like the water in a washing-machine cycle. On the eve of my last port of call Gary's recipe for a good party was one wash in the Indian Ocean, three rinses in San Miguel beer and a spin in Durban. The ship lurched from side to side making dancing all but impossible unless you wanted to end up in someone's lap. Many did. One of the engine room assistants told everyone to cheer up: 'Look on the bright side, there's no need to do drugs.'

Gunnes, one of the Swedish pursers, told us that a passenger had telephoned to ask if her stewardess would be able to join the ship to clean her cabin. There was a drunken silence as everyone waited for the punch line. The passenger had believed that the crew stayed on another ship that followed the *Vistafjord*, the purser explained. It wasn't a joke and the conversation was entered in the purser's log. She also told us about another passenger who called to ask if it was all right for her to leave her cabin. Why shouldn't it be? asked Gunnes. The passenger explained that there was a Do Not Disturb sign on her door.

Later, Gary told me about a couple in a $60,000 cabin on the previous year's world cruise. 'We had just sailed from New York and they had been invited to dinner at the captain's table. They were outside the shop on their way to the purser's office. We heard the man complaining to his wife: "We've paid all that money and we're asked to eat with the crew!" '

* * *

When I had enquired about visas from the South African embassy in London I had been told that I would have to sign a declaration that I would not write anything about the country. I didn't realize at the time how closely the townships of South Africa resembled the ghettos of Bradford or Poplar in England, the South Bronx in New York or Central Los Angeles.

As we berthed at Durban ships from a handful of nations that had in principle agreed to an economic embargo were docked in the harbour, their names conveniently painted out and a false name superimposed. A shoppers' shuttle whisked the passengers to a shopping complex where one could buy products from the local Body Shop or a nearby Woolworth's. Occasionally we were frisked or had to pass through a metal detector as we entered the shopping malls. Whilst Sally Ann, Martin and I ate lunch close to a beach there was a bomb scare. Maybe it was more like Belfast than Bradford, but talking to the few men and women with pale skins I realized that the majority of them would never in their lifetime go into the townships, like their counterparts in New York, London or Los Angeles who seldom if ever set foot in their local ghettos. Apartheid takes many forms. In the developed countries it is economic apartheid; in Afghanistan the apartheid is based on gender.

Three years before I had prepared to leave Poplar for New York. I was depressed by the stagnation and hopelessness and haunted by the eyes filled with crazed violence and the graffiti FUCK OFF PACKS scrawled across a shopfront in my local shopping precinct. It had taken me three years of travel to come full circle, halfway around the world, to realize that I didn't have to go much farther than my own doorstep to discover that my own society – so quick to criticize other societies – was diseased by the same ills as all those I had visited.

As some passengers disembarked from the *Vistafjord* for the last time, they exchanged the addresses of milliners and couturiers. All were busy making plans; there wouldn't be a spare moment between seasons. For those whose cruise wasn't yet over there were still more marathon shopping sessions and extravagant tours in Cape Town, Rio de Janeiro, Salvador, Belem and Barbados before reaching Fort Lauderdale, their final destination.

Sally Ann, Martin and I stood in line for a taxi to take us to the airport and back to London. A well-kept, full-bosomed, blonde passenger was getting into the taxi in front of us. The fair-skinned policeman leaned over into the driver's window, tapping the roof with his truncheon. He stared down hard at the black driver. 'Remember,' said the policeman venomously, 'if you don't take her directly to her hotel, I've got your number and I'll come and get you and I will break your fucking legs.'

I had heard similar threats in Poplar and New York.

15

FEAR OF LANDING

The Citadel, Brixton, July 1991

I left Kabul after my first visit a beleaguered city, on the brink of starvation. Back in New York I headed straight from my apartment to the nearest supermarket. It was late and the shop was about to close. I asked one of the saleswomen where I could find the milk. She pointed to a cooler, where I stood, bewildered by the choice, until she offered assistance. 'What are you looking for – regular homogenized?' she asked.

'Skimmed, please.'

'Will that be half and half, low fat, cultured low fat buttermilk, extra light vitamin A and D added, or non fat?'

'Non fat, please.'

'Lactose reduced non fat milk, calcium fortified non fat milk, or regular non fat?' she said patiently.

I chose regular non fat, but there was also real churned grade A, buttermilk, goat's milk and a variety of flavoured milks. I walked out of the delicatessen past shelves laden with every variety of muffin and bread: unleavened, rye, bran, wholemeal.

Returning from the rigours of the Middle East or Latin America I find it difficult to come to terms with the technology of the West: answering machines that can screen your telephone calls; VCRs that can be programmed by telephone; credit cards; magnetic money; automated pizza-making machines with up to seven toppings; vibrating slippers that massage with or without heat.

Every time I return from a battlefield, I come back mentally injured. I feel consumed by guilt. The guilt stays with me, it never leaves me; it's always there. It is the guilt of having witnessed man's inhumanity to man, the guilt of being impotent to prevent the misery and of being powerless to alleviate the suffering of others. It is the guilt of taking wretched pictures of other people's misfortune, and of my own privileged existence. It is the guilt of having survived whilst others died.

Friends ask if I have returned to painting. I sometimes feel inspired to paint but then I picture the screaming Kurdish children, the hungry eyes in Kabul, the children hoping for food and the long queues of people waiting for rations. I think of those fleeing from repression and those who are desperately looking for shelter where none exists. I hear the piercing screams of the war wounded, I smell the acrid smoke of a rocket attack and the stench of charcoaled bodies. I have not yet returned to my painting.

In one sense computer technology, robotics and satellite communications have brought us closer together. We live in a global village where everything is accessible from the latest in Paris fashions to the initiation rites of Papua New Guinean tribes. At 2 A.M. the Swiss franc can be traded in New York where international traders, eyes glued to green monitors, strive to find the perfect market: platinum is up; Hong Kong has a demand for gold; the dollar is unchanged in Frankfurt; the yen down in London; the French franc under pressure in Tokyo. The free flow of currencies and commodities never stops and they trade in a twilight zone of electronic pulses in which the national incomes of major states circle the globe at the speed of light. Symbols flash across time zones in a world that never sleeps. It is far removed from the slow brutal world of the underprivileged where people are beaten and property is smashed; where the young unemployed and the politically repressed feel powerless, while a steady diet of television displays the lifestyles of the rich and famous and exacerbates their feelings of economic impotence.

I am caught between two worlds. At one moment I am running towards a plane across open tarmac with no protection against random mortar attack, and within hours, on another continent, I disembark into a covered passageway, via an air-conditioned terminal and moving escalators, to queues at passport control. There are no rocket attacks here. But for passengers from developing nations Western democracy is not the democracy we know or experience. The Berlin Wall may have come down but the free movement of peoples between countries is limited; and those lured to the developed world by images of *Dallas* and *Miami Vice* soon find that they are trapped in a hostile and alien society where poverty, lack of jobs, poor pay and discrimination are the norm rather than the exception.

I still think of the *QE2*, the world cruise and life in Beverly Hills and Palm Beach. In Los Angeles the Four Seasons hotel has set up a Pet Amenity Program with a special room service menu for the prosperous pooch. Items include ground turkey, chopped steak, flaked tuna and a buffet of cheese morsels for cats. A video film for dogs, filmed mostly from a camera height of two feet, featuring a duck chase and a car ride, is provided to relieve canine boredom. The hotel management have said that their experience of catering for Sigourney Weaver's and Liza Minelli's dogs has convinced them that 'there's a real demand out there'.

After my return from Afghanistan in September 1989 I tried to get an assignment that would take me back to Kabul. I had been haunted by the memory of the children of Marastoon – the mental institution on the outskirts of Kabul – where they lived amongst insane and demented inmates. Surely I could do something to prevent the children from being socialized into the insanity that surrounded them. My chance eventually came one unusually fine Saturday evening in the early summer of 1990. I was sitting in front of the television with my parents, watching a programme on Northern Ireland. It inspired me to make a video. Without an intrusive camera crew, travelling and working as I usually do on my own, it seemed the perfect medium to show the plight of the children. It would also enable me to try to get the kids released from the asylum. I immediately wrote a letter to the BBC Community Programme Unit about my project and within six weeks I was back in Kabul.

Little had changed. Kabul was still under siege, surrounded and struggling for survival. The large bustling community of journalists that had been there when the Soviets withdrew was gone. I found a house to rent in the suburbs and immediately applied to visit Marastoon. The war was never far away. When you couldn't hear the rocket attacks there was the constant drone of the massive Soviet airlift resupplying the government. The political situation had not changed. The government still got all its military supplies from the Soviets and the mujahedeen their weapons from the United States mainly but also from the United Kingdom, Saudi Arabia, Pakistan and Iran. One side continues to fire indiscriminately into the towns and the cities, while the other bombs the mountains and the plains. Who fired first and who's defending whom has been forgotten.

For once I was determined that I would not just take pictures but actually *do* something. I would get the children out of the asylum and into a house of their own. The project took five months, the first two of which were spent writing letters begging for money. I also spent over a month with the United Nations as a consultant. I was asked to try to persuade Ismail Khan, the mujahedeen commander of Herat, with whom I had travelled in 1984, to allow the transport of humanitarian supplies from the government-controlled city of Herat into his sector. I also travelled into the countryside where communities were on the brink of starvation. The UN wanted to get supplies to them, but first we had to negotiate with the mujahedeen for the safe passage of the trucks.

Although one mujahedeen group allowed us to move into their valley, later, when we arrived at their headquarters, their commander had other ideas. He had decided to execute us. However, after gallons of Afghan tea, a little negotiation and a lot of grovelling, we persuaded him to change his mind. And in the end, I left Afghanistan with my life intact.

Consider the ironies. The United States is about to provide grants to the Soviet Union, while Moscow continues to spend billions of dollars a year on economic and military aid to the Afghan government. In other words, the United States will be indirectly financing the Soviets to continue their war against the US-backed mujahedeen. Or, to look at it in a different way, the US taxpayer is paying for both sides of the Afghan war.

My begging letters for money to get the children out of Marastoon fell immediately on sympathetic ears. The Norwegian Red Cross agreed to finance the refurbishment of a derelict house that had been given by the Afghan Red Crescent. In addition,

Princess Sadruddin Aga Khan made a donation that guaranteed enough money to support the children and the running of the house for two years. With both cheques in hand a Norwegian Red Cross official and I went to the Kabul money market and exchanged them for a suitcase stuffed with local currency. Within a few months these children had a new beginning.

It is impossible to describe here all the experiences I have had in the last four years. There were the 'daily news' assignments, to cover a British postal strike, for example, or disasters and plane crashes. Others took me to more exotic locations like Hong Kong, where in stark contrast to the fast-moving world of 21st-century skyscrapers I was sent to the 'Walled City', an overcrowded slum in Kowloon. Here some Chinese Triad gangs have their bases, and sweatshops operate between pornographic cinemas and unlicensed dentists.

Some of the events in the places I have travelled to continue to amaze and sadden me. Recently a new scheme has been introduced to stem the flow of illegal immigrants on the Mexican–US border. The Texas National Guards have been given a $3.5 million federal grant to fund a project where members of the force will actually spend their nights dressed as cactus plants. In Turkey, where it has only recently become legal to speak Kurdish and where the Kurdish national colours of red, yellow and green are still banned, I was told during my visit to Cizre that 'if we had traffic lights they'd probably ban those too'.

Often I wonder about our priorities when billions are spent on malfunctioning space telescopes and urbanites need biokinetic, thermodynamic, stress-reduction tools in synchro-energizing salons to cope with contemporary living. We worry about cholesterol levels while injured patients around the world can die for want of blood. The richest country in the world with only five per cent of the world's population uses over a quarter of the world's oil consumption and releases on average a quarter of the world's pollution and toxic wastes. As one US officer said early in the recent Gulf crisis, 'If Kuwait only grew carrots the United States would nowhere be seen.'

* * *

Through my travels, I have learnt that no country can exist totally on its own. No man is an island. We are all interdependent. Many of the people I met along the way had no material wealth, yet they offered me all they had; the gift of their friendship brought greater riches to my life than any shiny rocks that men may dig out of the earth.

I believe that despite all the suffering and misery we inflict upon each other, as long as there is laughter and caring and friendship, as long as we can learn not to judge but to try and understand each other's way of life, and to realize that the differences between us are what make life endlessly fascinating, as long as we can focus on our common humanity, there will always be hope.

I find it difficult to readjust to 'home'; nowhere feels like home and everywhere feels like home. Poplar, New York, Kurdistan, Kabul, Los Angeles . . . I remember returning once to London after a hectic two-week schedule. As always on my return I made a pilgrimage to my local café, the 'Cafe on the Hill' in Brixton, for my usual eggs, bacon and sausage 'twice'. I stood in front of the counter having arrived at Heathrow two hours earlier at six in the morning. Heather, the Scottish cook, looked at me. 'You look dead tired,' she said lovingly.

'I feel it. In the last two weeks I've been to Tehran, Istanbul, Los Angeles twice, San Francisco, Washington, New York and Miami.'

'I know the feeling,' Heather sympathized. 'Michael and I went down to Hastings on the Sussex coast for the weekend and we came back shattered.'

INDEX